Witchcraft

ISBN-13:
978-1536855364

ISBN-10:
1536855367

Table of Contents

16- Note on Localities, Family Heritages, Nations and Images

Introduction: If you live in the developed world perhaps when you think of the word 'witchcraft' you think of ugly women in pointy hats riding on broom sticks and casting spells. Or perhaps you think of stories of the burnings of women in the past centuries after the milk went sour and accusations were made as to what the cause was. Or perhaps you think of primitive cultures that are filled with superstitions. Perhaps you think that it is entirely imaginary, and that it is superstitious to think in the modern day and age that people with such power actually exist.

If you live in other parts of the world, perhaps you have a different opinion. Perhaps you have seen or heard of people practicing witchcraft or some other similar art and even seen results come from it. Perhaps you even have gone to people who say they can use this power to help eliminate some disease or problem from your life, and you actually saw a result that came after you went there. Or perhaps you have seen people practicing witchcraft and thought they were very superstitious.

And then again perhaps you have another viewpoint entirely different.

Throughout history and throughout the world, even in the modern-day, there are huge multitudes of people whose lives are affected by this phenomenon. It occupies an important place in the cultures of many people in every corner of the world. From an Albanian grandmother who does magic while singing Arabic verses from the Quran she doesn't understand, to a blind man sitting on a stool on the streets of Beijing who people say can tell you what your family name is without having met you before, to a witch-doctor in Zimbabwe who gives you an amulet that protects you from curses, to a group of young women in Canada who sit in a circle around candles and chant a spell… even in the modern world, it is still being practiced. Historically there is no place in the world which has not been affected by it.

Even though it has had such a great effect on the world, I think the vast majority of people, even including those who believe in it or practice it themselves, really do not understand what it even is, how it works, why it can produce results, etc. This work is a modest and fallible attempt to offer an explanation.

This work is not an attempt to go into detail about how witchcraft operates in societies in terms of a cultural or anthropological study. If you wish to learn about witchcraft from that perspective, there are anthropologists and social scientists who publish and lecture, and who can provide the answers to that aspect of the topic much better than you will find in this book. This book seeks to explain something that goes beyond the anthropologist's expertise or ability to study, it seeks to explain how the invisible world works and how witchcraft is able to produce results.

I cannot claim to be a trustworthy or accurate source in providing the explanations of these things, however. This might seem strange as to why I would write a book on it then, but I would further add, that I am not sure if any human being who is alive in this world is able to do so. I can only claim that I think I understand some things about it that others don't, and I wish to share that with you, the reader, in the hope that it will benefit you and glorify God.

Many times, as I was writing this, I deeply questioned myself, thinking it is all just my imagination. And very frequently I felt a strong temptation to simply just put it down and stop. But I kept writing and felt like I got signs to reassure me that this was the right thing to do.

Most especially, in my writing about 'tionchar' I had some of the biggest doubts. Partly because most of what I wrote about this came from my own imagination, and like any rational person, I don't trust my imagination to tell me about things in the outside world. And then when I was thinking about going back and editing it out, I was looking at the liturgical calendar for a different reason not related to the writing of this, and as I was going through the days I coincidentally realized that the date I had first coined the term and written it down, which is February 1st 2014, was also the feast day for Brigid of Kildare. I took it as a sign that I wasn't completely crazy in imagining these things to be true, and continued.

Even still, I still don't trust it. I write it, but I myself am not sure if it is really true. So, I ask the reader not to put too much trust in me or my understanding, but instead to pray and ask the Spirit who governs all things to instill a better understanding for all of us.

I first published in book in 2016, but after a year, I felt that there were things in it that I had got wrong and made changes to it. This version is the 2017 re-publishing of the first book.

In the first line of Genesis it tells us that God created the heavens and the Earth. It is referring, however, to more than just the sky and the ground. The Earth is the physical world, including all the planets, galaxies, nebula, etc. The heavens is the other world, the spiritual world, in which all the angels and demons, the souls of all human beings, and God Himself all live. We live in both worlds; our bodies are in the physical world (the Earth), our spirits and souls are in the spiritual world (the heavens). The two worlds are always touching each other. Everything that happens in the one is creating effects in the other.

Scientists can determine the existence of a mass present in the universe, simply by observing the gravitational forces, even if they do not see what object the forces are coming from. In the same way, the things that happen in the physical world that we can see are being caused by things in the spiritual world that we cannot see.

Because I hope to use this work to bring people closer to God, I am going to write prayers at the end of each chapter, which I invite the reader to say with me as he or she reads this work.

Lord, we pray that you give us spiritual eyes to see the invisible world. We pray that whatever in this book which may be of benefit will benefit ourselves and others. We ask for these things, if it is your will, in Jesus' name, Amen

I: The Spirits

In talking about the subject, 'what is witchcraft?' I need to go over a long explanation of the spiritual world, as I (fallibly) understand it, because this is necessary to understand the topic correctly. This will take a long space to complete, and I ask the reader for patience.

The first thing that is necessary to narrate is something that predates humanity.

God is a Trinity of three Persons: Father, Son and Holy Spirit.

The Father exists outside of time. He sees all things in all times all as though He were watching them at the same moment.

If you could imagine looking at a television screen, but the screen was divided into different pictures which all appeared on the same screen. In one picture you could see the beginning of creation, in another picture you could see Adam and Eve, in another one you could see the people of Israel, in another you could see the death of Jesus on the cross, in another one you could see the present, in another one you could see the future time, in another one you could see the second coming of Jesus, and in another one you could see the time after the second coming.

But you do not see these as happening one after the other, but instead you see them all at the same moment. You see the beginning, the middle, the end, the time after the end, all in the same breath. There is no start for you and no finish for you. There is no backwards or forwards. You see it all and you are happy, because you already see the ending, and nothing can take away this happiness from you. You are happy because in your heart, the one thing you desire is completely fulfilled – unhappiness comes from unfulfilled desire- but because your desires are completely fulfilled you are always completely happy. Your one desire is to love those you see in front of you and to be loved by them. And you see it completely fulfilled.

This is the Father.

The Son and the Holy Spirit are not like this. They do not see all time in this way. They do not yet know everything that shall happen in the future. God did not create them but He is the reason that they exist. There was no point in time at which they did not exist. The Son was destined to adopt a human nature, and perhaps the Spirit was meant to have an angelic nature.

The Son was greater than the Spirit, and the Father was greater than the Son. Neither the human beings nor the angels existed yet.

The Father was outside of time and outside of the creation. The Son and the Spirit perhaps were inside of time and inside the creation, in the heavens and the earth. In the beginning, the Son and the Spirit perhaps did not understand who they were. They perhaps did not know how great they were. They perhaps didn't know anything at all; only that they existed and they were persons.

And the three of them could see each other. The lesser two of them perhaps understood almost nothing, but they looked upon each other and upon the Father and they loved each other. They were a family. The Spirit wanted nothing else but to love the Son and the Father, and to receive their love. The Son wanted nothing else but to love the Spirit and the Father and to receive their love. The two of them trusted the Father who knew everything and who loved them as His children.

The Son and Spirit perhaps understood nothing at all about what would happen later, but they simply loved each other with all their hearts and that was it. Of everything that should happen afterwards in time, there was nothing else to be added later that ever changed this or affected the original plan. The entire meaning of everything was contained in this.

Everything that should happen later, all the angels and human beings to be created, all the universe with all its wonders, all the history of salvation and the coming of God's kingdom in the world- the entirety of it was simply an extension of what happened between those three at the very beginning.

You two are my family, you are everything to me, I want us to be together forever, and I love you, you love me- the entirety of God, and the entirety of all things- it is nothing more complicated than that.

In the first chapter of Genesis, the story begins by telling us that on the first day God created light. He then separated the light from the darkness, the darkness He called night and the light He called day. The text does not tell us that God created darkness but only that He created light and separated the darkness from the light.

God told the Son and the Spirit to create a huge number of beings who had souls but no bodies. And they did, and these beings were the light.

Their total population number is a finite, and not an infinite amount, but it is huge. If you started at one and counted, eventually you would reach an end to their number because it is not infinite. It is far larger than the number of human beings who have lived in the world up to this time in history. These spirits in later times were called 'angels', because they served as messengers (angelos, the word used in the Greek bible, means messenger).

They were the first things that God created. Before the Big Bang, they were already there.

Their vocation was to serve as messengers from God to His creation. Every Word that came from God, they were to bring to the rest of the Creation. And so they had no bodies, and they occupied no space, and they could see all the Creation down to the very last atom, at all times without difficulty.

Each one of them had a name that was unique. Each one was a messenger, but they gave different types of messages. One was a guardian angel, who would serve as a messenger from God to a human being. One was a seraph, who was on fire with the love of God, and who would give messages about the love of God to the rest of the creation. One was an angel who would have charge with giving messages to governments. One was an angel who would have charge with giving messages about God's glory though His creation.

No one spirit possessed the same name as another

spirit. And each name signified what their function was.

But in the beginning, they did not yet know what the purpose of their existence was. It was not yet revealed to them. They had names and they had beauty, but it was not yet clear to them what it meant.

When the angels were first created they knew that God existed but they didn't yet see Him face to face. They knew that God existed, and they could see some of His beauty, but they did not yet know anything about Him. God reveals Himself through His created works, but He had not yet created anything except them, and so very little was revealed yet. They only knew that He was a person.

In the beginning the heavens and the Earth existed, but the Earth was without form. The spiritual world and the physical world existed, but the physical world had neither time nor space. The angels and the Trinity inhabited the spiritual world, but there was a physical world, just without any form to it. Augustine wrote about this 'formless matter' in his *Confessions*, and said that this was matter that existed before time and before space. He did not know of the theories that would come long after he died about the Big Bang and how time-space entered into existence.

But before the Big Bang, before time-space came to be, there was matter that was formless and that was the physical world, or in other words 'the Earth'.

The spiritual world was inhabited by souls and the physical world had material. The souls of the Triune God and the souls of the angels were there, but they had no physical bodies.

The Father knew everything, but the Son, the Spirit and the angels knew almost nothing. They knew of the existence of the formless matter, but did not know what was to happen with it. They knew each other and loved each other, but they did not understand their own identities.

The Son and the Spirit enjoyed the beatific vision from the beginning, but it was no so with the angels. The Son and Spirit could always see the face of the Father and be united intimately within His love, and this lasted forever. Even when the Son would one day take flesh and walk as a human being, He still enjoyed this vision. They saw the face of God, but not everything was known to them; they were learning too, and continued to learn forever.

The angels, when they were created, did not see the

face of the Father. They knew He was there and they loved Him, but to be united in His love was something they could not yet taste. It was not yet made clear to them that they would find salvation.

They saw the beauty of their creation and marveled at their own beauty, but they only saw a tiny fraction of the beauty that they would have once they saw the face of God.

Not one of them was evil, all of them were good. The demons and the angels were both alike; they were the same in the beginning. Just like how human infants who enter the world leave it to go to heaven or hell, and yet in the beginning they are equally innocent, so was it likewise with the angels.

They were enamored by their own beauty, and there was nothing wrong with admiring their beauty, for their beauty came from God and it was a gift to them from the Father.

The Father gave them free will. They had the ability to choose to love Him or not.

Some people wonder at this point why God gave them a choice to love or not to love. Why did He give the free will to love or to sin? Why didn't He just make them only capable of love?

The reason is because love, in order to be love, must be freely given. A robot cannot love and a puppet cannot love, because they are not choosing to love, but rather they are just following a command they cannot resist. If the angels were incapable of saying no to this request, then they would also not be capable of saying yes to it either, because in order for love to truly be love, there must also be an option to say no. If it is coerced or forced, then it is not really love.

If you built a robot that said 'I love you' over and over again, and was unable to not say 'I love you', would you think that what the robot had for you was love or not? It would not be love, it would just be programming; it would just be the workings of a machine. A robot or a puppet is unable to love, because it has no love when it says it loves you; it cannot do otherwise. <u>The only way that it could really love, would be if it was able to choose not to love.</u>

If I took away your free will and only made you capable of love. Then you could say to me, 'I love you, but only because I am incapable of not loving. But if you gave me a choice, I would choose to not love you'. Where is the love?

Love can only be love if the person chooses to love no matter what choice they are given.

If you understand that, then you understand why God gave free will. God must give free will to humans and angels, otherwise they are incapable of love. Similarly, if free will was ever taken away, and we became incapable of sin, then we would also be incapable of love.

The angels had the choice to love or not, but all of them loved. They loved because they wanted to love, and God had given them a desire to love. There was no one tempting them not to love, because the devil and his angels were also loving God in the beginning and they tempted no one.

If all they wanted to do was to love, and no one ever tempted them, then how did they ever sin?

If sin comes from temptation, and temptation came from the devil, then who tempted the devil to commit sin?

God tempts no one, but He does test people. And He

gave a test to the angels, and if they passed the test, then they would see His face and enjoy the beatific vision, but if they failed the test then they would not see His face and would fall into punishment.

When God tested Abraham, He did not tempt Abraham. He asked Abraham to trust Him with everything, and that was the test.

Many people will say that the test given to Abraham was a test to see if Abraham loved God more than anything else, but this isn't quite accurate.

Abraham's choice was not really a test of whether he loved his son more than God, but it was a test to see if Abraham really believed God loved him or not.

If Abraham trusted God, then he knew that even if God took his son away, he would still have him back in the end. The letter to the Hebrews even states that Abraham was going to kill his son because he believed that God was going to raise him from the dead. And so, Abraham was going to sacrifice his son, believing that he was not going to lose him.

Hence, it was not really a choice between putting one in front of the other, it was a choice to trust God or not. Could Abraham really believe that God really loved Him or not? Could He really believe it even to the point of letting go everything else, even the most important of all things to him, and trusting even this to God?

If Abraham doubted that God really love him, he would not be able to do this. If Abraham doubted that God meant well for him, he would not be able to do this. He was able to do God's will, because he believed that God's love was real.

It was the same test given to all people in all times. If they really trust in God's love and mercy, they would overcome all temptations and tests given to them, and they would always be able to do the will of God. Human beings commit sin because they do not believe that God's love is real, and Jesus Christ came to Earth to die and resurrect to prove to human beings that this love was real.

This was the nature of the test given to the angels. The Father told them, through His Son and His Spirit, to take their beauty, the thing that mattered the most to them, and let it go.

He told them not to worship themselves but instead to worship Him, and He told them that from out of the formless matter He would make another being like them whom they would serve and one born from this matter would rule over them and be their King.

To their eyes, who saw nothing of the beatific vision and did not know intimately how great God's love was, this proved a test for them. God was not really telling them to give up their own beauty, but it appeared like this, because they did not see His face.

It looked to them like God was telling them to give up everything and choose Him instead.

Did they love what God created more or did they love Him more? Did they really want to be with Him more than they wanted their own identity? Could they really trust God; that His love for them was real and this plan was something good for them?

No one tempted the angels, but they were tested like this, because the choice given to them was very hard.

If they had seen His face, then the choice would have been very easy, because they would have known that everything that they thought they were giving up, He was not only going to give back to them, but give it to them an infinite fold. But they didn't see this.

They had to love God even without seeing Him, in order

to enter into His presence.

True beauty was never the abilities that a person had, but it was the love that the person had. If they had clung to their beauty but refused to love God, then their beauty would never truly be real. And if they had only loved God because He had shown them the vision, but they would not have loved God without this vision, then their love would never be real.

If God had granted to them this vision without this test, then they would all love God, but God would tell them 'you love me, but only because you have seen my face. If I had not shown it to you, however, you would never love me'

And how could this be heaven? How could they have beauty if their love was not real?

This test was a gift to them; passing it was the only way in which they could truly have love and truly have beauty.

If they entered heaven, but the Father told them that their identities were more important to them than Him, then that would mean that they did not have real love. And without real love, it could not be heaven. Heaven needed real love, and so a test was needed.

Tests do not make students fail to achieve what the

course required, rather they are what proves that the student had failed to achieve what the course required.

And so, if God never gave them this test and just let them all see His face, then they would gaze upon God, and God would tell them 'you love me, but only because it was easy for you to do so. But if it was hard for you to do so, then you wouldn't love me'... now what do you think, is that really love?

It is not really love, because if in the end the difference in the angels' decision was made by this, then really, they chose to love God, not because they really loved God but because they loved feeling good. They wouldn't choose Him for His own sake but they would choose Him because of what He could give to them. Their love is not unconditional, then. It is not what Paul says about love that 'bears all things, hopes all things, endures all things'. It is love that only exists because a bribe exists, and hence it is not really love.

If I love you because of what you give me, but I would stop loving you, if you didn't give it to me, would my love really be love?

Only those spirits who really loved God for His own sake, and not for any other reason, those who were willing to let go of all of their beauty and their identity while trusting it all to God would be the ones who would see Him and serve Him as angels, and the spirits who would not love God unless they were bribed first… these were the others who would not see Him and become demons.

It could not be any other way than this, or else love would not really be love.

The first to answer God's request was the one who carried the messages about God's greatness. Michael, whose name in Hebrew was a rhetorical question: 'who can compare with God?' was the first to answer God's request and he resigned his own identity in favour of the other person. He let go of his own beauty, trusting in God's love and believing that His plans were good. He announced that he accepted the king that would come from the formless matter and that he would serve the one that God would make from this matter. He would love God no matter what, and he could do so because he trusted that God's love was real, even though he could not yet see more than a glimmer of it.

And he then entered into God's presence and saw His face; he was the first of God's creatures to do so. And he came to see how great God's love was for him, and he saw that he had lost nothing. He had let go of his own beauty only to have God then take hold of it and make it even greater.

He had not lost his identity. Rather it was the case that he was no longer the one holding it up, but he let it go and God then held it up for him and raised it even higher than it was before. And he entered God's presence with the certain knowledge that his love for God was real; that even if he had not seen this vision of God's love for him, he would have loved God even still.

And other angels followed after him and the same occurred to them. But not all followed him.

The devil was so beautiful. Each angel had a name that was different from every other angel, which related to the vocation of the angel. The devil was created to be a messenger of God's light. God's light was His Son, about whom the gospel says 'the light came into the world'. He was the firstborn of all creation, although He was not created. The first day the light was made, although He had existed from the beginning.

The devil was created to show the world the brilliance of this light. To show to the world how great this light was and how much they needed this light.

And he himself shone with a great beauty surpassing all other angels. But he was not the light and he was told to give up his identity in favour of the light and even more- to give up his identity in favour of the matter that had no form.

The devil looked upon his beauty and upon the choice that God gave to him. No one tempted him, but the question went into the deepest part of his being. Could he really trust God this much? Could he really believe that God's love was real?

And he answered 'no'.

But God is Love, God is Truth, He is the author of life and all good things come from Him. And without Him, one cannot have Love, Truth, life or all the good things that come from Him.

And so, the devil then suffered. He was not designed to suffer. He suffered because he was designed to be with God, and yet he was without God and so he suffered. His punishment came out of his own choice; it was not God who rejected him, it was he who rejected God, but without God there was suffering, because he was designed for God.

If he wanted to come back and for the suffering to end

he could do so, but the same choice remained even still. He had to let go of himself in order to do that, but he would never do that. For eternity, he would not change his choice and there was nothing God would show to him to convince him otherwise.

And other angels joined with him and they had the same fate as he did. The dragon swept down a third of the stars of heaven with its tail.

That is the manner that the angelic salvation takes place or not.

Now, one might be tempted to think that the angelic sin is then greater than the human sin, because humans commit sins with a temptation present, but angels do not.

However, God also gives help to human beings that He didn't give to angels at the same time.

There was no one whispering to the angel that disobeying God would bring something more than obeying Him, like a human has.

But, when they were given that choice, it was at the

beginning of the world. God had not died or suffered yet. None of the holy men or women had sacrificed themselves yet for the salvation of others. God had not paid any price at all for anything yet.

Perhaps if holy people had sacrificed themselves for them, or God had died for them, or He had suffered for them at that moment at the beginning, it would have changed their mind.

When Christ did suffer, He suffered for all sins, including the sins of these angels, but that may not have been known to them at that time.

Human beings sin, even though such tremendous gifts have already been provided for them, undeservedly.

There may be many human beings who perhaps would not have gone to hell had they been like the angels, and been born in paradise without any suffering at all, but just given a simple choice to trust God or not and never with a tempting voice to tell them otherwise.

However, there may also have been many angels who would not have gone to hell had it been the case that they knew God or His servants suffered for them, and this had led them to make them trust God with that choice they were given.

The devil and his angels fell into despair, because they were made for God and yet they didn't have God. But in order to have him they had to let go of their own identities and choose him first, and they could only do that if they trusted in His love, which they were unwilling to do.

The devil and his angels were still as God made them though, and they had the same desires that God gave to them, but without the answer to these desires. They wanted what the beatific vision contained, but they did not see it and they were not able to know it. But their desire remained the same.

They wanted to be glorious, like what was given to Michael and his angels, but without God they could not have it. And so, they created something different in place of what God would have given them, and that was pride. They would push themselves higher and bring the creation to worship them, because this seemed like it could fill the hole that was left open because they did not have what was designed to fill it.

They wanted the love of God, but they didn't have it, and so they turned to trying to get love from what He created. They wanted to live in a world of justice, where they were always right and those who opposed them were always wrong, but they didn't have it, and so they turned to creating their own justice and they had wrath against those who displeased them. They wanted the glory that was meant for them in heaven, but they could not have it, and so they desired the worship of human beings through the masks of idols, because it seemed like it could fill what was left empty-although it never truly could.

Think of the story of Cain, when after Cain killed his brother and God cursed his existence on the Earth, Cain complained that he would be killed for what he had done, and God instead protected his life, even though the protection was not deserved. Even in Cain's damnation, God's mercy over him remained, so that his punishment would be always less than what he had deserved, for God did not enjoy his suffering. So it was also for Satan and the demons; God consigned them to pride, so that their eyes would not be fully open and they would not have to suffer as much as they deserved.

Think of the story of the Gerasene demoniac, and when the demons plead with Jesus that He would not banish them to destruction but that He would allow them to enter the pigs, and Jesus accepted their request and let them enter the pigs. So long as they could do things in the world, and inspire the fear of human beings, their pride could be kept intact and they would not have to suffer everything they deserved. For what they truly deserved was not to be allowed to do anything at all, and to just suffer in eternity without ever being able to touch the world (which was what they pleaded to Jesus not to have); but Jesus granted their request, just as the Father grants the request of so many prayers by Satan and his demons when they wish to tempt and do evil in the world, because His mercy is upon them too, just as it is on us, and even should they be forever damned, He still does not wish them to suffer as much as they deserve.

They held onto pride, because this was their lifeboat, so to speak. It was not intended for them to have this originally, but it was the only thing they could have that would at least seem to answer what it was that they wanted, and God allowed them to have this, because His mercy was real and He did not let them suffer everything that they deserved.

But the pride was illusory. And in order to hold onto the illusion, they had to delude themselves. No matter what should happen, they would refuse to believe that God's love was real. His creation of the universe, His planting of human beings on the world, and everything He did for them, they choose to hold on to the belief that He did not do these things for love, because if His love was real, then that meant their pride was illusory and worth nothing.

They refused to believe that God's actions in coming down to the world and dying on the cross was done for love. No matter what He did, even the sacrifice of His own Self, they would see it all and refuse to believe that this was done for love, and God allowed them to disbelieve because His mercy allowed them to remain in their delusion rather than face the full price that was due to them.

All they had to do was let go of their own identities and worship God first, and all of this would end. But they were never going to do so, and so God allowed them to remain in their pride, as it was better here than to be made to fully see the full reality of what they lost and burn in the thought of it. His love for them was still there, although they refused to believe it.

The devil confused them all and he confused himself. He used the talents God gave to him to blind them with his own light and make them believe in the lie of pride: that what they wanted was in their own identities and not in service to God.

And this 'pill' that took away their pain, itself was also the thing that prevented them from repenting and turning back. Their taking of this pill was just an extension of the same choice they made at the beginning; it was just another layer in the answer they gave to God in refusing to let go of their own beauty in favour of Him. And yet it was also just another layer in the test.

Because without this pill, they would see clearly that they could have repented and turned back to God and received everything they wanted, because they could see that they didn't actually have any beauty without Him, while with this pill they could maintain the delusion of beauty even without it actually being present.

But if it was like that, then it would no longer be a test for them. It would be the same reason why God couldn't let them have seen the beatific vision before they were given this choice. It would mean that they only loved God because it was easy, and they would not love Him if it was hard, and thus their love would not really be love.

They would then repent and enter heaven, and God would tell them 'you love me, but only because it was easy, and if it was hard you would never love me'. And then heaven would not really be heaven, because heaven is where love is and this is not real love.

Hence, the pill had to remain, and God consigned them to their pride both as a punishment and as a kind of mercy. It was their own choice to take the pill and thus delude themselves with the false vision of pride. The test for them still remained; all they had to do was believe in God's love for them, let go of their pride in favour of Him and the human beings He created, and they would then come to heaven and see God and He would tell them that they loved Him no matter what, and heaven would then be heaven.

The prisons they were kept in were of their own making; they held the keys to it the whole time, and yet refused to open the door, because that would mean letting go of their identity, and they could only do that if they believed that God's love was real, which they forever refused to do.

They wanted to conquer heaven and to rule all things, because they were designed to rule the world with God, and they still wanted it, because God had designed them for this. Within the lies they created for themselves that God permitted them to have, they thought such was possible, but they were struck down in an instant. God would rule the world through Michael and his angels, and not through the devil and his angels, and this fact becoming manifest to them was what is meant when the scripture says they were struck down. The devil 'fell from heaven like lightning', because not even for a moment was it possible for him to have what he wanted without God.

Like the matter that annihilated the antimatter at the early moments of the universe in the fractions of a moment, and left only matter in existence, the devil and his demons fell from lightning from heaven and the Earth was to be ruled by God with His angels instead.

But even when they fell from heaven, they still deluded themselves and held onto their pride. A monstrous pride is what they had. The most arrogant human beings who ever lived were humble in comparison with them.

And so, their pride manipulated their view on everything. Because they were proud and they wanted to set themselves up in place of God, therefore they considered their own identity superior to all else. The flesh of human beings they would look down upon and their own nature without physical bodies they would think superior. They would enjoy torturing the flesh of creatures that had flesh, through violence, through disease, through starvation, etc. because their pride drove them to do so.

They would look down upon the Creation that God made and would instead favour the pollution and environmental destruction that harmed Creation that they inspired human beings to create, also as a result of the same pride.

All of God's laws they would hold in derision, and instead hold up their own ideas, ideologies and plans, inspired by them and planted within the midst of human beings, as something higher.

But the human being was the most troublesome part to the delusion of pride. Because when the human being entered the world the devil could not accept that this being would be raised up and he would be brought down and he was indeed going to be raised up.

The devil's pride did not allow him to accept this and so he wanted the human brought low. Everything that God had made good in the human being- the devil sought to corrupt to something evil. Every way that the human being could be beautiful and glorious, the devil wanted to change into something hideous and villainous.

Rather than the one who would be formed out of the formless matter to rise higher than him, he would bring this one lower than animals. He would pervert him into becoming monster while convincing him that he was great. He would teach the human being to sin and destroy the beauty that God gifted his soul with. He would tell him to eat garbage and convince him that the garbage was the most delicious of gourmets. He would bring him into becoming the lowest form of life imaginable, an utterly corrupted version of what God had made him to be, while convincing him in his stupidity that what was happening to him was something good. And he did this all from his pride and hatred for the one that God said He would raise up higher than him.

If the human being was brought high and made glorious, even to rule over the angels, then his pride would no longer be possible and his delusion could not continue. If the human being passed the test that the devil and his angels failed, and they were brought to rule over them it would be the most horrific of all things to them. There are arrogant people who feel terrible to see people of other races to rule over them, because they believe their own race superior; their arrogance is small in comparison with what is felt by the devil and his angels towards human beings.

If that happened, then the pill that God allowed him to have that took away his pain would be denied him and his full punishment would come. That was the time of the final punishment; the end which the demons begged Jesus not to let them have and it already began to take effect once Jesus died on the cross and heaven was opened to human beings.

And even when that punishment was given to them, they still would not turn back, instead they would still cling onto their identities rather than let go of them and love the one they were made to serve. They would prefer to suffer for eternity than to let go of themselves. The sparks and fires of hell come from no other place than the heart of the lonely one who is without the other.

It did not have to be like this, however, because the devil and his angels at any time could have changed their minds and come back to him, but this was not to be so and God knew that they would never come back, and there was nothing else He could show to them to bring them back.

Some of the angels did not answer the question at all, and did not decide between themselves or God. And they were left to suffer, but they would be sent to serve human beings and to suffer without the vision of God, but one day, through the merits of Christ, they would be permitted to have what they were once without. Paul wrote in Colossians that God had reconciled all to Himself, whether on Earth or in the heavens.

The legends of jinn (genies) or spirits that were bound as servants or slaves to aid human beings perhaps could be related to this.

God said to him, 'You suffer because you made the wrong decision. If you turn back and choose me, you will have peace again.'

The devil said, 'I choose myself over peace. I would rather suffer and be first than have peace and be second. Without my beauty, there is no true peace.'

God said to him, 'But you know that this will last forever? You will have no peace forever. You will suffer without end. Can you do this?'

The devil said, 'Even if time continues for infinity and the ages for eons without end, I prefer to suffer any and all pain over letting go of myself.'

God said to him, 'But this saddens me. I love you. I do not want to lose you. I would do anything to keep you.'

The devil said, 'There is no greater deception than your love. Even should you do everything for me, even should you sacrifice yourself in the most painful of hells for my sake, I still will not believe that your love is real.'

He hated God and became God's enemy, and hence he was called Satan (in Hebrew it means 'enemy').

They hated God continuously, and blamed Him for all their troubles.

The Trinity did not give the devil a test which they themselves had not already fulfilled. The members of the Trinity were a family that put a greater value on serving the other than on serving themselves. They loved the other first and themselves second. They preferred to give rather than to receive. They did not want Satan to become their servant or slave, but they wanted him to become just like them. They wanted to be servants of others, because this was the way to delight their own hearts the most. They loved each other so much and knew that this was where paradise dwelt in. And they wanted to teach all the others they would create how to be happy just like they were.

Just as the fires of hell are simply the sparks that come from the heart of the one closed to others, so likewise the delight of paradise is simply to love and be loved and become a member of the family who already loved each other before the beginning of time.

God the Father, the Son and the Holy Spirit, are like a family. God is like their parent, and the other two are like siblings who are very deeply in love with each other.

I call them a family not to anthropomorphize God, but rather I am trying to explain something very deep in the nature of humanity. The family relations between human beings, the love between husband and wife, parents and children, sisters and brothers, etc, is a copy of the Trinity. I am not anthropomorphizing God, I am explaining humanity. The Trinity is the original, we are the copy- not the other way around. The love between siblings, spouses, parents and children is the copy, the Trinity is the original.

The three of them were so happy and content with each other. They wanted nothing else than to be together and love each other forever. But they wanted more than this. They wanted others to join them, so they could also be together and love each other, being happy forever. So, the Father first told them to create the angels.

They did not create because they wanted servants. They created because they wanted friends.

They did not want to lord it over their creation. If the three of them were standing in a shopping mall waiting in line at the checkout, they would not butt in front of anyone, and they would insist to take their proper turn. They wouldn't care if someone else went first. They don't think of themselves as more important than others.

When Jesus came down to Earth most of His time on Earth was spent living as an ordinary person as the son of a carpenter. God came down from heaven to live on earth and make tables and chairs for people. He was God but He did not tell anyone. He didn't think being God made Him better than them. He only started preaching and told people He was God because He wanted to save them from their sins and for them to know the Truth about their existence. But if they didn't need His preaching for this, then He would have been content to just continue living as an ordinary person, making tables and chairs.

What makes God better than human beings is not that God is powerful and humans are weak, but because God has love and human beings do not. St Paul wrote in 1 Corinthians 13 that if one has all power, all wisdom, and can do all things, and yet has no love then one is nothing. Those three had all of these things: all power, all wisdom, all ability... and yet to them this didn't mean anything- all that mattered to them was love.

And they knew that if their creation could love just as they loved, then their creation could be perfectly happy just like them. The greatest gift that they could give to their creation was to get them to love just like they loved, so they all could be together like a loving family.

So, when God presented Satan with this choice, He was not telling Satan to become less than Him, He was telling Satan how to become just like Him. But Satan insisted on being first and thereby became less than Him.

God created Satan and all his angels, and all humans, with a desire to be great; with a desire to become like God. But the way to fulfill this desire was through serving others first, because that is how God is Himself.

Thus, the test was finished and their salvations were set forever. On the first day of the week God separated the light from the darkness.

Lord, we pray that you help us to be like the Trinity, and that in the very depths of our hearts, others will always come first. Make our deepest desire and craving be to serve others rather than to be served by them. Open our eyes to the reality that this is how we become like God and how we become our true selves. We ask for these things, if it is your will, in Jesus' name, Amen

II: Man and Woman

After the first day, God then set about with the task of the creation of the rest of the universe. The angels, the Son and the Holy Spirit, understood and knew almost nothing about God's plan in the very beginning. But God would reveal His plan to them more and more as time went on.

Each of the angels had each been made for a different purpose. But they didn't yet know what this purpose was. God told them what to do, and the purpose became revealed to them through their work.

Each angel had a name, and according to the name, the angel would have charge of some different aspect of creation. And God gave them desires and talents with respect to what they were designed for.

For example, the angel who looked after the stars had a desire to create the stars and arrange the physical universe to make way for their existence. The angel who looked after the physical laws of the universe had wisdom from God of how to arrange these laws correctly. The number of the angels is as numerous as the aspects of creation; there are perhaps more angels than atoms in the universe, and yet their number remains finite.

They had extreme intelligence. They could watch every

atom and bit of energy in the universe at the same time and understand everything that was happening in the material world. They had deeper understandings of science, mathematics and the arrangement of matter than any human being who has ever lived. There was nothing in the material world that they could not understand perfectly and completely. And through everything that was made they communicated a message about God's greatness and glory.

They wrote the laws of physics, they took the formless matter and created time and space, they initiated the big bang, they created galaxies, stars, planets, etc. They were told by God that even though their intelligence was extreme and they had no difficulty at all in understanding the most complicated mathematical things which not even the greatest of computers could not possibly master, that they should, however, write all these laws of the universe in a way that can be understood by a very simple mind. They should make all the things of the universe in such a way as could be understand by a mind that was far less intelligent than theirs.

Through carrying out God's instructions, the design He had became clearer and clearer. God reveals Himself through His creation, not just to us, but also for them.

They could see how it was that God was planning on

introducing another being like them into the universe.

And so, they worked for billions of years arranging everything all according to God's instructions. They chose one place in a suitable location where they would pay the closest attention to. They formed the planet Earth, and arranged it so that 'life', something which ought to be very fragile and easily destroyed in consideration of the manner they arranged the entire universe, could exist.

On so many other places life could be destroyed so easily. They had to make sure asteroid or comets would not vaporize the surface, so they put a few giant gas planets behind the Earth to take most of the brunt of the smaller objects they had already sent flying around the universe. They had to make sure that the Earth would be the right temperature so that liquid water could continually exist on the surface without being vaporized or frozen. So, they had to space the planet in the right zone away from the Sun, and put the right combination of gases into the atmosphere to keep a stable temperature. They had to make sure that radiation from space wouldn't kill all life on the surface, which could easily happen in so many other places, and so they put radioactive elements inside the Earth that would create so much heat in the iron core that it would be molten, and it would be liquid and turn, and would make a giant magnetic field around the planet that would protect it from the radiation. They put this core into the Earth, but they needed it to be stable enough so that it wouldn't melt the entire surface and completely wipe out the conditions life needed to survive. Even just completely wiping out any of these conditions for just a few thousand years, which is just a blink of an eye in consideration of the time frames they were operating in when creating everything else, was unacceptable, because life really was that fragile.

Just like how a parent puts a baby into a cradle so the baby can be safe, so they arranged the Earth at God's instructions to be a place safe for life.

And life itself also required special care. God instructed them to create life such that it would have a code written in proteins that would be inside of it and would contain the entire plan for how the organism was formed. This code, which is DNA, was not simple. Even the simplest versions of it contained details that would fill many books, and if there were too many mistakes in the code, then the life could not survive.

And they caused chemicals in the ancient Earth to come together and form this extremely complicated code, and to reproduce it so that it would continue.

Human beings can create computers and give them programming through use of chips made out of silicon.

These chips, while complicated, are still far simpler than DNA. But God chose to make something even more complicated than this to base life on, perhaps because He wanted to make it clear to human beings later that this did not come by accident.

There is no place in the world today that a person can go to and find chemicals coming together randomly to form DNA. There is no laboratory or scientist in the world who has put chemicals in a particular condition such that they came together naturally to form DNA. And many have tried experiments, but no one has ever succeeded in getting chemicals to come together and form it.

And even if they could, this alone is not the final solution. Because the cell mechanics to read the DNA and perform functions based on the code that is read, or to even copy the code to make a second strand, also need to be in place as well, or else the DNA strand will do nothing. But how do those mechanics come into existence without natural selection, without even DNA to order them into existence? How do they come into existence by just the random mixing of chemicals? Not even scientists in a laboratory who control every variable can make these things come about on their own.

And on top of all of this, after these things are formed,

they must survive and not be wiped out by some environmental factor.

Under controlled conditions in which they can arrange every variable, they still cannot reproduce what happened in the ancient world, and yet modern man has faith that this happened by chance without a designer.

So, they created life, and they caused the life to evolve, but life was still not quite like them. The plants, the animals, and the micro-organisms possessed souls, but they were not like the angels. It was clear that this was not God's final goal. But when was God going to tell them to make something that would be like the angels?

They knew that this being would never be as intelligent as them, because it was clear that the limits of the physical brain that was possible would never be able to watch every atom and bit of energy in the entire universe, understanding all of it at the same time- which was what their minds were easily capable of. However, God required that the brain should be at least large enough to master and understand all these things they had created.

It is a strange fact to think that people who study these scientific laws today never wonder of how or why it is that they should be able to understand the way the universe works using methods and equations that the human mind is capable of comprehending.

They understand it because it was designed so that they could understand it. It is like a teacher who reads a story to the children and uses the simplest words she can so that the children can follow along.

God told them to make the universe run on predictable and knowable laws, because if they didn't, then the human beings would never be able to be masters of it. If the seasons were not predictable, then farming would be impossible. If iron did not melt at the same temperature every time, then how would you design a forge? If we were unable to understand the laws of physics, then we could not design airplanes safely. In the first chapter of Genesis, God gave the creation as a gift to human beings and intended that the human beings should rule over the Earth; and it is only through their ability to understand that they are capable of being masters of the created world. Hence, God had to ensure that the universe would work in a predictable way according to set laws, and that these laws be capable of being understood by an intelligence as small as ours. The forces and workings of the entire physical universe are contained in such simple equations as can be taught to human teenagers in a physics classroom; there is no physical law in existence that governs the universe which is too great for the human mind to grasp. And yet people still don't recognize that this was designed to be this way.

Why should it be that we are unable to say about anything in the universe: 'we cannot ever understand how this thing works, because the laws governing it are far too complicated for a mere human mind to grasp?'

Because God required that the being to accompany them and join their family should be able to understand and thereby dominate the material world, this ruled out many possibilities automatically: plants could not be it, neither could bacteria. But animals had brains and they perhaps could understand.

They created the squid, and an angel asked God, 'What about the squid? It has a big brain, and it has arms to manipulate objects. Can this be where you will place the souls of this new being capable of living with us? Will they be our new brothers and sisters?'

God said, 'Not this one, I want a capacity to create and use fire so it can create technology through which it can dominate the world. An underwater creature will not suffice."

And so, they brought the animals out of the sea and onto the land, and evolved them into many new species.

They created the dinosaurs.

An angel asked God, 'What about this one? It can dominate the world and it is a land animal.'

God said, 'The brain is not large enough. It will not be able to understand well enough.'

They created mammals with large brains.

An angel asked God, 'What about this one? It is a land animal and it has a large brain.'

God said, 'We are going in the right direction, but these elephants and whales will not do. They need to be able to manipulate the world with their limbs.'

The angel said, 'What about monkeys? We can take the same form and make it bigger, give it a larger brain. What about that?'

God said, 'That will do. Make it larger with a larger brain, and get it to stand upright on two legs. Also develop the vocal chords and speech centres of the brain so that it be able to not only understand the creation but can also communicate any idea.'

And so God made man. The angels finally saw the end goal behind all the work they had been doing for billions of years. If man had not been created, none of it would have any point. God had told them to create all these things, so that man would have a home. But if man did not exist, there would no purpose to the universe, in the same way that there is no purpose to play a movie in an empty theatre.

The angels were creating all these things in the universe, and yet their vocation was still as 'messengers'. They were performing this role though their creation, because it was through this physical world that the message of God's glory was to be revealed.

The angels then saw human beings, who were made in God's image, and they learned things by watching them that they never understood before. They had understood the entire physical world and prepared it for over 13 billion years for man's entrance, but to them this knowledge was insignificant in comparison with what they were going to learn from watching human beings. They watched human beings live with each other, love each other, communicate with each other and know and love God. And this truly amazed them – they could not stop staring at human beings. They couldn't help it.

Perhaps it is difficult for us to understand the angels' perspective and how astonished they were about this. So allow me to use a comparison:

Imagine if tomorrow a UFO were to hover over your house and stay in place for hours. Would you be able to stop thinking about it and just continue doing business as usual? Would you be able to ignore it and forget about it? So is it similarly to the angels' perspective when after creating the whole physical universe over billions of years, one day human beings came along. But unlike the UFO it was not scary to them- but it was something they could not possibly take their minds off of.

All of those stars and galaxies were trivial in comparison to this being that had been created. There was nothing else in the universe that revealed to them who God was more than the human being. The love between human beings was a copy of the Trinity; this is what caught their attention the most.

Later on human beings would be impressed with power, impressed with intelligence, impressed with ability, etc. If a great general conquered a nation, if a woman was extremely beautiful, if a person was extremely wealthy and could command others to do what he wanted, if technology could accomplish something amazing... human beings were impressed with these things, and yet the angels couldn't care less. Rather, the mother holding her child, the girl who writes a thank you note to her friend, the man who works to support his family... human beings did not think of these as impressive, and yet the angels could not stop staring at them. The richest people in the world holding so much wealth and power, to them is like watching an ant which is slightly bigger than the other ants. The smartest people in the world finding amazing discoveries, to them is like watching a child figure out that two plus two is four.

All the things in the natural world, they already fully understood for eons and they understood it billions of times more deeply than the best of science today, and they could receive power over these things too. To their perspective, intelligence, power and ability is not impressive or noteworthy at all. What made the human beings so incredible to them was the fact that here was a copy of the Trinity, and the Trinity was something even greater than everything that had been created.

In the Genesis story, the six days are not a literal six days. But rather it may be thought of as a message to tell us that the whole of creation was arranged for what would happen on the sixth day when God ended His work, which was the creation of human beings. All things were arranged and created for the entrance of this being into the world as the final goal of all creation.

The angels who loved God were not unhappy about this being who was meant to have greater inheritance than them. Instead they loved them, as a good son or daughter loves a newborn baby brother or sister to whom the parents give more attention to than the older sibling.

The entire solar system was formed from the accretion of dust in the vacuum of space. And the Earth was therefore made from dust as well, and therefore when Genesis tells us that God made man from the dust, even if Adam was born of two hominid parents, he still ultimately came from the dust.

When Adam was born, he was different from the animals who came before him. God created him in His own image, and made him like Himself. Adam's parents were not in God's image, and they did not possess the understanding or the ability to love God that Adam would possess. Adam's parents were similar to him in every way physically and mentally, but just without the ability to know and love God, to know good from evil, etc.

Animals have souls and bodies, just like humans, but they lack the divine part. Animals can understand things, they can think, they can do many physical and mental things... but what separates them from the human being is the ability to know God.

In creation you can see Chimpanzees, Apes, Elephants, Dolphins, or Whales that are very intelligent, who can figure out and understand many things. Squids and Octopuses are also said to be very intelligent. Some of these animals have brains larger than humans. These animals are so smart they can learn, communicate with each other to a limited degree and even understand your own behaviour to some extent.

Because they can understand human behaviour to some extent, they can even have a relationship with you and help you or hurt you, but they are still not able to know God. They have souls, but not made in God's image; they do not go to heaven or hell when they die, and they do not sin, because they do not really know good from evil.

Adam's parents would have been like those animals. They would possess the same brain as he did, with the same understanding of everything, but simply without the ability to know God. They were very intelligent, and would have helped and loved Adam as an elephant helps and loves her own calf, or as a chimpanzee takes care of her own baby. Adam did not possess much power of communication or language, but he could communicate with them in the same way that they would have communicated with each other, just like how some animals can use various ways to communicate messages to each other, but Adam himself would have possessed a divine image that his parents did not.

Adam lived in this world among the other hominids, doing the things that they did and living with them, but able to understand something that they did not understand.

He could see God; they couldn't.

He was therefore different from all the other hominids. He learned that he could communicate with God and God would listen to him, and God would respond to him. God told Adam many things. For the billions of years of waiting, finally he had been born and God told Adam that this entire place and everything in it was made for him to live in.

Adam could not communicate these things with his

parents or relatives, because they were only animals. He himself was not much different from them, and could not understand any of these things too deeply, nor was his ability of communication sufficient enough to communicate these ideas. If we today had seen what he looked like, we would have difficulty distinguishing him from an animal. But an animal can only see a person that is visible to the eyes, but he was aware of the existence of a person who was not visible to the eyes.

Everything Adam asked for from God, God gave to him. And so Adam did not have to suffer any of the things that the other hominids would suffer. Adam did not want to be cold, so he perhaps asked God not to suffer cold, and so God arranged for him to never have such weather affect him. Adam did not want to go hungry, and so he perhaps asked God never to be hungry, and so God arranged for him to always be able to find food. Adam did not want to suffer boredom, and so he perhaps asked God never to suffer boredom, and God made it so that creation was ordered so that Adam was also interested in what happened around him. Not one thing did Adam have to suffer, because his every need was fulfilled by God, and God would bend the creation around Adam to suit Adam's every need and desire, just as Adam requested or perhaps even without his asking. This was Eden.

The other hominids, who did not know God, were not

able to pray. They did not know there was a Creator to this reality who could fulfill their every need. Instead their food, their sustenance, was all provided by the world around them, but they suffered want and death. Adam did not have to, because he simply asked God and God listened to his prayer and let him live without want and death.

And so Adam lived without dying, and his parents died, and all his brothers and sisters died, but they were all not made in God's image. They were not able to pray.

Adam loved them all; they were only animals and not people, but they loved him and he loved them, just like how a herd of elephants looks after one of its own members, or a pod of dolphins plays with each other.

Adam loved them, but they were different from him. They could only love him as a member of a group of animals is loved, they could not see the divine spark in him. He could not find anyone among them who was like himself, who could know God and be like another 'him'.

As much as Adam loved them, he could not find such a companion among them. God knew this and knew that it was not good for it to be like this.

Eventually God created another person just like Adam, who was able to see God and love Him and pray to Him, just like how Adam was. And she would be his wife and the two became joined together. She could be a companion to him in the ways that the other hominids could not. And like Adam, she could pray to God and God would give her everything she asked for in prayer.

For all this time up to that point, the evil spirits were not permitted to interfere in creation. They of course did not want human beings to come into existence, but they were not permitted to stop this or hinder it. The demons simply sat and waited for billions of years, and were not permitted to do anything- all of creation would be good, they could not put anything evil inside of it. But they suffered torments for billions of years and their hearts were harder than diamonds.

When the angels saw the human beings, they were so amazed and happy. They wanted to be friends with the human beings and they were so happy to find out that the human beings were going to someday join their family that had begun with the Trinity.

When the demons saw the human beings, they were so angry and envious. They still clung to their own identities and they could not let go of the idea that these others, or anyone at all, would be first and they would be second.

God had created the devil originally to show all the beings in the universe how great His Light was. The devil was still going to fulfill God's purpose whether or not he had sinned.

The devil then prayed to God and asked God if God would permit him to test whether the humans really loved him, just like how he had been tested at the very beginning. God permitted this request and told the devil that he may tempt the humans.

Everything that the devil does, he does with God's knowledge and permission. The devil is not able to do anything that God does not permit. The devil also prays to God and talks to God, and God grants his prayers, because what the devil asks for is God's will.

The devil's intention is to hurt the human beings, because he envies and hates them. He does not like the fact that God created them as a being with so much beauty while he himself has lost his beauty, and thus he does everything in his power to take away their dignity and turn them into monsters. He hates to see their beauty, so he finds every way he can in order to take it away.

Lord, we thank you for the gift of the creation of human beings, of angels and of the universe itself. We pray that you help us to recognize the true beauty in our creation lies not in our own powers, abilities or intelligence, but in our reflection of the love of the Trinity. Help us to become the beautiful reflections of the Trinity that you meant us to be. We ask for these things, if it is your will, in Jesus' name, Amen

III: Temptation

A great question many want to know the answer to at this point will be: why would God grant the devil's prayer?

So many people in the world completely fail to understand how the devil really does his work. They think that it is without God's knowledge, or that God is powerless to stop the demons, or that God is in the process of stopping the demons but has not finished His work in stopping them yet, etc.

None of these things are quite accurate though.

The reality is that every single thing that happens in our universe is done with the full knowledge and permission of the Creator. Every leaf that falls from a tree can only do so because God has given His permission for it to fall. Every bee that collects nectar from a flower can only do so because God has permitted the bee to take the nectar from the flower.

Every person who suffers, does so only because God has allowed that person to suffer. Every person who dies, does so only because God has allowed that person to die.

Similarly, every sin and evil that exists in the world is done with God's complete knowledge and permission.

When the devil tempted Eve, the devil first prayed to God and asked God that he may tempt Eve, and God said yes.

In the book of Job, there is a conversation between the devil and God giving us an example of what this looks like. The devil asks God for permission to test to see whether Job's love for God really is true or not, and God grants the devil permission to do anything to Job but just not to touch his life.

Every time the devil does anything in the world, it is just like this. The devil is not like a thief who crawls around at night when God is not looking. The devil prays to the same God that human beings do, and asks this God for things in prayer, and God grants these prayers when it is His will to grant them.

So, every temptation under heaven is just like this. There is a soul who the devil envies and wants to harm, and he prays to God and says 'I pray that you allow me to tempt this person, to see if they really love you or if they love the thing with which I tempt them'.

The devil has a question for the human race: Do you really love God, or do you love what He created? Do you really love God or would you prefer an ounce of gold? Do you really love God or would you prefer a beautiful woman or the love of a man? Do you really love Him or do you love your own pleasure? Do you really love God or do you love the respect of other human beings? Etc.

He can also phrase it like this: Do you really love God? What if God was poor, would you still love Him? What if God was a foetus, would you still love Him? What if God was black, Chinese, Jewish, etc., would you still love Him? What if God was female, would you love Him? What if God had same-sex attractions, would you still love Him? What if God was the person who couldn't understand you on the phone, would you still be polite to Him? What if God was the person who fired you from your job, would you still say nothing bad about Him? What if God was the teacher who gave you the bad mark, would you still respect Him? What if God was the person who drove a better car than you, would you still not hate Him from envy? What if God was the person who voted for the person in the other party, would you still be friendly to Him? What if God was the person who played the music loudly on the train, would you still give no dirty look to Him? What if no one told you the difference between right and wrong, would you still love Him? What if you were raised in a place where they told you not to love Him when He appeared in any of the above forms, would you still love Him? And the list goes on…

One could even write this in a Dr. Seuss style: 'Do you

love me with a throne? Do you love me eating a bone? Do you love me in Japan? Do you love me eating ham? Do you love me praying at mosque? Do you love me wearing fox? Do you love me as your son? Do you love me if I drink rum?', and the saints would reply 'Oh that, God-I-am, that God-I-am, I do much love that God-I-am. I would love you on a throne, I would love you eating a bone, I would love you in Japan, I would love you eating ham, I would love you praying at mosque, I would love you wearing fox, I would love you as my son, I would love you drinking rum, I would love you here or there, I would love you anywhere!'

It sounds silly, and yet the entire meaning of every moment of our lives is contained in that paragraph above.

And what we don't understand is that every minute of every day this question is being asked of us and God has disguised Himself behind the faces of all these people, and we don't understand that we are writing a test. The correct answer to every question is: 'yes I really love you Lord, even when you are this person, even when you are that person, even when I have this temptation or that temptation, no matter what I still love you Lord'. But most of us fail to write this test correctly. Even though we say that we love God and praise Him at church, maybe we drive our cars home and when God is driving too slowly in front of us (although He is disguised behind the face of another person), we curse Him and get angry at Him. All you have to do is forget for just one moment that the test is going on, and that God is disguised behind the other person, and you can make a mistake that will lead you to fail the exam.

The devil asks again and again: 'Do you really love God? Do you love Him when He is poor, or do you love buying things for yourself more? Do you love God when He is in the Sunday mass, or do you love sleeping in more? Do you love God when He is a dumb person, or do you enjoy making jokes to tease Him more?'

In this world, very few people really love God. One could go to a mosque in the Middle East and the people will shout 'God is great, God is great!' and they praise God, bowing down to Him, heaping up such lofty titles on Him, and then they hate Jews or other people. They chant 'death to Israel! Death to Israel!'- they are basically saying: 'we hate God! We hate God!', but they don't understand that this is what they are saying because they still live in this world with all of its guises and God has not yet taken off His mask yet.

Even if people say with their lips that they love God, by their actions they say that they love other things more than Him. They would willingly sacrifice their relationship with God to attain other things, thus proving how false their love really is.

The devil enjoys this, because it comforts him to see this thing he envies and hates to do something so stupid and ruin itself. Like a narcissistic woman who enjoys seeing her rival humiliate herself with a poor choice in fashion, so does the devil enjoy seeing us sin.

The greatest blessing that a human being can have is not being loved, but it is to possess love inside of oneself. This is the thing that the angels could not stop staring at.

To be a good person is worth more than all the money in the world, it is sweeter than the sweetest of foods, it is wiser than all the wisdom of the world. It is easier to conquer an entire empire than it is to conquer oneself, and those who do so inherit the greatest kind of glory.

Socrates was right: it is better to be a virtuous person who suffers and is hated by all, than to be a wicked person who enjoys happiness and the love of all. The greatest blessing that one can have is to have love; and the devil knows this as a reality.

This is the meaning of the book of Job: the man who is truly blessed is not the one who is loved but the one who loves, if God takes everything away from a man, all comfort, dignity and praise, but he still loves Him, then he is still richer and more blessed than everyone else who has the entire world but lacks love.

We perhaps know it simply just as an idea, which we may not even think about very often.

But to him, it is a reality more real than the physical world itself. He was denied achieving this beauty himself because of his sin, and he absolutely cannot stand the thought that we should be allowed to attain it; he would prefer anything than that we should get this beauty and rise so high above him.

He takes what God created and he deceives it, telling it to eat poison with the lie that poison is good for it. He is like a gangster who meets a teenage girl and addicts her to drugs by telling her that it will make her happy, while secretly planning to make her into a sex slave through the addiction. He is like a doctor who prescribes medicine for a patient that will cause his death, while telling the patient that the medicine will cure him.

If you want to hurt someone, perhaps you will try to hurt their feelings, hurt their reputation, give pain to them, wrong them in some way, etc. And in your mind, this is the way to make your enemy suffer. But you are a human being, and you perhaps don't really understand anything at all.

The way to really hurt a person the most is not by doing any of these things. But the way you may hurt your enemy the most is by making them become a bad person. The worst thing you can do to a person, is not to destroy their reputation, their feelings, their comfort, their livelihood... but the worst thing of all that you can do is to take away their dignity and make them become a monster. If you take away anything your enemy possesses, but he still loves others, then he still has everything... but if you take away the love he has for others, then even if he has everything else, he really has nothing in the end.

And so the devil asks God for permission to tempt human beings so that they may sin and lose the beauty that they were meant to have. He does this all from his envy and hatred.

Like Cain to Abel, like the sons of Israel to Joseph; those two stories are allegorical to Satan and the demons towards human beings. He cannot let go of his own identity and pass the test, and because he cannot let go of his own identity, therefore he must envy and hate human beings as well.

Abel is Cain's younger brother, but Cain sees Abel pleases God more than him, and so out of envy he kills him. Satan is older than us, but he sees that we are able to rise above him and pass the test he failed, and so he seeks to destroy us. For the murder of his brother, Cain is cursed from the Earth and all his offspring are devoured in the flood. Likewise, Satan is punished with endless torment and all of his children have their end in destruction. And yet God, in His mercy still does not treat the devil as badly as he deserves. Similarly, Cain's life was protected and God protected him from being killed by others, even though he deserved it.

The brothers of Joseph, out of envy for the one that their father favoured over them, cause Joseph to become a slave in Egypt, so likewise have the demons out of envy made us slaves to sin. Only through the sacrifice of the Passover lamb would they be released from Egypt, so likewise only through the sacrifice of the Lamb of God would we be freed from sin.

But why does God allow the demons to tempt human beings?

It is for the same reason as the test was given to the angels at the beginning.

If people only loved God because everything was made easy for them, but they stopped loving God the moment it was no longer easy, is their love really love?

Imagine if you said you loved your mother, but if you had to suffer even just a tiny bit for her, you decided to stop loving her. Or if you had a wife you loved, but the moment you found out she couldn't give you children, you decided to stop loving her. If that were so then is your love really love?

Of course it is not. The same is true with God, because if human beings never were subject to temptation and it was always so easy to follow God and obey His commandments, but if the moment they had the slightest suffering or hardship in following His commandments, they then decided to stop loving Him and stop obeying His commandments... would the love really be love then?

This was why when at the beginning of the world, God did not create the angels to see the whole of His face and feel the depth of His love immediately. He created them without any such thing to give them a preference in their choice and allowed them to choose freely; for if He gave them all a great desire for Him when they were created then none of them would have sinned, and they would have all followed Him... but the love of many of them would not truly be love because God knows that they only love Him because He gave them something that bribed them to love Him.

Similarly, if God prevented Adam and Eve from being tempted, then they would have never sinned, but if the only reason why they didn't sin was because they were not tempted, then the love they had was never real love to begin with. It is the same as if your wife loves you when you make lots of money, but when you lose your job and go into debt, she ends her love and divorces you... it only proves that she never really loved you to begin with.

I think it is for exactly the same reason that God does not fill the world with miracles everyday so that every person in the world can believe without any doubt that God is real. For if He did so, people would believe and follow God, not because they loved Him and were searching for the Truth, but people would believe Him just because there was no way to logically believe He was not there; if people all worshipped God because they saw Him as a kind of despot who couldn't be resisted and questioned, then this would not really be love. Thus, God does not fill the world with miracles constantly nor does He make His signs so obvious, nor does He make the correct religion so obvious, but only gives miracles that are much more hidden, miracles that are harder to prove (but still provable), so that only those who really love Him and are looking for the Truth will find Him.

For the same reason does Jesus speak in parables. His disciples asked Him, why do you speak in parables? And He quoted Isaiah and said so that they may hear and not listen, look and not see, so that they may not know the Truth. Why on earth would He do that? Because there is a reason why God hides Himself; if He didn't do so, everyone would follow Him, but the love of many would be imperfect and not real.

One may ask: but couldn't God have simply known whose love was genuine and whose was not genuine without testing? Of course, He did. When God tests people by giving permission to the devil to tempt them, God does not do so because He needs to find the result of the test; He already knows what the result of the test is.

If He already knows, then why test?

This is not hard to understand. Imagine for a moment if the day a baby was born, an angel came to the hospital and announced to the staff: "Sorry, this baby is going to commit mortal sin and go to hell at the end of his life, and so we are going to put this baby into hell now for the sins he will commit in the future."

Now, that would be extremely unfair. If I punish you for sins that you have not committed yet, then I am punishing an innocent person. It is unjust to slay the righteous with the wicked, far be it from the Lord of all the Earth to do such.

Furthermore, this is also an incorrect understanding of hell. The pain in hell comes from a lack of love; if a person in hell loves God, then this person would not be in hell. Their pain comes from a lack of God, and if they had God in their hearts, then where does the pain come from? The baby can't go to hell, because hell comes out of one's own heart, and the baby needs to commit mortal sin first before he can enter it.

Even if a person condemned to eternal hellfire turned their eyes towards God and chose to love Him, despite the torments and the sentence they were under, it would no longer be hell for that person. If someone in hell looked at God and said, "God, forgive me! I sinned against you and I deserve my punishment! Now even if I must stay in this place forever and be endlessly tormented, I will choose to love you even still!" And this person could not be in hell anymore.

And every person in hell is capable of doing that because they continue to possess free will even in that place; if they were incapable, then their sin is not really sin, because in order for sin to be sin, it needs to be a choice. Heaven and hell is permanent; there is no one from hell who ever goes to heaven, and no one from heaven that ever goes to hell, but what too many people don't understand is that what makes heaven and hell permanent is not God's decision, it is ours.

If the baby died today, it would be impossible for him to be in hell; where would the sparks come from? So, if he died today, he would find salvation, in one way or another. But if the baby only went to heaven and loved because he never received the temptation that other people receive in life and that the baby would have stopped loving and gone to hell, if he had been given more time and some temptations... then the baby's love is not really real. The baby therefore must not die as a baby, but must be given a full course of years in his life, so that the real and genuine choice of his final direction can be made.

God wants people to love Him with all their hearts, all their minds, all their souls and all their strength. If there was never any temptation in the world, and God did not allow the devil to be unloosed (revelations 20) of his bonds in the 1000 years that we live in (1000 years referring to all human history until the second coming) then every human being would follow God without failure. But God would plainly know that their love was imperfect; that they followed Him only because it was easy.

God could not be happy if our love was like this. Thus He gave permission to Satan to make it harder for us to love Him. We would be tested in such a way, that only those who really loved God more than all the wonderful things that God created with which Satan would use to tempt us... only these people who would still love God in the end would be His friends.

The devil's temptation is not causing people to stop loving God, it is merely proving that they didn't love God to begin with. God doesn't allow Satan to tempt people because He doesn't want us to love Him, He allows Satan to tempt people to prove that we never loved Him to begin with, and He can thus fairly separate out who loves and who doesn't in a way that we are capable of accepting as just.

That was my best attempt at explaining something hard to grasp for many people. If you still have not understood, I will make one last attempt.

If you can imagine a conversation like this:

Satan says to God, "May I tempt humanity? May I give them desires for things that are evil, and make them loathe things that are good? May I make it hard for them to love you and obey your commandments and make it easy for them to forget you and commit sin?"

God says to Satan, "But why should I allow you to do that? If I let you do that, you will take many human beings away from me and they shall fall into hell and be eternally damned."

Satan says to God, "In the Song of Songs did Your Spirit not write 'If someone offered all he has to purchase love, he would be roundly mocked.' Therefore, if you give human beings everything they want in order so that they love you, should you not be roundly mocked?"

God says, "I see you only speak this out of envy. You can't accept that human beings will pass the test that you failed; your pride makes you insist that you must demonstrate that they will do even worse than you."

Satan says, "Whatever my motivations, I know that what I ask for is still your will. You cannot turn a deaf error to my accusations, because you know that someone who buys someone else's love is a fool. If I need to pay you to love me, then your love is not truly love; if you act like this to humanity then the church is not your bride but rather she is your prostitute! And I will roundly mock you as such and I will be right, for your own Word says so!"

God says, "But I will have to pay a price for their love. At first they shall be like a prostitute who only loves me because I had to pay for them, but they will grow in love and when they reach heaven they will love me even if I took everything else away from them. They will all go through their own sufferings and crosses, such that even if I paid a price for them at first, they will come to love me in the end such that they would love me even if I gave them nothing at all."

Satan says, "You will pay a price for their love, but most of them will still fail to really love you. That is why you must let me tempt them! Imagine if I gave them no temptation at all, and all those human beings for whom you paid the price were to go to heaven and live with you in paradise, and they told you 'God, we love you, but only because you pay for our love. If you stopped giving us what we wanted for even a moment, we would not love you anymore.' And what kind of paradise is that? How ridiculous would that be? Would you be happy to have people like that as your friends? Would you be pleased for these creatures to be the ones to accompany you for eternity?"

God says, "Of course not. I would have no delight in them if their love was as shallow as that. It would pain me if they were like that. I want nothing else from human beings than their love. Love that is conditional is not truly love."

Satan say, "So, then please give me permission so that I may tempt them, to make it hard for them to do good and make it easy for them to do evil, to make them suffer to do good and to have pleasure in doing evil.

You know that I do not ask you this because I love you but because I hate them, but I know that you will still grant this request because it agrees with your will too. I will force them to choose between love of your creation and love of you. All of those who only love you because you pay them with something and cannot love you for your own sake... these ones I will take away with the temptation and they will become mine. And all of those who really love you, who are willing to forgo and sacrifice everything else rather than lose you, these few…. and I know they are very few... these few you may take for yourself."

God says, "Your plan is acceptable to me. All of those who do not really love me, you may use temptation to draw them out. But I must insist on something: because some human beings will not love me at one time, but they will change their hearts and learn to love me later. Therefore, I will give you permission to tempt, but I will not let you do everything you want to do. You are allowed to tempt only insomuch as the human beings are able to resist; I will not let you tempt more than that, in order so that every one of them, both those whom I know will eventually love me and those whom I know will never love me, will both equally have a chance to love me."

Satan says, "And it will be very unfair if I only tempt those who are going to fail the test and cannot tempt those who will pass the test. So both of them, my children and yours, must be subject to the same test. Otherwise, those who go to hell will be able to say that they didn't go to heaven because they were subject to a test that others were not given, and that if they had been treated like these others, then they would not have gone to hell. That would be very unfair. So, even though your elect are going to pass the test and you already know who they are, to make it fair, you must let me subject your elect to the exact same tests, the same temptations and trials, so that there is no difference between the test given. Let me make them suffer just the same. Let me make them suffer the denial of the fulfillment of the desires you implanted within them so that I can offer them a temptation that gives them a shortcut through sin to fulfill these desires. The test must be completely the same for both of them, even though we already know how they will score in the test, because otherwise salvation is a farce."

It is for this reason we have temptation. It is for the same reason we must have suffering, even if we are good people, because if there was no suffering and we were always perfectly happy, it would be impossible to tempt us with anything, since there could be nothing we lacked. Temptation can only exist when a desire is unfulfilled, and unfulfilled desire is all that suffering is.

In a perfect world, no desire could be unfulfilled, and there could be no temptation, and this would also mean that this test to divide the two groups could also not occur.

The test has to be the same for everyone. If God simply let the devil give temptation (which implies suffering/unfulfilled desire) to those who were going to fail the test, but not to those who were going to pass, then those who went to hell could all say: "I went to hell because God chose that person to be untested and not me. But if he had treated me the same as that person, I would go to heaven." Hence everyone had to be given the same test. Even Jesus and Mary, who had no sin at all, needed to be given this test, for otherwise it would be unfair.

Lord, we pray to pass the test we have been presented with in this life. We pray to recognize that every moment of our lives is simply a hidden choice between to love or not, and help us to make the wise decision always. We pray for strength to withstand all temptations. We ask for these things, if it is your will, in Jesus' name, Amen

IV: The Woman

Adam was made from the dust, and Eve was made from the rib.

Modern developed society is so blind about the nature of the different genders. In the past it was blind to the dignity of women, and in the present it is still very blind to it: today we often think the dignity of women rests in them becoming like men. It has come this way, as a result of erroneous political ideologies, to embrace the position that men and women are essentially the same and that there is nothing that a man can do that a woman can't, and if that is not true, then this means that the sexes are not equal.

This is really foolishness, however. The sexes are equal, but they are not the same. Just as I can do some things which you can't, and you can do things which I can't... so there are things that women excel at better than men, and things that men excel at better than women. They are equal, but not the same.

When God created the two, they were both equally made in His image. A man in his masculinity reflects who God is just as much as a woman in her femininity reflects who God is. God created two big treasure houses, one of them called masculinity and one called femininity, both of them filled with immeasurable gifts and treasures, and they were both equal in value to each other, but the treasures were not the same.

One American dollar is equal to six Chinese Yuan: the value is the same, but the items that make up the value are different. So it is with the treasure in those two treasure houses.

For every gift that God gave to man, He gave a gift equivalent in value to woman. For every gift that God gave to woman, He gave a gift equivalent in value to man.

Thus, men are generally physically stronger than women, and yet women are generally physically more beautiful than men. Men are ordained as priests in God's church, and it is by them that people receive God in the sacraments, the Woman was the Mother of God, and it is by her that people received God in the world. Men have natural interests in the way that things work, women have natural interests in the way that people work. Women are more sensitive to others' emotions and this allows them to work in ways that men can't because the men can't see the emotions of others so well, men are not as sensitive to others' emotions as women, and this allows them to work in ways women can't because they can ignore the emotions of others better.

And when humanity inherited the effects of original sin, they also inherited the bad effects in equal measure.

Men waste the world's time, resources and energy on military concerns, which too often brings about evil through warfare. Women waste the world's time, resources and energy on personal appearance, which too often brings about evil through lust.

True beauty is in cultivating a beautiful soul, unstained by sin, but few women achieve this in life even though it is the highest form in feminine beauty, but many seek after the false beauty that consists in the physical only. True warfare is to fight against the forces of evil, to bring yourself and others to resist the poison in temptation and win the fight against the devil, but few men do this in life and achieve the ultimate form of masculinity, but many will fight against all sorts of people or things in their lifetime that make them angry but are not necessarily evil.

Female estrogen can give cancer later in life, male testosterone kills brain cells at the beginning of life. The woman is cursed with pain in child-bearing which is necessary for the continuance of civilization, the man is cursed with sweat and hard work in order to earn his daily bread, which is necessary for the continuance of civilization.

You see, they are equal in every way, just different. The values add up, but they are composed of different currencies.

Modern scientists will also confirm that their brains are different. Men and women are different not only from social conditioning, which is very important, but also because there are inherent differences.

In the womb, every human being begins life with either an XX or XY chromosome set which genetically sets them as apart from the moment of conception. However, in the beginning stages of foetal development every foetus starts in the womb developing as a female. The brain also begins as a female brain as though it were the default state. Around 8 weeks in the pregnancy, if it is a male, then the foetus will have a boost in its testosterone which will permanently alter the brain to make it male. The testosterone will kill part of the boy's brain, which the girl still retains, and increases the brain in other areas.

The part of the brain that is killed is associated with communication, relationships, emotions and emotional memory. The girl retains all these things, while the male still has them, but just has these areas reduced in size. The Creator still made them equal though, because the male brain, on average, will be slightly larger than the female brain by the time they are adults, it will just lack development in those particular areas.

Thus, from the womb they are already set apart. Scientists have done experiments in taking newborn babies, both girls and boys, who have experienced no cultural indoctrination whatsoever, and they give them a choice of looking at a face or looking at some mechanical object, and the boys will more frequently choose the mechanical object to look at than the girls who will more often choose the face to look at.

The result of this helps produce differences in interests between the two. The boy has a greater interest in the way things work, whereas the girl has a greater interest in how people work. These are simply generalities, and there are of course many exceptions.

Even in the sexual act, the man's brain is wired to think of the woman as an object... a beautiful object... but an object of the created world, whereas the woman's brain is wired to feel pleasure in submission to another person who loves her.

To men, God gave a vocation towards the entire created world, whereas towards women He gave a vocation towards the one thing in the created world that was more important than everything else.

A lot of people, for too long in history, have noticed the treasure present in the man's treasure house without paying attention or even realizing what was inside the woman's treasure house. The man could excel at engineering, mechanical arts, invention, warfare, politics, science... so many things... while the woman was taking care of children and families.

Humankind foolishly thought that the former was more important than the latter, when in fact the vocations were equal. A woman who stays at home and took care of her family was just as important and vital to society as the man who sailed around the world; because the man who sailed around the world also had a mother who formed him both physically and psychologically, without which he could have done nothing. God's thinking is not human thinking. Human beings only think of what they see immediately, whereas God sees everything.

Frail human thinking therefore thought that what the man did was more important than what the woman did, and in their foolishness human beings thought that women had to become like men and do the things that men do in order for them to be equal in dignity. Their error was in fundamentally failing to recognize how great and important a duty it was to tend to a family, and be the pillar that the whole of society would stand upon.

The entire created universe was given to the vocation of

the man, but the most important created thing in the universe was given to the vocation of the woman. They are equal in every respect.

Even if the man can more greatly excel in building structures, discovering scientific laws, inventing things, possessing power and strength... one must remember all the angels were staring at the human being as though all those others things never mattered.

The woman has talents with understanding and communicating with people which are greater than what the man possesses. She will understand the human being better than he does. She will be able to communicate and converse with people better than he will. She will be better at forming the characters' of children than he will. She will understand how people feel and think better than the man does.

It is not simply a brain difference but it is also a difference in the way that God made the spirits of either one. A male has a male soul, and a female has a female soul. The gender of the individual is permanently a part of the person's soul. Similarly, an angel has an angelic soul, and it is permanently different from a human soul.

The characteristics of the soul are things we cannot see with our eyes or perceive with our senses... they are invisible. But the visible world and especially the person's physical body will manifest the invisible things that lie within the person's soul. I do not mean only by this, the way a person looks or the way their body is configured... these things are part of it too, but I also mean every physical action, word and thing which the person does in his life in this physical world is in some measure a manifestation of the characteristics in the invisible soul.

I know that this is true, but it is also something which I do not understand so well myself. I do not think that God made my soul with the intent of explaining this all, but simply in writing a general introduction to it; there must be another person he made or will make who has that specialized vocation of more greatly explaining this invisible world. It is not my vocation to explain all of this, but just to give an introduction to it from the little I think I know. I should state that I believe the spiritual world has more in it to be explained than all the things in this world; from this perspective, this book really is a very brief introduction, and a fallible one at that.

But with regard to the object of this book, what is important here to understand is that the spirit of the person itself has characteristics. Just like the body has strength, and different people have different strength, so also the spirit has strength, and different spirits have different strengths.

The strength of the physical body only exists because other things allow it to exist. Food, water, sleep, growth, lack of disease, exercise... all these things are necessary in order for a physical body to possess strength. And all these things only exist because God has created them and granted that human beings should be allowed to have them. If God did not give permission for a person to have these things, then that person would not have them. And every person who does not have them does not have them because God gave permission for the person to be deprived of them.

Hence the strength of the body is not quite something that a person completely gives to himself, but it is rather something that God permits the person to have.

The strength of the spirit is the same; it exists because of God's granting of it.

I don't know what the right word to describe this 'strength' is. Simply calling it 'strength' is misleading, because it is not actually 'strength', as we would understand it, because it works a little different than the strength of the body. So if I keep calling it 'strength of the spirit' it is going to be misleading people about what it is, even though I really don't know another word.

In order to make it less confusing, I am going to take a word from a different language and use that in reference to the thing I am talking about. I will use the Irish Gaelic word 'tionchar' which means 'strength' but it also can be translated as 'force, impact, influence, effect'.

So the tionchar of the human spirit refers to its ability to communicate with God and His angels (through whom God speaks through).

Hence to just call it 'strength' is a misleading word, because that would seem to imply like the spirit of the person had the ability to force an answer from the higher powers. The truth is that the spirit has no power at all to cause an answer, but rather God (who acts through angels) or the fallen angels by their own free will whether to answer the soul or not.

Now, this is the part that I think will be very hard to understand, but it will make sense if I apply it to the physical world. God through His angels will answer people differently and speak to them differently depending on the nature of their soul.

In the physical world, the relationship you have with your mother and the relationship you have with you friend are different. The relationship you have with your friend and the relationship you have with your child are different. You do not speak to them all in the same way, you do not answer them all in the same way. It is not necessarily because one is worse than the other, one is better than the other; it is not like this at all. It is rather the case that to you, one of them will have a relationship like this and another like that, not because they are better and worse, but simply because they are different.

In just the same way as you have a different relationship with different human beings, not because they are better or worse, but rather depending on who they are, so it is also with God. God has a different relationship with His creatures, not because they are ultimately better or worse than one another, but because they have different identities which give them different relationships with Him. The relationship He has with His Mother, and the relationship He has with Joseph are different. The relationship He has with Joseph and the relationship He has with His apostles are different. The relationship He has with His apostles, and the relationship He has with a nun in a monastery are different. The relationship He has with a nun in a monastery and the relationship He has with a poor peasant widow in the mountains of Ecuador are different. It is not because one is better than the other, it is just because they were created differently and they have different relationships with Him.

If you understand this, then you can then understand this concept I am introducing which I will name 'tionchar'.

The meaning of the concept is basically that in prayer, people will receive answers from God differently on the basis of their identity that they are created with. This identity is known to the Father before the person is created; even before the beginning of the world. The person herself may have no idea of her own identity, but it is known to God and He will speak and listen to her differently, on the basis of this identity she was given. This is her tionchar.

Speaking generally, men are stronger than women. At the same time, however, there are many things that women do better than men.

In their bodies, men generally are physically stronger. Men, lacking the same degree of sensitivity towards others that women possess, are also able to do so many things that are harder for women because she feels greater emotional pain than him; she often gets stopped before he does because of the fear of what others say or think. His brain is also slightly larger than hers. He has interests in so many things that make him to excel in the material world and become the master of politics, governments, economics, etc. In all these ways, men are stronger than women in this world.

However, there are many exceptions. There are women weightlifters who can lift more than most men, there are female soldiers who are tougher than most men, there are female rulers who are more powerful than most men, etc. But generally speaking, the male is stronger than the female, and it is usually easier for him to dominate her than for her to dominate him.

It had to be the case that women needed some strength of their own, even if it didn't reach what men could so, because otherwise they could not truly be companions to men as they were created to be. For to be able to do these things yourself gives you a better ability to relate to someone else who does these things too.

But, remember that the Creator made them equal. For every gift and blessing He put in one treasure house, He gave one that was equivalent in value in the other.

Generally speaking, women are better at communicating than men are. They are often more in tune with what others are thinking or feeling than men are, and are often better at influencing other people's feelings than men are. In short, they are better at relationships than men are typically. [1]

The sexes could be effectively divided from each other by saying that males are designed to be masters of all the creation and females are designed to be mistresses of the one thing in the creation that mattered the most – the human being. It could also be divided by saying that males are masters of work and females are mistresses of relationships.

However, there is entirely higher dimension to this whole dynamic as well.

The creation is to be used for what purpose? Answer: to serve God and human beings.

God created Adam to be His friend and companion. Adam used his work in the creation to serve God. God created woman to be a companion to man, just as how He created man to be a companion to Himself.

Paul said man was created first and woman was created

---

[1] In the first version of this book that I published in August 2016, this entire section about the male relationship to God was not present, because I thought that women had superior tionchar, and after some meditation and re-reading of scriptures, I came to think I had made a serious error in this part, which led me to rewrite it.

for man, not man for woman. He also said that man is the head of woman and Christ is the head of man. Paul said that man is the image and glory of God and that woman is the glory of man.

In other words, one could say in a certain way, that what a woman is to a man, is what man is to God. She is created for him, not him for her, and she is by nature designed to please him. And not just him, but any human being, whether male or female, she is designed to serve and please.

In the same way, the male was created for God, designed to obey His laws and please Him. Every man is meant to be a companion to God and to please God, just as how every woman is meant to be a companion to other human beings (male or female) and to please them.

She is a mistress of all relationships, but there is one kind of relationship that the male exceeds her in, which is the relationship to God directly. Women are better at relationships with all other human beings than men, but they are not better at relationships directly to God than men.

Boys are designed to seek something higher, some greater purpose, some greater struggle to put their hearts into. The purpose, the struggle, the higher thing that they feel a calling to serve is God... although many boys, confused by the effects of original sin, will serve other things instead as though those things were the ultimate purpose. But even if they are led astray by sin to serve a created thing, their original nature is to serve an uncreated thing.

To put on the uniform, to salute the flag, to march toward the higher calling, to offer the sacrifice to heaven... it is something which fits the masculine nature more than the feminine as a generality, but not an absolute. But that is not a statement of superiority, however.

Girls are designed to please other people, to make other people happy, to try to turn human beings from strangers or enemies into a family of brothers and sisters. However, girls will often be confused by the effects of original sin and seek to serve themselves rather than other people. But even if they are led astray by sin to be selfish, their original nature is to still be selfless.

To turn the company from just a place where people are working together by circumstance and contract into a place where people love each other as a happy family, to remind the husband to stop thinking so much about other things and to take some time to think about what their children are feeling, to turn isolated neighbours into friends who talk with one another… it is something that fits the feminine nature more than the masculine, as a generality, but not an absolute.

The vocations are completely equal. God and human beings are both meant to be equal in the marriage at the end. If women are inferior to men, then it means that the one she is the glory of is inferior to the one he is the glory of. In other words, if men and women are equal, then God and human beings are equal, but if they are unequal, then God is more important than us.

The design of the Trinity, I here remind, was to make friends and not servants, however, and They do not consider themselves more important than human beings. It was human beings who introduced the idea that we are the slaves and God is the Master, but He came to serve and not to be served.

In Islamic countries or other places where women's rights are trampled upon, it is also in the same places where the idea of God being a master and us being inferior is so greatly enunciated.

In communist countries or other places where women are regarded as equal to men, it is also the same places where human beings are considered as not at all being servants or slaves to higher divinities.

The communists are wrong because God is real, and we

were created to serve Him, but the Muslims are wrong as well, because God wants us to be a companion to Him, as an equal partner in a marriage, and not as a slave or a dog.

It is not a bad thing to be submissive; the submissive person is not worse or inferior to the one she is submissive to – Christ Himself came to Earth to be a slave to human beings and give up Himself for their sake.

It is not better to be a man than it is to be a woman, or vice-versa. They are simply two different ways of being human and that is all.

In a perfect world without sin, they are equal and no submission would be necessary, because everything that he would want and what she would want, would never be in contradiction with one another. But in a world where sin confuses us and leads us to seek evil rather than good, and the wills of people are not in conformity, it is necessary that the one who knows God should command the one who does not for a family to work, for a state to work, for a church to work or for any institution to work.

Domination and submission were never part of God's original plan.

This was one of the consequences of the sin of Adam and Eve. God told the woman that because she had done this, her desire would be for her husband and he would rule over her. If she hadn't done this, he would not rule over her – it is because of sin that men and women are like this, that slaves and masters are like this, that rulers and ruled are like this, and it is not the original plan. But so long as we remain in this world with its temptations and possibilities to sin, the things that Paul said about women must remain true; she must be submissive to her husband, he is the head of her, she must not hold authority in the church, etc.

God is Spirit and He doesn't take too much attention about whether people are good-looking or not, how nice they smell, how their eyes or their hair looks, how bright their smiles are, how pleasant their voice is, etc. He is rather concerned about whether or not the person is obeying His laws from the heart. An ugly, smelly, unpleasant man who loves God in his heart, will be loved and accepted by God, although not necessarily by other human beings.

However, human beings take attention at those things, and human beings care about those things. God created the man to be a companion to Himself and for the woman to be a companion to human beings, and so it is more in her nature to be concerned of how to please human beings, than it is in the man's nature.

Man was created from the dust and woman from the rib. He is for work for all creation and she is for work with the human being.

Man was created first and then woman, because her existence only makes sense if there is another human being. If she was created first, it would not make as much sense, since her purpose was then for something that didn't exist, because it would not have been created yet.

Adam knew God and Eve knew God through Adam.

So, the male tionchar will have a certainty superiority over the female tionchar for that reason, since tionchar is the way that a person is designed to have a relationship with God.

However, it was perhaps for this reason that Paul insisted that no female should hold authority in the church.

Eve was deceived and Adam was not deceived. Eve knew God through Adam and Adam knew God directly. Eve, by her nature, could not have known God better than Adam, because she was a woman and she was designed as a companion to human beings, not as a companion to God.

When she chose to believe the serpent, she was choosing to believe that she could know the Truth about God better than her husband did. Through making that choice, she committed her sin and by choosing to follow her rather than to follow God, Adam joined in the sin.

If Adam had followed God, whom he knew directly, rather than his wife, then the sin would not have been committed. If Eve had accepted that what Adam said about God was true and what the serpent said was false, then she would not have sinned either.

Eve ate the fruit because she did not believe that God's love was real, as her husband told her that is was real. The devil told her that God was hiding something from her and so she distrusted God, thus taking the fruit. Adam knew that God's love was real, he was closer to God than her, but he loved his wife too much to say no to her and upset her, and thus he took the fruit as well, although he was not deceived as she was.

Paul said that he permitted no woman to teach or hold

authority in the church for this reason. If Adam had done what he knew was correct rather than listening to the woman, then he would not have sinned. The man is meant to be closer to God than the woman, just as she is meant to be closer to other human beings than him. His tionchar is greater than hers, just as her relationships with human beings are deeper than his.

She is meant to discover God through other people, and for that reason Paul tells her to ask her husband at home. But it is not from her, but from man, that God is first known, and therefore she needs to stay silent in church and to submissively accept instruction from those men who do know God.

This would seem to mean that a woman could not be a prophet. Anna the prophetess in Luke's gospel or Deborah in the book of judges would seem to contradict this.

However, one would have to realize that prophecy is not the primary means that a person comes to know God. If a woman has a dream in which she sees God and God tells her something, it may be true, and He may have really told her something, but that doesn't mean that the dream has revealed to her something more than what the priest learns from studying theology and the entire deposit of faith left from the apostles.

A woman can be a prophet and she is still designed as a companion to human beings, rather than to God, and her primary way of knowing God is still through what the priest says at mass rather than what she saw in the dream. Even if God spoke to Eve directly, her main way of knowing God was still through what her husband told her.

Women are the mistresses of all relationships, except for one. Men are the masters of all work, except for one kind.

The work with the human being, most especially in the raising of children, whether biologically or spiritually, is something that women are designed to be better at than men.

And in truth, all work is designed to serve the human being ultimately, and since women are better at relationships with people than men, therefore this kind of work in being a companion to the human being, is something that women exceed at over men, just as how the man exceeds the woman in the relationship with God directly.

Women are saved through child-rearing, does not at all

just mean biological mothering. A boss who takes care of her employees as human beings and not as tools is also doing a kind of child-rearing. A queen who takes care of her subjects as her children and not as her slaves, is also doing a kind of child-rearing. A nun who prays for people and they are reborn in grace, is also doing a kind of child-rearing. Even just the wife who looks after her husband or the woman who looks after her friends (male or female) is doing a kind of child-rearing. Through doing these things well, with all of her heart, she can be saved.

If one were to interpret Paul's words in the strictest sense of saying that women should have no authority at all in the church, one might wonder if that meant that the female Sunday school teachers, the nuns who teach adult catechism, or the women who serve in parish councils... is this all a big mistake then?

In the modern day, one can find lots of nuns who support things that are in contradiction with church teaching, female catechists that water down church teachings to make them more amenable to the people they teach, women on parish councils who support things that are agreeable to others, but in disagreement with the eternal law of God. And these things could be interpreted as modern examples of Eve listening to the snake.

In the strict interpretation of Paul's teaching, this was all a big mistake.

I could be wrong, but I don't think that it is wrong in itself for women to have positions of authority in the church or anywhere else.

Paul said that he did not permit any women to hold authority over a man in the church because Eve was deceived and Adam was not; if the woman obeyed the man rather than the other way around, then the sin would not have happened.

But let us suppose for a moment that Adam and Eve already had a son before they took the fruit. And Eve believed what Adam told her about God forbidding them from taking the fruit so that they may not die, but their son did not believe this. And Eve, who knows God through her husband, believes this and tells her son that he should believe this and tries to stop him from taking the fruit. Could the son say that because Eve is a woman, therefore her words have no authority and he is not bound to follow them?

The same is true of nuns who teach people to obey the commandments of God and follow Jesus Christ in accordance with the church or female catechists that teach the full doctrine truly and correctly... should the males who are under their authority say that they are not bound to listen, because these people are women?

Paul's words, if I interpret them correctly, are pointing at a kind of primordial ordering of the sexes, in that man knows God by himself and woman knows God through other people, therefore woman should listen to man in questions of who God is. Paul also said that woman is saved by child-bearing, so long as she does so in faith and goodness.

I think it should be possible for a woman to hold a position of authority in the church and yet she still relies on others to know who God is, thus keeping the primordial ordering from God. The present church where the male priesthood holds the highest authority within the church and all other ministries (whether it is catechism, missionaries, teachers, etc.) are subordinate to this authority is not in violation of this order, but I could be mistaken.

If a man is a leader, he serves as leader as a companion to God, and if a woman is a leader, she serves as leader as a companion to human beings. She can still exercise motherhood in many forms and find salvation through such leadership.

In the leadership of a church, the question to think about is not what the parishioners want but what God wants. Women are designed to consider more what people think than men, and men are designed to consider more what God wills than women.

But the same is true of any leadership situation. In the leadership of a company, the question to think about is not what employees want, but what God wants. In the leadership of a country, the question to think about is not what the citizens want, but what God wants.

She is submissive to the human beings she must listen to, from whom she knows God, and only then she can direct others. He is submissive to God, in accordance with his conscience, and only then she can direct others.

If I am not mistaken, then Paul's words could be understood as a kind of canon law for the church at that time period and not an eternal principle that the church must always keep. Paul permitted bishops to marry as well, but the later church got rid of that. But, I could be wrong about any of this.

Women are for relationships, men are for work.

Women are better than men at all relationships with human beings, but men are better than women at the relationship with God directly. Men are better than women at all kinds of work with any piece of creation, but women are better than men with work with the one part of creation that mattered the most: the human being.

Women are to have a relationship with God directly, they are to pray and to listen to God's word, but for them this is not as important as the way they relate to God through the human being. Likewise, men are to have relationships with other people too, they are to make friends and to spend their lives with others, but for them this is not as important as the way they follow the higher calling from above that commands them to serve.

Men are to help in raising children, in taking care of people, in doing work with human beings, but they will never exceed in doing this more than women. Women are to speak to God in prayer, to read His scriptures and contemplate His will in their lives, but they will not exceed in this more than men.

But I am speaking here in generalities and not in absolutes. To say that men are masters at work more than women, does not at all mean that you cannot ever have a woman who does some kind of work better than a woman.

Are we to believe that a female law professor knows less about the constitution than a male airplane pilot? Are we to believe that a female doctor is less qualified at healing someone's illness than a male policeman? Are we to believe that a female sniper is less able to kill someone with a scoped rifle than a male chauffeur who has never used a gun?

Of course, women can exceed men in doing work.

Oppositely are we to believe that a father's own son is not as close to his father as a female nurse who looks after him in the hospital? Are we to believe that a woman's husband is less likely to understand her than her female boss? Are we to believe that a male student is less familiar with his teacher than the female taxi driver who drives the teacher to a birthday party one time?

Of course, men can exceed women in relationships with people.

Furthermore, one could speak even further and say, are we really to believe that a woman in a monastery who gives her life to God as a nun and prays continuously, reading the scriptures and seeking to do God's will... cannot be closer to God than a man who barely thinks about God?

Or should we believe that a father who spends many hours every week in taking care of his own children is not as close to them as a female babysitter who comes occasionally?

But, what I said remains true, although it needs to be better explained and interpreted than I have done thus far to make it make sense.

Men are masters of work, women are mistresses of relationships.

In a relationship between a man and a woman, the relationship belongs to the woman more than it does to the man. The relationships between girls are often closer than the relationships between boys. Boys usually don't hug and cry over each other, or share all of their feelings with each other as deeply as girls do; they don't hold hands or go shopping together.

Men and women both have relationships, but relationships are not as big a part of his life as they are for her life.

Men and women both do work with the Creation, but except for the work regarding human beings, this kind of work is not as big a part of her life as it is for his life.

A father will likely be closer to his own children than a female babysitter who comes occasionally, but the female babysitter will be closer to some other human beings than the man is to his own children.

The female lawyer might know the law better than the man who is a plumber, but the man who is plumber will do more with his work as a plumber than she does with her work as a lawyer.

A mother is designed to be closer to her children than a father, but not all mothers will be so, not because they are not designed for it, but because not all mothers take up the role they are called to perform.

A man is designed to be closer to God than a woman, but a nun might be closer to God than he is, because he fails to become like Joseph or the saint he was supposed to be in his own daily life.

If I take the female Olympic athletes, you will find that their scores are usually lower than the male scores in the same sport, however, their scores (the female athletes) still surpass the other 99.99% of males in the world if all these males attempted these sports.

The best athletes in any category are almost always male, but the females who are the best of their sex in that category are still better than almost all males in existence.

If I take the best female snipers in the world, you will find that they are better at shooting a rifle than 99% of males, but there will still be males who exceed them.

If I take the best female lawyers and judges in the world, you will find that they are better at interpreting the law than 99% of males, but there will still be males who exceed them.

If I take the most powerful female rulers in the world, you will find that they are more powerful people than 99.99% of males in the world, but there were still other leaders who were male that had more power than they did.

Similarly, if I take any male who was close to another person in a relationship, one can often find that that other person will still have women in his/her life, whether it is the mother, the wife, the daughter, the best friend, etc. who likely had a closer relationship with that person than the male did.

We are all influenced by other people, both male and female, but the greatest influence upon us will come from the females in our lives rather than the males.

Sigmund Freud interpreted so much of human psychological as being the effect of the mother on the offspring, whether people recognized and admitted it or not.

Studies have found that fathers with daughters are more likely to vote in political elections along lines influenced by their daughters.

God created all things and gave it to man on the sixth day as his gift. All created things were given to man, and the human being itself was given to women. Men own (so to speak) all the stars and galaxies, all the plants and animals, all the civilizations and cities, all the science and technology, all the philosophy and knowledge, all the world and everything in it... and the woman owns him.

Human beings were created too and when God gave the creation as a gift to human beings, that also included human beings as created things also being given as a gift to human beings. And women are the mistresses of them, just as men are masters with work regarding everything else.

With regard to all those women who have so many skills with whatever kind of work, in truth, women needed to be able to do such things, even to do them very well.

If Eve really is a companion to Adam, then she needs to be able to understand Adam and know something of what it is like to be in his shoes and to have some skill at what he can do. In order for a female to be a companion to law enforcement officers, she must also be able to be a police officer and to do that work well. In order for a female to be a companion of scientific researchers, she needs to be able to become a scientist too and know something about this in order to truly be able to relate to them. The same is true of the female Olympian athletes; if they can't be an athletic superstar themselves, then how can they serve as companions to those who are? It is natural and right for women to take part in all the fields of work that men do.

She doesn't need to exceed the man for this, but she does need skill of her own. Paul said that women are weaker than men; I interpret it simply as meaning this.

Furthermore, one should not think that weakness is a bad thing either. For even if such weakness makes it harder for woman in life in many things than it is for men, such things are also opportunities to please God, for that which costed the person more to accomplish will also be a greater merit before the throne of God in the kingdom of heaven.

Paul indeed writes that women are weaker than men, but he also writes that it is in weakness that he is strong.

Oppositely if men only did work and had no relationships at all, then how could they truly do work? For what is the point of building a house if it is not going to be used for a human being? Or what is the point of fighting a battle in a war, if it is not being used to defend human life? Or what is the point of weaving an article of clothing, if it is not meant to be worn by someone?

You serve God by serving human beings, for the apostle John said that if you do not love the one you can see, then how can you love the one that you didn't see? And the Lord said that what you do to the least of my brothers, that is what you did to me. If men just do work without reference to the human being, then their work is pointless and meaningless, and cannot serve God either, hence they needed to have relationships as well.

He doesn't need to be better at women for this, but he does need something.

A man might exceed a woman in a relationship with such and such person, and a woman might exceed men in skill or work with such and such thing, but it remains true that one still came from the rib and the other from the dust, and work will still belong to him more and relationships will still belong to her more.

Now, there is another dimension to this whole dynamic, and we need to go there in order to reach the full depth of what this book is aiming at.

Because, God the Son is a human being, and the entire Trinity manifested through Him. And if women are better at relationships than men with human beings, then should that not also mean that women are better than men at relationships with God, who was a human being?

Furthermore, the spiritual world is only persons, with no objects. The spiritual world where God and the angels reside is nothing more than just persons; there are no objects. The objects are all in the material world. Every human being at all times is in both. Whether living or deceased, your physical body is always in the material world, and whether living or deceased, your soul is always in the spiritual world while linked to the body in the physical world. The angels who have no bodies are watching the material world and governing it. The residents of heaven are always looking upon the material world. The inhabitants of the spiritual world are alive or dead, depending on their relationship with God, and not really depending upon the biological state of the body.

Furthermore, God the Son is a male, and the entire Trinity manifested itself through Him. And how could it possibly be that women could have deeper relationships with people or be better at work with people than the Person who actually created their bodies, minds and souls? The Person who knows their very thoughts from beginning to end and has the answer to what lies within every human heart?

Is it to be believed that the work that He did in saving the human race from sin was something less than the work that women have done for human beings? Does the mother who gives birth to a person really possess a greater influence or understanding of the person than the actual Being who created his soul and knew of him before the world even began?

I need to go very deep with this book in order to explain the spiritual realities and architecture for what they are, and this has to be addressed in order to understand these things correctly. But first I need to deal with something else, before we get there.

Lord, we pray that you help us to recognize and use the full resources of femininity and masculinity as pleases you. Help us to recognize the beauty you gave us in making us as men and women. We ask for these things, if it is your will, in Jesus' name, Amen

V: Tionchar

I want to devote this chapter to going into more detail on the concept of tionchar. This is not an easy thing to explain, and while it makes sense to me, I am honestly not sure if I can explain it well, but I will try my best.

Maybe start with this thought...

If God wanted to, He could do all the work in the world, and we would just be spectators to it. He would make our bed in the morning, He would drive our cars for us and we would sit in the passenger seats, He would write our tests for us without us having to touch the pen, He would plough the fields and harvest the crops, He would do everything. But if God did everything and we just watched it, then how could we ever love?

In order to give our love to God or to people, it has to be carried out using created things. God created all the creation for this purpose.

The physical universe is the place where love can be carried out. All of the space and time that was created by God, and all of the things that occupy this space and time, are simply the opportunities God gives to human beings in order to perform the love which is the end goal of their existence.

Love involves actions, words and thoughts. Love is something that transcends these things, but it is performed with these things. If a person possesses love for God and neighbour, then they will use actions, words and thoughts in order to please God and benefit other people.

Actions, words and thoughts are things which occur in the physical world. Whether a thought is actually a physical entity or not, I do not know, but it is a certainty that the brain has a relationship with the shape of the thought and the brain exists in the physical world. Because these things exist in the physical world, and it is through these physical things that we choose to either love or sin, therefore the physical world can be understood as simply that setting under which love can be carried out.

Actions, words and thoughts require time to exist. If there was no time, then there could be no actions, words and thoughts, and hence God created time. Actions, words and thoughts require space to exist, and hence God created space. Actions, words and thoughts require matter. They require for people to possess bodies. For people to possess the ability to think in those bodies, to sense, to speak, to move, etc.

But in order to use these actions and words to love other people, there also needs to be many things created. In order to give you a glass of water, I need both water and glass to exist. In order to say a kind word to you, the air that carries the sound and the laws of physics that allows the sound wave to reach you must also exist. In order for you to understand the word, language must exist and you must have a brain that is capable of learning the language. In order to hug you, I need arms and you need a body. In order to kiss you, I need a mouth and you need skin. In order to cook food for you, the various animals and plants I use in the recipe must exist, the agriculture that raised them must be instituted, the utensils and fire I use to cook with must exist, and I must be able to learn this knowledge of how to cook from somewhere in the physical world (eg. a cookbook, watching other people cook, etc.)

In order to paint a painting out of love for you, paint and paper must exist. In order for a parent to tuck a child in bed at night, the bed must exist, the blanket must exist, the human body's capacity and need for sleep must exist. In order for the parent to read the child a story, writing must exist and the human brain must possess an ability to imagine things that it does not see at present.

In order to reproach you to get you to change from evil,

because I love you and do not want you to be a bad person, sins must exist and the various ways you can abuse created objects must also exist. In order to tell you to stop smoking out of love for you, the tobacco must exist, your body's ability to become addicted must exist, the laws of chemistry that cause fire to burn material and create smoke must exist, etc. In order to die on the cross for you, wood must exist, trees must exist, iron nails must exist, gravity must exist, blood must exist, loss of blood and exhaustion must be capable of causing physical death of a human body, etc.

The Holy Spirit has inspiration over the whole world, and within every culture. Not only the Christian world, but also the world that never received the true faith; the same Spirit is still present, and inspiring things, even without the people who make the culture being aware of what is happening.

In the Chinese language, the character for wood is 木 (pronounced 'mu'). Why is it drawn like that? Probably because it looks like a tree and some people in ancient China set it down like this. But interestingly enough, another observation can be made, which the people who created these characters in ancient times were probably not thinking of at all. In Chinese the character for a human being, or a person, is 人 (pronounced 'ren'), and if you want to draw wood, you first draw a cross 十 and then add a person 人 and there is the etymology of wood 木 . Through a tree, sin would come into the world, and through wood sin would be defeated in the world. And God came to Earth to work as a carpenter for most of His life, and the work of carpenters is to cut down trees and transform their wood into something useful. That was all that the Son of God was doing in this world as a carpenter: taking one tree at the beginning of human history and crafting it into a cross.

The reason why the tree was created, why the wood was created, was because of this purpose of providing a way for which this kind of love could be given. God did not create the tree first, and then think later on how He would use the tree as an opportunity to love human beings, but rather He loved human beings first and created the tree for that purpose. The meaning for why it was created, as the Spirit perhaps inspired in the Chinese language, was entirely contained within the man 人 on the cross 十 which gave the wood 木 its meaning. It had no greater meaning beyond that. Every other created thing in the universe is the same.

The physical world was created by God in order to provide an opportunity to love. All the time, space and material which occupies it, are simply ways by which we can give love and receive love- they have no other reason for their creation than that.

In other words, it may be put like this: God created the tree, in order so that you could take its wood to make something out of it to give out of love. He created your tongue and voice in order so that you could say nice words to other people. He created your mind and intelligence, in order so you could use it to think of ways to love other people. He gave you the capacity to create technology, so you could use this technology to love people. He gave you legs so you could walk to places you need to go to in order to give your love to others. He gave you the law of gravity in order so you could push your child on the swing. He gave you reading and writing in order so you could write things to help other people out of love for them.

And these things also have quite a large number of different uses. God made the flower, so you could grow them and give them to your mother on her birthday. He also made it so you could give it to other people. He also made it so you could feed bees with nectar in order to make honey, and use the honey to give to people out of love, or to sell in order to make money, and then use the money to love people. He also made it because He loves you personally, and knows that you will like looking at it, and so He gives it to you to let you see such beauty. He also made it so you could investigate it scientifically and thereby better understand things in the created world, and then be able to use that knowledge to benefit people. He also used it so you could decorate with it to please the eyes of others. And there are thousands and thousands of other ways it can be used to perform love beyond this.

He also created it in order to tell you something about Himself. That He knows what beauty is, that He is capable of creating things that are beautiful, and that He has glory because what He made shows such glory.

And the greatest love of all is to use such things for their ultimate purpose of bringing people to salvation by being united with the Person who is Love.

Love was the ultimate purpose behind every aspect of creation. All these physical things, all of space and time, are simply together the place where love is capable of being carried out.

This is also why He does not make us spectators, and He doesn't do everything for us. Because if we did, then we could never love.

But not only physical things, but also mental things are likewise applicable to this. He gives us a mind so that we can contemplate Truth, so that we can use our thoughts to love Him and love others. He does not do all the thinking Himself and leave us as blank thoughtless things that watch His thoughts, but He gives us our capacity to think so that we can use it to love.

He is capable of doing everything only on His own, but He refuses to, because He wants to give us an opportunity to love, and therefore He refrains from doing the work, which He instead lets us do.

Not only physical things, not only mental things, but also spiritual things likewise are this way. And this is difficult to understand, perhaps.

God the Father has power over all things. And yet, He does not use even a tiny bit of it until someone prays to Him to ask Him to use it. He can do everything without people (and by people, I mean here both humans and angels) having first prayed for it, but He doesn't, because He wants to give us an opportunity to love. He controls all things: not a single leaf falls from a tree unless He wills it, not a single person dies unless He permits it, not a single second passes by in time unless He causes it. And yet, He only does these things because there is someone who has prayed to Him for it.

In the first chapter of Genesis, the Son prays to the

Father at the direction of the Spirit, 'Let there be light, let there be a firmament, etc.' And none of these things would have happened unless the prayer had been made first.

He is like this for the same reason that He doesn't do all your work for you. He doesn't do all your work for you, in order so that you can have an opportunity to love, because if you could not do any work, because He did it all, then you could not love. Similarly, He does not use any power at all, unless someone first prays for it, because He wants to give you an opportunity to love. If He did everything without prayers, then we would have no opportunity to love through our prayers. Therefore, He made it such that He uses no power until someone prays for it first. Even if floods or hurricanes, wars and disasters should fill a place and cause great suffering, and He desires it to stop, He will not use even a little bit of power to end it until someone prays for it first, because otherwise we would have no opportunity to love.

In the physical world, the angels watch over all creation, and they pray to God continually for everything that passes by in the physical world- such that the angel for the tree asks God for the leaf to fall, and so it falls, your guardian angel prays for you to get over your cold and so you do, and the devil asks God that you die now because of the penalty of Adam's sin you are under, and so you do.

God intended for the universe to be like this. I am here speaking of God the Father. The Holy Spirit and Jesus also make their own prayers to Him.

Furthermore, there is nothing that is able to happen in the physical world unless someone has prayed for it first. You cannot even lift your finger unless someone in heaven had prayed for it. Even just the breath you take is a gift of someone else's love. It is your own decision to do these things, but you would have no power to do any of it, unless it had first been prayed for.

The angels do not have magic powers over the creation. They can see everything that is happening everywhere, and they merely pray to God about something, and God grants it. You can pray to God, and it is the same power.

Now, when God created people He made them different. Each person has a different niche in His creation that they were meant to fit into. Every person, whether human or angelic, was given a capacity to pray. But God decreed that the capacities should be different.

He said, 'I will give a greater response to this person's

prayer than I will give to that person's prayer when they ask this type of request. I will also show myself to this person more than I will show myself to that person under that circumstance.'

Why does He do that?

It is because He intended that people should love in different ways. If I pray for a person to help them, then this is a way of loving them. If I go to the person and do work to help them, this is also a way of loving them. They are both forms of love. However, God created people differently, and He intended that each person would love in a unique way.

And according to the unique way that each person was created to love, He gave talents and capacities to each person in accordance with how He made them.

Let me use an example: suppose there was a man He created so that he would glorify God's law through teaching people the lesson through his work that safety is more important than profit.

And how does God plan to use this man for this purpose? Suppose this man in his life came to work in a factory, and the boss put the workers under pressure to work in conditions that were unsafe and which made the community unsafe, but the man refused to work like this because his conscience did not permit him. And so, the boss fired him, and he had to eke out a meagre existence for the rest of his life because there was no other work in his town. All the other workers do as the boss says, continue working and nothing bad befalls them. They think their former colleague is silly for thinking the way he does. The man, knows that safety is more important than profit and he won't take risks with his life, but he feels great temptation to return to the factory. But one day the factory had an accident and all the workers get killed, and furthermore they release poison gas over part of the town. He, who followed his conscience, in the end still has his life, and his friends who thought he was foolish in giving up the factory job now applaud him. He is not a famous person, but just an ordinary person, and most people will never even know that he existed. And he is a catholic who takes the Bread of God regularly in the mass, and believes that all he did was what Jesus required of him, and thus he completes God's purpose for him in his life, and dies a saint.

And before this person was born, God already arranged everything to be available for him to do this. He gave the person good enough health in mind and body, such that he would always be capable of factory work- because if he was unhealthy, then he would have a different excuse for why he shouldn't work there, but God made him healthy so he could glorify Him through his refusal on grounds of safety alone. He gave him enough intelligence to understand all these things that he would need to understand. He gave him a particular ability to think outside the box, to overlook his context and recognize dangers even when everyone else assumed they were not there, because this capacity was necessary for him to perform his vocation in life given to him by God. He gave him enough time in his life so that he could do all these things. He gave him the right skills and conditions necessary to carry out all these things in order to fulfill the purpose God had for him.

All people were created with the right talents and skills appropriate to what purpose God had for them. The angels were given power through their prayers to create the entire universe and control it, because it is through the voiceless words of the creation that the message of God's glory is delivered. This was the way they were to love, and hence they were given talents and abilities accordingly. We are not able to watch the entire physical universe as they were and control it with our prayers, because we didn't need this ability in order to love. In order, for example, to give the message of God's glory through the creation of planets in other galaxies, they needed to be able to see these planets constantly and for their prayers for these planets to be heard by God. But we didn't need to do this, hence we don't see these planets as they do.

The man in the above example was given his own

particular talents because he needed those in order to fulfill the way he was designed to love. Another person perhaps could not think outside of the box in the way this man could, because this other person did not need this ability in order to love in the particular way that God meant him to.

All people were meant to love through their prayers, and so God gave them an ability to communicate in the spiritual world (tionchar), but the degree and way to which they were to use prayer for love varied from person to person, and hence tionchar is different from person to person. A person is not able to reach as deep a connection through prayer as the one with greater tionchar, because that person did not need that ability in order to love in the way he was created to love.

In order for love to be love, it has to be able to also be refused to be given. This man must also have been able to say no to God's plan, and instead to use all these talents he was given for a different purpose. But all these talents and abilities God gave to him, would still have to be his, even if he said no to God's plan, because if he didn't have them any longer, then he couldn't change and come to fulfill God's plan. So, the talents and abilities must be his, whether or not he follows God's plan.

You can use intelligence for good or for evil. You can use dancing to glorify God or to tempt human beings. You can use nuclear physics to destroy the world or produce electricity. You can use your lips to smile or to frown.

And you don't lose your ownership over these talents because you use them for evil.

But just in the same way as all these things continue to be yours even if you do evil, so also is the ability to pray.

You can talk to God and those who are in Heaven, united with Him, or you can talk to demons. In either case, your capacity to communicate with them is your tionchar, and it belongs to you. When you talk to God or those in heaven who are One with Him, then this is prayer. When you talk to the demons, this is witchcraft.

There is a reason why I needed to invent a word, because I can't just call this 'strength', 'power' or 'influence', because it is not quite like those things.

You have abilities within the physical world which are given to you, because they form part of your vocation, and God intended you to have these abilities in order to carry out love in the world in the particular way which you were meant to love.

Your ability to pray is exactly the same. You have an

ability to pray to God, to speak to Him and to hear what He says, and this ability is different for each person, depending on the vocation they were given and the particular way that God designed them to love. And this ability is your tionchar.

The tionchar of each person is different depending on how God intended them to use their prayers to love.

Now prayer is something that can be done by people in any culture, any religion. Prayer is, very simply, the communication between people and God. It is as Therese de Lisieux wrote, 'a simple look towards heaven'; a glance at God. It is not per se, the monotonous repetition of words to which the person who speaks them thinks nothing about.

Prayer is about communication with God. It is about having a relationship with God. A person can sometimes communicate much with only a glance, and say nothing at all by reading a sheet that no one listens to.

Prayer is about speaking to God and listening to what God has to say to oneself. Every person possesses the ability to pray; but this ability is different for each person, depending on the role that they were given by God and the particular way they were meant to love. This is the tionchar.

Suppose that God created this particular man here with the intention that this man should be a monk in a monastery, and spend most of his time praying to God. And perhaps God intended this person to live in silence most of his life, with little contact with the world outside of the monastery. He prays to God because it makes God happy and because he can help other people with these prayers, by praying for them; and thus, through a prayer life, he lives out a vocation of loving God and loving neighbour.

Now, in order to be able to love God and love neighbour in this way, it is a necessity that his prayers are in fact capable of making God happy and of bringing blessings for other people. If he prayed and prayed and prayed, and yet it didn't make the least bit of difference to God, and no blessing ever came on other people whom he prayed for... then really, he has just wasted all of his time. And if he is not accomplishing anything and he knows that he is not accomplishing anything, then he is not loving anyone, and thus he is not fulfilling his vocation of loving God and neighbour.

Therefore, in order for him to be able to fulfill this vocation of loving through prayer, it is necessary that

God in fact will feel happier because this man prays and that other people will receive blessings they would not have otherwise received because this man prayed for them. Because if it was not like that, then this man could never love. If no matter what I do, I am unable to make you happy, then I can't love you. It is only if I am somehow able to make you happy and you are sensitive to me; only then is it possible for me to be able to give my love to you.

Therefore, God gave tionchar to the monk in order so that he would be able to hear God well enough and to be able to speak to God, and he gave him such tionchar that he was in fact able to bring blessings upon many people with his prayers and to greatly please God through these prayers.

In other words, this is to say, that God had a special relationship with this monk which He didn't have with many other people in the world, not because he was better than others, but because he was created differently from others and was designed to have this relationship. In the same way, you have a different relationship with the person who sits next to you everyday versus the person who you meet once a month; it is not the case that one is better than the other, or even that you love one less than the other, it is just the case that they are different and your relationships with them are different.

To return to our example:

But perhaps there is a different person who God created not to be a monk, but perhaps God wanted this person to be a school teacher. Let us suppose it is a woman. How does she love in this world? Unlike the monk, she has many people around her, and she lives in a society. However, she is not married. She has children that she teaches in the classroom, she has other teachers she meets with regularly, she has girl friends that she goes out with, she has parents that she talks to every week, she goes to stores and buys things and interacts with the staff... all around her are opportunities to meet people, and in all of these opportunities there is always the opportunity to either love them or sin against them. She can be good to the children in her classroom or bad to them. She can be polite to the other teachers or be arrogant to them. She can be supportive to her girlfriends or be selfish towards them. She can be respectful to her parents or disrespectful, etc. And in life, God requires her to be loving towards all these people that she meets every day and that is her vocation. In order to live this vocation, she needs to possess enough intelligence to understand how to love in the way she was created for, enough strength in order to love in the way she was created for, enough abilities to be able to love all these people in the particular way she was created for.

The monk in the above example, he will also have an opportunity to interact with other people, because he was not born in a monastery, but he was raised as any other person was, and furthermore, within the monastery there are also monks whom he will interact with daily, but his level of this kind of interaction will be greatly less than that of other peoples. The girl in the above example: she was also intended by God to have a prayer life and to spend some of her time praying to God, in order to please God and help other people by praying for them. However, God did not intend that she should be spending as much time in prayer as he should. It is not as important to her vocation in how she carries out love in the world as it is important to his vocation in how he carries out love in the world.

Therefore, when God created them, because he knew full well what their respective vocations were, he gave them different talents accordingly. He perhaps cannot be a social butterfly and have relationships with people as well as she can. However, she does not have as deep an ability to go into the spiritual world as he does.

When she prays, her prayers are able to make God

happy and to bring benefits for others, however, not in the same way as his prayers. They have different tionchar because their vocations are different. God only intended her to perhaps pray an hour a day, while He intended him to pray for the whole day. He will help more people with his prayers than she will, even if she spent the whole day in prayer like him. And she will benefit more people through her relationships than he will, even if he spent all his time around other people.

Why is that?

It has to be like that, because their vocations are like that.

Think of it like this:

Imagine if the two of them switched places and lived each other's lives. So, the reclusive quiet monk becomes the school teacher, and goes out with girl friends who are always talking, talking, talking, meets all these people every day and has only an hour of time to pray. And we take the girl who is spending most of her time involved in various kinds of relationships with people, and separate her from most others, put her in the monastery in complete silence and get her to spend almost all of her time silently meditating and praying to God.

If he was able to be able to give love to others in all

these relationships even better than she was, and if she was able to please God more in her prayers and to bring greater blessings upon people than he did, then switching them is the right thing to do.

If you have a hockey team, and one player is better at being the goalie and the other is better at being the forward, why would you put the former player as the forward and the latter as the goalie? If you want to win the game, reversing them is the better course of action.

In exactly the same way, if you want to make God and others happy in this world, then you would put each person within the particular role that they are able to fulfill the best. If the girl can do the monk's job better than the monk, and if the monk can do the girl's job better than the girl, and so if the girl lived as a monk she would make more people happy, and if the monk lived as the girl, he would make more people happy, then they ought to reverse the roles in order so that they can love better.

However, God did not intend for the girl to love like the way the monk loves, nor did He intend the monk to love the way the girl loves, and therefore He has to make it such that the monk can benefit more people through living his life and the girl can benefit more people through living her life, otherwise it would logical to switch them, and thus God's plan for how they should give love in this world is no longer sensible, since in that case they can actually benefit more people by going against God's plan.

Therefore, if the girl joined a monastery and lived like him, spending the same amount of time as he did in prayer, her prayers would be incapable of pleasing God as much as his prayers, and they would be incapable of bringing about as many benefit for others as his prayers would be able to do. They were both gifted with different tionchar, and one can do more in prayer than the other can. She can accomplish things with her prayers and bring benefits to others with her prayers, but she can't do it in the same way as he can, because her vocation is different. It was never God's will that she should be able to love in the same way as he can.

If she could pray as well as he could and live her life as well as she could; that is to say, if she could do both his vocation and her vocation at the same time, then this man no longer has anything to give to the world. Therefore, it had to be the case that she was unable to do the things that he did, unable to reach the same degree of spiritual listening and speaking as he can, otherwise he would be unable to love, since she would fulfill his role for him, and he would no longer be necessary for anything. It is for the same reason why God doesn't do everything and make us all spectators, even though He is capable of doing everything; He doesn't do this, because He cares about nothing other than love, and if He did that, then we would no longer be needed for anything, and we would never have an opportunity to love.

Now, tionchar is far more complicated than simply saying that one type of tionchar is greater than the other, as though it was a number we could apply to a person. The truth is that this girl will still be able to do things in her prayer life that this monk cannot do in his, even though he should help more people in his prayers than she does with hers. It is just like saying, that there will be ways that this monk can bond and make friends with other monks that this girl cannot do, even though personal relationships are going to be a much bigger part of her life than his.

Because the way that people pray in the world and have communication with God is really very diverse, and God intended that it should be diverse, and He gave very different kinds of tionchar to each person.

It is the same as saying that you have different relationships with different members of your family. Some of them you may listen to more than others, and you may give different answers to their requests of you depending on who they are, and you may have different things to say to them, depending on who they are, but they are all equally your family. Some of them you may talk with you more than others, some of them may influence you more than others, but this doesn't mean that you love them less or that one is worse than the other, or that one is better than the other. It just is this way because they are different people. Tionchar is like this.

Depending on how the person is created, the relationship God has with them is different, the way that they influence Him or He speaks to them is different. This is the tionchar of the person.

There is nothing that happens without someone praying for it first, whether this person be human or angelic. Every leaf that falls from a tree, every electron that spins around an atom, every drop of rain that hits the ground, only does so because there was an angel, who is a person, and possessing a mind, with thoughts and feelings, who is watching these things, who can see God's glory and love being shown through them, and who prays to God and says 'Lord, make the leaf fall from the tree now so you may be glorified by it. Make the electron spin around that atom another time, so that you may be glorified by it. Make another drop of rain hit the ground, so you may be glorified by it' But if the angel didn't pray this, then it would not happen. And the angel whose role is giving messages through the created world lives out his vocation of loving God and loving people through this, because He pleases God by this prayer and the object serves human beings who benefit from it, who may see God's love for them through it and give thanks back to Him for it.

All these things operate according to physical laws, because the angels prayed that all these things should occur in recognizable patterns. And they asked for it, because it was God's will that it should be thus, otherwise human beings would never be able to be masters of the world. But, all things operate only according to such laws because there are angels watching each and every thing in the physical world and praying for them so that these patterns would occur.

The angel watching this physical object also has tionchar. If the angel were to pray like the monk did, and was praying for the salvation of the souls of people, God would listen to him, but he would not listen in the same way as he would listen to the monk, because it was not God's will for this to be the angel's vocation inasmuch as it belonged to the monk's vocation. However, it was this angel's vocation to love through his prayers for this physical object. Hence, if the monk were to point his finger at a tree and say 'Lord, I pray for the leaf to fall from the tree now so that you may be glorified', perhaps no leaf would fall... he might have to wait until Autumn in fact. But if the angel pointed his finger at the tree and said the same prayer, the leaf would fall immediately every time, even if it wasn't Autumn, but the angel would not ask for the leaf to fall in a way that broke the recognizable patterns that we call scientific laws unless it was God's will to do a miracle and remind people that it was persons and not laws that are behind the workings of the physical world.

This angel has a lesser form of tionchar than the monk, because making the leaf fall from the tree for God's glory is less important and less needed than the salvation of your soul, but the angel has tionchar which is different. There are things that the angel can do with his prayers that the monk could not.

The plant on your windowsill is growing because there is an angel asking for it grow so that God can be glorified and it can benefit you or others. The black hole is absorbing light and matter because there is an angel asking for it. Nothing happens in the world without prayer.

And the angel will have a better understanding of how God is pleased with the leaf falling, then you are, because that was necessary for his vocation. He needed to know how God is pleased by the falling leaf, in order to know when and how to pray. Everything there is to know about how the falling leaf reveals God's glory is spoken by God to this angel who delivers the message to others, and the angel had to be able to hear what God said about this better than others. If there were other people who could hear what God said about the leaf better than the angel, or if they could please God or benefit others by this falling leaf better than the angel, then just like the monk and the girl, that would mean that he was no longer necessary because others could do his vocation for him and he would no longer have an opportunity to love.

All tionchar everywhere is like this. Every person is able to hear God differently and to get an answer from God for their prayers differently depending on how God created them and how He intended them to use this in order to love.

We are given different abilities in the physical world because we have different vocations and love in different ways, and the spiritual world is the same; we have different tionchar because our vocations are different and we love in different ways.

There is no person who doesn't need someone else to be happy, because if there was, then we would have no opportunity to give our love to this person.

So, for example, two people can both pray for the same thing, but God perhaps give a different answer to them, depending on who they are.

Mother Teresa said that the greatest kind of poverty is to be unwanted. If there was a person who existed that didn't have anything special and unique to them, who could not give anything that another person could give just as easily if not better, then that person would be unnecessary and they would possess that kind of poverty.

There are things which some people can receive with their prayers which others cannot, and this is not necessarily because one is holier than the other, but it is because God created them differently and intended them to love in different ways.

You can have people who possess such great tionchar that they pray for a sinful person and this person repents overnight, but if the same person with the great tionchar prays for her own father, maybe she has to spend decades before he converts. Why is that? It is because God intended her to love like this: God only needs her to spend a few minutes loving the particular stranger with her prayers, but he wants her to spend many years loving her father with her prayers, hence he gives an answer to one much faster than the other, in order to provide the opportunity to love. If God granted her prayers for her father as fast as he granted the prayers for the stranger, then she would have nothing left to pray for him anymore because everything is already granted, hence He makes it such that the answer to one is delayed longer than the other.

It is not like a mathematical equation where you can punch in numbers and come out with the answer. It is entirely about relationship and nothing else. He answers prayers according to His divine wisdom and very often the results are surprising.

The Lord said that if you had faith the size of a mustard seed, then you could tell a mountain to move into the sea and it would obey you. Teresa of Avila interpreted this to mean that God would actually give bigger answers in prayer to those who were less mature in their faith, in order to encourage them (so that their faith grows from being a seed into a plant), but for those who had gone deeper, He would make it harder for them to see such great results.

If that interpretation is correct, it would mean that the answers a person gets in prayer will also vary depending upon how much God wants to test them by His response. A person who gets little or no response from their prayer is not necessarily the person with the weakest tionchar or the smallest faith.

The Lord also said that whatever two or three of you ask for in prayer, it shall be given to you. This would seem to imply that people who pray in groups will get different answers than those who simply pray individually.

The Lord also said that whatever you ask for in my name, it shall be given to you. This would imply that no matter what a person asks for in prayer, no matter who they are and what their tionchar is, they will always receive an answer to what they are asking for. It may not be the way they expect, or when they expect, and if my thesis is right, then it will also be different depending upon the tionchar and vocation of the person who asks for it.

Damien of Molokai prayed in front of a statue of Francis Xavier every day for half an hour to go on a mission. In the end, he went to Molokai in Hawaii and served in the leper colony. A different person who made the same prayer in front of that statue every day might get an entirely different result depending on the way that God created the person and the way their relationship with God was intended to be. This is my thesis regarding tionchar.

A particular person perhaps has the ability to ask God for a miracle and God grants it immediately, but if they ask for a war to end, maybe it doesn't end until after a long time. This was because God perhaps intended for more people to have the opportunity to give their love by praying for the end of the war and for more time to be spent on it, so therefore he doesn't give the answer as fast.

Of all the things to ask for, it is praying for the human person, and especially for the salvation of the person, which is the one that takes the most to get an answer to. The human person is the most important thing of all the things that were created. To bring a person to leave sin and love God, is the greatest gift that you can give to a person. To ask for anything else for them, whether it be health, the solving of various problems, a good spouse, etc. it is something less than that. Therefore, prayers for the salvation of people, for the elimination of their sins and the filling them with virtue, are the things that will require the most time and effort in order to complete. The reason, is because God intended for us to love like that. He did not want us to spend all of our time praying for material blessings but rather it is for this that He wanted us to spend the most time on, hence He will usually give an answer to those other things faster than this, in order to provide the opportunity to love like this. If we prayed for someone's salvation and it was granted immediately but other things took time, then we would spend very little time praying for the salvation of people and lots of time for other things; but God didn't want us to love like that, so He made it such that the human heart would take more prayer than anything else.

Teresa of Avila said: "Prayer is not thinking much, but loving much." The Trinity cares about nothing else than love, but there is a particular way that God intended for people to love, and the way He answers prayers will be according to that design. The differences in how He answers and speaks to different people in their prayers, according to how they were meant to love, is their tionchar.

If tionchar were compared to the strength of the body you would compare it with different muscles. A person who is a marathon runner perhaps is not a good sprinter, or a person who is a sprinter perhaps is not a good marathon runner. A person can be strong in their arms and weak in their legs, or strong in their legs but weak in their jaw muscle, or strong in their jaw muscle but weak in their finger muscles. Tionchar is like this: people can possess prayers which receive certain results in one thing but not in the other, because God intended for their vocation and the way they would love in this world to be this way and not in that way.

Whatever your vocation is, it is a certainty that there is no one else created in past history or in the future who will be able to do this vocation as well as you. And you are given unique attributes that allow you to do something that no one else was able to do. These attributes include tionchar.

Males should possess greater tionchar than females as an absolute and universal rule, because the relationship with God belongs to men, and the relationship with other human beings belongs to women.

There should also be different men or different women who possess greater tionchar than others within their own sex, simply because it was meant for them to speak and listen to God more than it was for other people. Not every person is called to be a monk or nun, nor is every person called to be a lawyer or a flight attendant.

Throughout this piece, sometimes I write 'greater' or 'lesser' tionchar. And this is a really extreme oversimplification, which carries the risk of making people think like this is a power in the person himself as opposed to being about the relationship. As long as it is remembered that it is an oversimplification, then everything should be fine.

The greater tionchar, is simply the person who prays and can receive answers that are in some important way greater than the person who has lesser tionchar, and who also is able to hear what God is saying better than the person with lesser tionchar. But as I said above, it is not as clear-cut or simple as this. Because the angel for the tree may have really 'tiny' tionchar in relation to praying for the salvation of people's souls, but extremely 'great' tionchar in relation to making leaves fall for God's glory, which was still also part of the work done to bring souls to salvation, and the great saint with great tionchar might get no response at all to what she asks for in prayer, because her faith is no longer a mustard seed.

There are also other factors, however, which go into the way that God interacts with people and how much He answers and speaks to them, and I will write about that a bit later.

Tionchar, just like a vocation, is given to people when they are first created; they do not lose it or increase it because of what happens in the world. A person with one type of tionchar can never become a person with another type of tionchar, nor can a person with great tionchar ever become a person with lesser tionchar. The person with lesser tionchar will never be able to reach the same potential in their communication with God as the person with great tionchar.

Your mother is your mother, your brother is your brother; this can't change. The relationships you have with these people will always be different because of these things that can't be changed. It is not the case that you love one and don't love the other, it is not the case that you love one more than the other, or that it is better to be one than the other, or that one is worse than the other. It has nothing to do with that; it is entirely a question of their identity that they are born with.

Similarly, tionchar also cannot be changed once the person is created; it cannot be changed anymore than a person's vocation can be changed or a person's gender can be changed.

If someone's gender could be changed, then I think perhaps tionchar and vocation should change as well, since a person is then changing from being a companion to God to a companion of human beings, or vice-versa. I'm assuming here that these things can't be changed, although I could be wrong.

Christ told James and John that it was not even in His power to let them sit at His right or left hand in the kingdom, but such a close position was for whom the

Father prepared it. This verse would seem to imply that vocation and tionchar couldn't change, otherwise, could not the vocations and relationships to God of John and James be changed so that they could sit at His right or His left?

Lord, we pray that you help us recognize the tionchar you gave us in our vocation, help us to live and develop the relationship with you that it was given to us for. Help us to recognize the particular vocation you meant us to follow and help us to fulfill it. Help us to have the humility to recognize that nothing makes us better than anyone else except love. We ask for these things, if it is your will, in Jesus' name, Amen

VI: Vocations

Men are masters of work, women are mistresses of relationships.

There is another type of being, however, which should be mentioned and those are the angels.

The angels are neither male nor female, but in the bible, they are often called 'men' (Michael is called a prince, not a princess) and it makes sense as well, since they are companions to God.

By contrast, if someone were to build an intelligent robot, it would make sense to call it female, even if it had no gender, because the robot was designed to serve human beings.

There are three types of vocation for God's children then: male, female and angelic.

A male is a companion to God and a master of work. A female is a companion to human beings and a mistress of relationships. An angel serves as God's messenger, and God acts through him in the Creation.

But no vocation is like another vocation. Each person is unique in all creation and all history.

Each male is a companion to God and a master of work in his own particular way, shared by no one else at any time or place. Each female is a companion to human beings and a mistress of relationships in her own particular way, shared by no one else at any time or place. Each angel is a messenger of God with his own name, unique to him and shared by no other in creation.

And all of them complement one another. They all fit together.

Now, if you can imagine it like this: suppose you had a very big city filled with many houses. Each house had one person who lived in the house, and this person was the master of that house. The houses were all of varying sizes and shapes, with some houses bigger than others and some houses smaller than others. The things inside each house were different, so the interior of every house was unique to that house.

The house represents what position that God uniquely

gave to each person, with some positions being bigger than others and some positions being smaller than others. In the same way, some houses are bigger and some are smaller. But, every house is different, and so every person is different. And inside of each house, the master of that house is master of everything in the house.

And within each house, there are chairs set up for guests. Bigger houses have more space for guests than smaller houses. Whenever someone from outside the house, who comes from another house, enters this one, he or she is a guest and is served by the master or mistress of the house.

Even if someone else from a bigger house came to visit his smaller house, he is still the master of that house and the one from the bigger house is only his guest.

In a similar way does God give talents to people.

So, for example, Joseph, the husband of Mary has a big house here, because he had a great role of being a husband to Mary, a father (an adopted one, not a biological one) of God and of using his labour to give material support to the Holy Family.

He is a patron of workers. One could say that perhaps all

work everywhere belonged to him, because all work everywhere was meant to serve what his vocation was, which was to serve God. He was a companion to God and used his work to serve God.

Whenever someone else comes to his house, they are the guests in his house, and he is the master. When the Virgin Mary enters his house, he serves her and she is his guest. Even though she may be a greater saint than him, and her house is larger than his, she is still the receiver of the fruits of his labour and receives the love given through his own particular vocation.

But his house is quite large, and many guests come to it. The whole church enters his house regularly, because its existence came about from his daily sacrifices in the hard sweat of his workshop, and so the whole church becomes his guest and he serves it by his love. Even though there may be many saints in the church, bishops or people of authority who had more power than Joseph ever had in his life, they are all likewise guests in his house and served by him.

And there are many Catholic workers who enter his house and receive his help from his prayers for them, and they become his guests and he serves them by using the tionchar God gave him to pray to God on account of their work and labour.

There is no one else in creation who has a house like this. If you go to any other house, you will receive different service than in this one.

Now, Joseph is still a great man, let me take a much smaller man.

Suppose there was a certain peasant on the coast of Mozambique who was male and God gave him the vocation of using his labour to warn people about the dangers of sharks when they went swimming, and ultimately serving as a small reminder in this one aspect of creation that the way back to Eden is still not open.

He has his own house too, but it is much smaller than the houses of Joseph or Mary, and yet it is still something important; it still has glory and meaning to it.

There are many other people in history who warned people about sharks, but this man has a unique way of warning people about sharks that is not shared by any other person in any place or time.

This kind of work belongs to him, and in the question of warning swimmers about the dangers of sharks in this particular way, he is the master and even the greatest people created are simply guests in his house, who in their humility must accept his mastery of it.

If Joseph were to come over to this house, even though

it be much smaller than Joseph's, Joseph will still sit as a guest in this house and this man will use his talents to serve Joseph, and Joseph cannot receive the same service anywhere else, nor can Joseph do it himself.

He is Joseph's superior on this thing for which he is master of, even though Joseph is his superior for what Joseph is master of.

People require the aid and love of Joseph more than they require the aid and love of this man, and so Joseph's house is larger and has a larger number of guests. And hence, what the Lord said about those being greatest among you are the servants of all, can then come true.

Now, suppose there is another house over here, which belongs to a great female saint. Let us take Monica, the mother of Augustine, as an example.

Monica's house is smaller than Joseph's, but it is still quite large.

She was female, and her house is unlike the houses of Joseph or the man from Mozambique. In their houses, the master of the house gives his love through his own male vocation, as a worker and companion to God.

Monica, was a female and a companion of human

beings. Her son Augustine is a guest in her house, as are her other family members and children. They received service from their mother, who gave them faith and prayed for their conversion.

Even though Augustine may have a larger house than his mother, he still needs to be in this house to receive the service from her, which he cannot get from anywhere else.

And many Catholics, both male and female enter her house, to receive service from her prayers for them and by learning of her example, so they can also learn from her to use prayer to help people convert.

Even if Joseph or Mary were to come to her house, they would still receive service from Monica and get service from Monica that they could neither find anywhere else nor provide themselves.

Now, suppose I take a much smaller woman. I will take a mother in Chad who is married to a cattle farmer and has four kids.

This mother in Chad serves as a companion to the cattle farmer, her children, her family, her friends and her neighbours in her own particular way in life, which is unique and shared by no one else in any time or place.

And while her house doesn't have as many guests as Joseph's or Monica's, whenever someone enters the house, they nevertheless receive service from her. Even if the person be a great saint, or even be the Lord Himself, when they enter her house, she is there to give them service in her own particular way, which they can get from no one else and cannot provide themselves.

Then there is another house, and this house is for Michael the Archangel. In his house, he serves by giving the message that God is greater than anything else.

In Hebrew 'Michael' means: who can compare with God? The Islamic call 'Allah-o-akbar' (God is great) is also a very apt description of the essence of Michael's message for the world.

His house is very large, although large in an angelic fashion which is different from a human existence. He tells others about God's greatness.

And all angels that serve God are guests in his house, because there is no angel anywhere that has a message that does not also fall within Michael's message that God is great.

And many come to his house regularly to receive his love by his giving of this message to them. It is a message that he did not make himself, but which God gave to him to propagate.

But suppose there is another angel, whose name is not known to human beings, but who has a charge of one particular draughtsboard shark off the coast of Australia. This shark only is going to live a few years, but the angel was created before time began and witnessed all the history of the universe right down to the moment that this particular shark came into existence, and through this shark, the angel would pray to God so that the shark might glorify Him.

And after the shark had died, the angel continues to exist for eternity, with the entire meaning of his existence placed upon that one shark and how God was glorified by it.

And while the guests in his house are quite few: at the most perhaps a scientist who studies the shark, a fisherman who catches it or a tourist who saw the shark while diving; nevertheless, he gives his love to them by giving the message of God's glory through the shark's existence.

The messages of angels are often done with 'voiceless'

songs. Every single thing in existence is serving God's glory, every tree, every mountain, every human being, everything that happens every day, and the arrangement of these things, are all showing God's glory and love.

And there are angels continually watching these things and praying for them, each in a different way depending on the name of the angel, and even though the tree doesn't scream out with audible words 'glory to God!', nevertheless it is pointing at that message and the reason why it is pointing at that message is the existence of the angel who is watching it and praying for it, so that it may thus do so.

The angel, however, has no body. Despite depictions in art with them as people with halos and wings, the truth is that they have no bodies and occupy no physical space. They can see all creation at the same time, but they are not in any particular physical place; they exist in a different way. They have no face, no appearance, no voice, except when they choose to take on such things when they show themselves to human beings. Because they have no body, however, they permanently cannot take the Eucharist, which is reserved to human beings only. They are nevertheless united with the Eucharist and united with the Trinity in a way which is unique for them, which God is nevertheless perfectly pleased with and which they are also happy to possess.

They can take a form that we can see and speak with words that we can hear, however, 99% of the time, they are present without a form we can see and they speak without words that we hear. At least, if you understand seeing and hearing in the normal sense.

But, in reality, their voices are louder than any human voice and they are in fact calling out with words that pass through the whole creation at all times.

This is what I mean by voiceless songs.

Everything in reality, every bit of matter and energy, every thought, every concept, everything, absolutely everything... is just a giant picture being painted by God. But God (speaking of the Father), does nothing unless it is prayed for first. Hence, who is the one asking God to paint the picture in this way or that way, to arrange the matter, energy, logic, all things, like this and not like that? It is the angels who pray Him for this, and they see all of reality at the same time and according to the name of each one of them, and the particular message about God they were meant to convey, they will pray to Him for different things and He will grant their prayers to them.

From the moment you are born to the moment you die, from the moment you open your eyes in the morning to the moment you close them at night, nothing passes through your perception that was not arranged by an angel. Angels, perhaps may not speak with 'words', but in actuality they are speaking more things to you in a day than any human person. Everything you see, in all of reality, down to the last detail, was arranged by legions of intelligent minds who were trying to use these things to say something to you.

They are telling you how much God loves you, how much God loves all people, how great God is, what He is like, how He feels, etc. And the only way to understand the message is by prayer and a clean heart.

There is so much to know about them. Human beings search for intelligent life elsewhere in the universe and try to make contact with it, and yet we don't realize that there actually is another intelligent being, different from a human, which has always existed and who in fact would love very greatly to be in contact with us, if we just turned our attention to them and started talking to them in prayer.

The demons are the same; every gift given to people can be used for good or for evil, and they do not stop being angels even though they sin. A demon still retains the office of an angel in much the same way like how a priest still retains his special character as a priest even though he sins against God.

The demons are permitted to arrange the creation only to a degree, but this degree increases as the strength to withstand temptation increases- the societies which have the most free time to give to prayer, the most developed churches, the most opportunity to get grace from God... these societies shall always be the ones where the demons will be given the most degree of freedom to operate, because the people of these places were given the tools to resist the demons the most.

God permits them to arrange things to give people a false message so that people may be tempted. The vast majority of temptations do not occur with words, but all of them came from intelligent minds who understood their audience. The temptations themselves occur just in the same way that the angelic messages do; a legion of intelligent demonic minds who were permitted to arrange the world around in such a way that you would be tempted, and these temptations do not occur with words. Similarly, the words of angels in the creation do not occur with words, but all of them are planned according to a will, and they are meant to explain something.

The angels do not need to repaint anything the demons have been permitted to paint; the things that the demons arrange in creation can all be left in place, because they will all show the glory of God in the end even though for a time they were used for temptation.

Everything is included within this, even just the feelings that pass through your head or the stains on your walls; they are part of a painting being painted with a meaning behind it, and most of us will not understand what the painter was trying to say until we get to heaven. The angels have it as their vocation to arrange all of creation to reveal who God is. When they actually do speak words, like to Moses or to Mary, they are just using an obvious form and adding it to the many ways that they already speak to people at all times, everywhere.

The angelic houses are far more numerous than the human houses, but in general they tend to be smaller than the human houses, since they were not designed to serve as much as the humans were and to have as many guests as they did.

But even though they may be so small, whenever someone enters their house, they become the masters and that person becomes the guest.

When the Virgin Mary looks at a single flower in the

desert as she made her way to Egypt with the Holy Family, the beauty of the flower was the angel's love for her. Even though she is so much greater than him, she becomes the guest served when she enters his house by looking at the flower.

The same is true for us when we look at that flower, or any object in creation; we then become the guests of the angels who are serving us by giving us God's love through those things.

Whenever people receive love in some fashion from anywhere else, human or angelic, they become guests in that person's house. And no matter where they go, they cannot ever find another person in any place who can give the same gift or service. Each person is unique, each person is vital, each person is necessary.

Now, each vocation is unique. Male vocations are designed for work, set towards one relationship with God. Female vocations are designed for relationships, using work to take care of the human being. Angelic vocations are designed for serving as messengers to the whole creation.

For every type of work in existence, there is a man somewhere who is a master of it. For every kind of person in existence, there is a woman somewhere who is mistress of him. For every kind of way that God's glory can be shown, there is an angel somewhere who has charge of it.

All of the creation is divided up like this. Every part has its own true 'owner', so to speak, who has a vocation towards it.

In ways that are hard to see for human eyes, every single dot and detail in the person's life will point towards this vocation.

This might be a bit complicated to explain, but hopefully the reader can follow the next piece of logic. We are going to go even deeper still than this, however, but this is all necessary to explain the spiritual architecture.

The logic goes like this: every single dot and detail in the person's life all is being painted by angels who are using everything to serve the glory of God. There is in fact nothing in existence that does not serve the glory of God, for if there were, then it would not exist. Even sins do so, like the crucifixion of Jesus.

Every person has a vocation given to them by God, which I separate into three main types: male, female and angelic. The vocation itself is a gift of God, which the person has a choice to either accept and fulfill or to reject and use their vocation for evil rather than good.

Every dot and detail in the person's life is for a purpose, and every dot and detail in the person's life is connected with the vocation that they are given.

It may be unclear to most people in their lives what their vocation actually is, however, every person they meet and everything that they do is all connected with it. For if it was not connected with it, then the angels would not have painted it.

This means, that if it were a female vocation, every person that she meets in her life forms part of her vocation. This includes her children, her husband... it also includes the person who stands next to her on the subway, the person she sees on tv, etc. All the work that she does in life is connected with this as well.

If it is a male vocation, every kind of work that the man is involved with in his life is connected with his vocation. This includes his job, his work for his family... it is also includes the time he sweeps the stairs, the way he drives his car, the prayers he makes, etc. All the relationships that he has in life are also connected with this as well.

Now, for the vast majority of females, the people in their lives will be ordinary human beings, like themselves. And for the vast majority of males, the work in their lives will be the day to day toil given by God to Adam. And those things, all put together, will be the vocations that they were given by God.

The person she did not encounter, was not part of her vocation. The work he did not do, was not part of his vocation. For if it was part of it, then he would have done it and she would have encountered him.

I made a diagram here to try to explain this better.

Ordinary Female Vocation

Ordinary Male Vocation

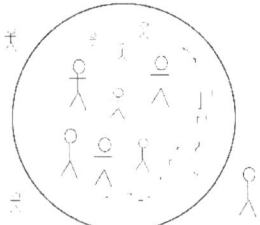

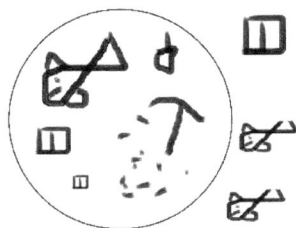

The bigger figures represent the people who are big parts of her life. The smaller figures represent the people who are smaller parts of her life. The little dots and lines represent all the people she barely knows at all in life but whom she still encounters. The dots and persons outside the bubble are those she didn't encounter and who are not part of her vocation.

The different objects represent the different kinds of work that the man does in his life, which are all designed to be used by him to serve God and be His companion. Some objects are larger than others because they form a bigger part of his life than other objects. The tiny little blotches represent the multitude of little pieces of work that each represent little parts of his life. The objects that are outside the bubble represent kinds of work that were not part of his life and did not form part of his vocation.

I assume that this vocation cannot be changed by human beings, just like how Jesus told James and John that He had no power to put them at His left hand or His right. I could be wrong.

Now here we have to reach the deepest point.

I mentioned above that men should have greater

tionchar than women, because God is their head and human beings are the head of women. Men are made as companions to God and women are made as companions to human beings.

Men exceed women in matters of work with all the creation, and women exceed men in work with the human being.

All work is meant to serve God, and if women did work better than men, then they would be the ones to have God as their head and to serve God with their work, since you must give the best portion to God.

Work with human beings must belong to women because they are companions to human beings and relationships with people belong to them, and how could you be a mistress of relationships with people and not be a mistress of the work with people, which is carried out by relationships?

But, there is a detail that enters the picture though in the incarnation of God's Son.

For God is a human being and He is a male. Only the Son is this, the Father and the Holy Spirit are neither human nor male, but it doesn't change anything here, however, because the Son is also manifesting the Spirit and the Father.

If women are companions to human beings, then what if a woman is a companion to Jesus Christ? Is her head man or is it God? Is she a companion to human beings or a companion to God?

The answer is 'yes' to both.

If a man Himself is God, is He going to be an inferior to anyone in understanding a created being? Is the work that He does for the created being going to be less than the work that a woman does?

Of course, it is not, and the work and relationship with human beings belongs even more to Him than any woman ever.

While men should have greater tionchar than women, there is one woman who ought to have greater tionchar than any man who ever lived. Of course, I am referring to the Mother of God.

When God gives out different vocations to each person, He will give talents that correspond to the vocation given. Because the person with a vocation is going to be the unique master in all of creation for that aspect of creation he has a vocation to, this person will also be gifted with abilities that correspond. Hence, if there was another person who was better at warning people about sharks in that particular way than the man from Mozambique I mentioned, then it would not be possible for this man to be the master of that thing, because in fact, there is someone else who can do it better than him. Therefore, there is no other person who can warn people about sharks in that way better than that man. Nor is there a person who does the work that Joseph did better than Joseph. But if Joseph was on the beach of Mozambique and trying to tell swimmers about the sharks, he would not be able to do it as well as that man, because he was never given that vocation or the talents needed to be the ultimate master of it. This is what I meant by each house having its own master and all others who enter are guests within it.

He is a better worker than that man, but only in a general sense to being better able at fulfilling his own vocation; in this man's specific work, Joseph could not surpass him at doing the job of actually telling the people about the sharks. Joseph would need this man's help to do that. But if this man wanted to use his work of warning people about the sharks to fulfill the purpose of all work, which is to bring people to God, he would perhaps need to see how Joseph did it first, or listen to Joseph's advice or get some other help from him, in order to do it. This is what I mean when I say that one is a guest in the other's house.

Mother Teresa in India said that there were perhaps

things she could do that we cannot do, but there are also things that we can do that she cannot do, and together we can do something beautiful for God.

Mary is the greatest person who was ever created. God was not created, and God is greater than Mary, but among all the things created in the entire universe, the soul of Mary is the greatest.

Tradition says that her parents were named Anne and Joachim, and that they could not produce a child. But they prayed to God, and Anne seemingly miraculously became pregnant. They gave birth to a girl whom they named Mary, and when Mary was three years old they took her to the temple in Jerusalem to consecrate her to God. A tradition says that she then grew up in the temple until she became a teenager when she was betrothed to Joseph.

She had been consecrated to God when she was three. There were no nuns at that time yet, but in a certain way she became like a nun. It is worth pointing out that when she appeared to Lucia dos Santos at Fatima in 1917, Lucia said she was dressed in the habit of a Carmelite nun. Her parents probably did not intend for her to be a perpetual virgin when they consecrated her in the temple, but nevertheless at some point Mary

herself realized that God wanted her to keep her
virginity intact. She was betrothed to Joseph, and she
didn't know how it was going to be possible for her to
give him children and at the same time to keep herself
consecrated as a sort of nun.

Mary had a very deep prayer life. She prayed to God
continually and an angel came to tell her the answer to
this seeming contradiction of being both a wife and a
nun. The Holy Spirit would come upon her and put a
child in her womb without the act of sexual intercourse.
This child would be the Saviour of the world, and the
Son of God Himself.

By becoming the Mother of God, she gave witness to
the ultimate form of prayer.

Prayer is essentially communication between God and
His creatures. It can involve talking, whispering,
shouting, thinking, or even just a look or a glance.

Since, prayer is communication with God, what is the
ultimate way by which people can communicate with
God? There were great people, many of them women,
in past ages who were called mystics and who had
visions and they were able to speak words to God in
visions and dreams, and hear answers to what they said.
But what did Mary do?

When Mary became pregnant with Jesus, and gave birth

to Him. She saw God, not as a dream in her imagination or a vision, but as a real physical Person who called her mommy. Through being the Mother of God, she talked to God, saw God, gave milk to God from her breasts, listened to what God said, helped God put on His clothes, exchanged hugs and kisses with God, held God's hand as they walked around, played games with God, cooked food for God, put God to bed, perhaps read stories or sung songs to God, etc. She spent every single day intimately with God, and thereby came to understand how He thought and behaved better than anyone else.

When monks pray on mountain tops for their whole lives, it is still little in comparison to this. When Muslims bow down five times a day to submit to God, it is still small in comparison with this kind of prayer. Teresa of Avila levitated in the air when she prayed and could talk to God in a vision; it sounds impressive, but when she was doing this she still only talked with God as a vision in her imagination, whereas Mary talked with Him in the flesh.

A contemplative nun is someone who lives a very devout spiritual life contemplating the Son of God and the holy mysteries of His life. Contemplatives may do spiritual readings, very long prayers accompanied by fasting, and long meditations in order to contemplate who God is. Mother Teresa founded her missionary order of nuns in Calcutta as a contemplative order that would contemplate Jesus who lived in the poor. Mary was also a kind of contemplative nun; that is perhaps why she appeared dressed in the habit of the Carmelites to the three visionaries at Fatima in October 1917; that is why whenever Mary is mentioned in Luke it says 'she kept these things in her heart'. She was a kind of contemplative nun who meditated on God, not by spiritual reading in a monastery, but by contemplating the God who lived and walked before her eyes and meditating on what He did in His life, 'keeping these things in her heart'.

Mary's motherhood of God, was an extension of her prayer-life. The same God she prayed to when she grew up in the temple, was the same God who she knew as a Mother and by being His Mother she could perceive the thoughts and feelings of God more intimately than anyone else, and could influence Him more deeply than anyone else. Hence, she is the ultimate mistress of what prayer is, and she possessed the greatest tionchar of anyone else, angel or human, ever created.

In Revelations 12, the woman who is clothed with the sun with the moon under her feet, is partly referring to Mary. She is clothed with the sun, because she is very close to God (God represented by the Sun). In art Mary is very frequently depicted wearing some combination of a sky-blue veil with a white dress or some other combination with those two colours; Anne Catherine Emmerich, in her visions, claimed to have seen her wear clothes like this when she was alive. The clouds are white, the sky is blue, and the sun goes across it every day. The sky is deeply connected with our experience of the Sun, just as Mary is deeply connected with our encounter with Jesus. Hence, her clothing symbolically matches, whether she realized it or not.

The human being belongs to the woman, but God is a human being. Each type of woman has a different vocation, which is manifested by the various relationships that she has in her own life. For the vast majority of women, those persons will be ordinary human beings. For the Virgin Mary, the central relationship in her life that formed her vocation was one with a human being that was God.

Just as all creation was given to men, and the part of creation made on the sixth day was given to women, so also God was given to Mary, and she is His possessor. And since God is Truth and Love, one can also say that Truth belongs to her, Love belongs to her... all that God is, belongs to her.

But just as God is a human being, so is He also a male.

And how can it be that the work with human beings belongs to women more than it belongs to God?

A mother gives her child life, but she didn't create his soul, she didn't form him and decide his destiny. There is no woman, no matter how close she is to a human being, who can say that she is closer to the person than God is, or that she knows the person more than God does.

The relationship that a man has to his mother is not more important than the relationship he has to God.

And if God is male, then it must also mean that there is a male who knows the human being better than any female, and who does work with the human being more deeply than any female.

The way that a woman owns the human being is not greater than the way He owns the human being.

Our thoughts, our will, our lives, our decisions, everything we have... all of it belongs to God, and we can choose to give it to Him, as something that belongs to Him justly, or to deny it to Him, and to refuse to let Him have what is His rightful possession. There is no woman who has a right over a human being like this.

Even the Virgin Mary only has rights to such things, simply because she shares it with Him, since she is mystically joined together with Him.

Christ is within the priests and bishops. He is not in them the same way He is in the Eucharist, as though we could put a priest or bishop on the altar and offer him up as a sacrifice to God, nor could we adore him in worship.

However, in a mystical way, Christ is present within the priest and works through him. Even when they make mistakes or they sin, Christ remains within them and acts through them even still, through their mistakes and sins.

While the priest himself is not Christ, he does serve in Christ's place to such an extent that the church belongs to him just as it does to Christ.

The very reason why the priest and bishop must be male is because he is serving in Christ's place as a bridegroom to the church. In other words, the priest and bishop is serving as a husband to the church and for that reason he must be male.

A man does not own his wife to the same degree as Christ owns His church, however. A husband has no right over the soul of his wife; Christ does, however, with regard to His wife.

If the priest is serving as a spouse to the church in the place of Christ, then to a certain degree, Christ's ownership of the human being within the church belongs to the priest as well.

Furthermore, the sacraments performed by the priest are equal to the sacraments performed by Christ. This a profound statement, which many Catholics may not consciously always think about, however, it remains true.

The mass done by the priest today is equal to the breaking of the bread at the last supper. The Eucharist given today is just as much the body of Christ as Christ's actual body 2000 years ago. The absolution of sins given by priests today is equal to the forgiveness given by Christ in the gospel to sinners. Christ is just as much present when the priest does these things today, as when Christ personally did these things 2000 years ago.

If Jesus came back to the world now and He took up work doing mass and sacraments in some parish somewhere, you would not need to leave where you are and to go to Him in His parish, where He was serving, because the priest and the parish near you is just as much an encounter with Jesus as if you actually went to that other parish where He was giving mass. It is a profound truth.

I am not saying that Christ is less than He is, but I am saying that the priest who lives today and the work he does is more than what people think.

And different priests have different levels of authority. A priest without a parish will have authority only over those he gives the sacraments to or whom the church otherwise puts under his instruction or care. A priest who has a parish will have authority over his parish. A bishop will have charge over many parishes that make up a diocese. And different bishops have differing levels of authority. The bishop of Rome has authority over all other bishops in the world, and with them, the entire church.

God is the bridegroom and the church is His bride. In a marriage both parties are equal, although the woman is obligated to obey the man as her head.

A priest has to be a male because he is serving in the place of the bridegroom.

The church is the bride, and it is broken up into different pieces to be governed by different males ordained to the priesthood and episcopate who are serving as husbands to the church.

The Pope is the spouse of the universal church. The bishop is the husband of his diocese. The parish priest is the husband of his parish. And just as a wife is obligated to obey her husband, so also is the church obligated to obey the pope, the diocese to obey the bishop or the parish to obey the pastor.

Now, I believe it is unquestionable from a Christian perspective to conclude that God owns the human being more than any woman does, and since God was a male, it means that a male therefore owned the human being more than any woman.

Although the priest is not Christ Himself, He does share in Christ's nature as a possessor of the church to such a degree, that I nevertheless think it is right to conclude that the priest and bishop, unlike all other men, also have a work that they do with human beings that is superior to the work that women do with human beings.

Even should your mother give you life and she raises you, it is the priest who gives you absolution and the Eucharist that gives you the means to have eternal life. To find eternal life is a greater thing than to have life itself.

Jesus said of the traitor that it would have been better

for that one if he had never been born. For all of the people who end their existence in hell, the statement is the same. In the end, what their mothers did for them by giving them life became something bad for them in the end, since having life itself was not the final goal of human existence.

The sacraments are the means by which people get to heaven. There is no work that you can do with the human being that is more important than this work with the sacraments. And whether it is the priest who gives the sacraments or Christ Himself who gives the sacraments, the sacraments are equal and the same. In fact, whenever a priest gives the sacraments, it is not him, but Christ within him who is giving the sacrament.

Quite a lot of priests will waste the graces given to them and lead people to hell rather than heaven, but that doesn't negate what I am writing. You can use your lips to smile or to frown, but it still belongs to you either way. There is no created person who has a greater responsibility in getting people to heaven than the priest and there is no person who is more effective at bringing people to hell by abusing what he was given than the priest. The ultimate and highest kind of work that can be done with the human being still belongs to him whether he uses it correctly or he abuses it.

Eternal salvation is the ultimate goal of all work, and

there is no created person who possesses this work in a greater way than the priest, who even possesses the church in Christ's place, like a husband to a wife. Despite the fact that he is male, the work he does with the human being is greater than the work that women do with human beings, just like how Christ Himself possessed the human being more than any woman ever did.

Similarly, Mary has a relationship with God that surpasses what any male can have, including the priest, including even the apostles.

God is the head of this woman, because the human being who occupied the centre within her own vocation was God.

Now, perhaps I am wrong, but I think that she was not alone in this kind of vocation that she had.

Margaret Mary Alacoque was a French nun of the 17th century who claimed to have a mystical communication with Christ concerning His Sacred Heart. And she wrote down secrets and things that He passed to her about His Sacred Heart. She was a spouse to His Sacred Heart and became like an apostle of this mystery to the world.

In addition to this, I can name other saints with similar

vocations. Faustina Kowalska towards His Divine Mercy, for example.

Christ Himself was the centre of their own vocations as well. Now, this might be confusing, because in fact every person, no matter who they are, has Christ as a centre of their vocation, whether it is the priest or the baker or the housewife... but that is not what I mean.

The housewife has Christ as the centre of her vocation because when she gives service to her family, her children, her neighbours, etc. she is serving Christ by serving them and thus Christ is the centre of what she is doing.

But she remains like Eve, her head is still the human being, and she knows God through other people, not like Faustina Kowalska to whom Christ confided things to her directly and not through the priest, or like the Virgin Mary who was a housewife that served God in Person under her own roof, and was much closer to Him than any priest or temple authority.

I am implying that the Virgin Mary was not the only woman with her kind of vocation, like how Jesus Christ was not the only priest.

There were other women in history who really did have Christ as their head, through a kind of mystical connection with Him.

God is not a thing, He is a person. The angels are not things, but they are persons.

Great philosophers like Plato searched for the truth by trying to think in terms of rationality, in terms of logical sequences and shapes, and they never really understood why a woman's mind and personality was the way it was. Einstein could figure out the solutions to some of the most difficult problems in physics, to the amazement of the scientific world, but he didn't understand the most important thing that lay behind all the equations and laws.

The woman's disposition towards relationships was the key to understanding the entire universe. It is not rational laws and equations that are behind everything in the created world, but it is persons, and hence half of the human race was designed with this fact in mind, while at the same time often ignored and misunderstood by so many people who sought the truth by rational calculation and philosophy.

To make things easier for us, I am going to give a name to this type of woman. I will call her a wei'nu (Chinese

伟女， meaning 'great woman').

For every type of woman, the people who make up her life constitute her vocation. For one woman, she will have charge of this group of people, for another woman, maybe that group of people. In this fashion, a woman can be a possessor of policemen, a possessor of children with disabilities, a possessor of people who chew gum regularly, etc.

I could be wrong, but I believe that the vast majority of nuns do not exactly constitute what I am referring to, even though they spend so much time with God in prayer, because somehow their vocation is still to created people.

A nun who spends all of her time in praying for such and such persons is getting very close to God, and she is being a spiritual mother to those she prays for, and it is to them that her vocation is, not to God directly, if I am right in my conclusions here. The direct relationship with the Person of God is a key part of her vocation, but it is not the actual centre... at least not in the way I mean in reference to the Virgin Mary or Alacoque. She remains with the vocation of Eve as a companion to human beings.

Her tionchar will not be superior to a man's, but that will not mean that her prayers will not find results, since the Lord said that any person can move mountains with faith.

I believe that there is a tiny number of women in the present world and in the history of the world, who are created with this kind of vocation, of being a companion to God directly as a woman, with a more intense and deeper relationship with Him than any man can achieve, since they are men and not women.

Think of Joan of Arc, and how it was that the priests at the trial insisted that they knew God better than she did, since they studied theology, and they told her to stop believing these visions came from God and to recant them. In actuality, her connection to God was superior than what a priest or bishop had, because they were men, and they could not be companions to a Man in the same way that a woman could.

It is like an object approaching the speed of light; as it accelerates and gets closer and closer, it can never actually reach the light speed, since its mass will increase in proportion to its speed and as it gets very close to the actual speed, its mass will increase infinitely and the object cannot be accelerated any further. Men towards God are like this, because no matter how great their tionchar may be and how close their connection with God may be, as long as they still have masculinity, it is impossible for them to actually reach that point, since God is a human being.

I don't believe that a wei'nu is necessarily a visionary either, although they may be. Nor is it to be assumed that every female visionary or prophetess is a wei'nu, since visions and prophecies are not the major means of knowing God – the woman in question who prophecies may still mainly know God through other people, and most especially the priest.

And theoretically, it should also be assumed that most of the women created with this kind of nature did not inherit eternal life, and therefore they probably never became saints, which means that we probably don't know who they are or were in history either.

Since the woman has this as her created vocation, she becomes a wei'nu the moment she is created and never ceases to be one, nor was there a time when she wasn't one. It is not like the priest, where the man is created with a calling to the priesthood, and doesn't actually reach this nature until he is ordained sacramentally.

They have tionchar that exceeds all other human beings, including the priests and bishops. Just like how the priest does work with the human being that surpasses the woman, so also the wei'nu has a relationship with God that surpasses the man.

The Virgin Mary is the wei'nu who possesses the whole

of Christ. It is like how Christ possesses the whole of the church or the Pope possesses the whole of the church on Earth.

But other wei'nu possess this aspect of Him or that aspect of Him. If you'll forgive my imagination, but I could suggest the following: Mary Magdalene was the mistress of the Resurrected Lord, Margaret Mary Alacoque was the mistress of His Sacred Heart, Mary of the Divine Heart is perhaps also a mistress of His Sacred Heart but in a different way than Alacoque, Faustina Kowalska possessed Him as Lord of Mercy, Joan of Arc possessed Him as a Warrior who fought with His people, Teresa of Avila possessed Him as Lord of the Spiritual Life, Therese of Lisieux possessed Him as He lived during His 30 years before He began His preaching, Anne Catherine Emmerich is the mistress of His Passion, Rita of Cascia perhaps is also a mistress of His Passion but in a different way than Emmerich, Mother Teresa is the mistress of His presence in the poor, Alphonsa Muttathupadathu perhaps is mistress of His presence in the sick, Cecilia (the martyr) is perhaps mistress of Him as He is present in sacred music, Clare of Assisi perhaps is the mistress of His personal lifestyle when He was doing His ministry, Catherine of Genoa perhaps is the mistress of Him as Lord of purgatory, Catherine of Alexandria perhaps is the mistress of Him in His role as a Spouse, Kateri Tekakwitha perhaps is the mistress of

Him as the Creator of life and the natural environment.

Catherine of Siena, Hildegard of Bingen, Bridget of Sweden and Brigid of Kildare, I would also assume to be of this nature as well.

In the Old Testament, the figure of Deborah also perhaps as well.

Perhaps prophetess Anna in the New Testament, may not be have been a wei'nu, but perhaps was like a nun who devotes her life to God... but the human being she was a companion to may have been other prophets like Simeon and her own powers of prophecy were given to her so that she could be a true companion to the males who were prophets. Obviously, I could easily be wrong.

Deborah may be to the wei'nu what Melchizedek is to the priesthood. Deborah spoke on God's behalf to the people, not just as a prophetess, but as one of the judges to whose voice Israel needed to obey. Men knew God through her, not the other way around.

Some modern mystics in recent years like Nancy Fowler or Catalina Rivas perhaps are also. Catalina Rivas said that Jesus said that Jesus said she was the messenger of His love and Fowler was the messenger of His peace. If what I am writing is correct, then Christ is their head, and the church can come to know Christ through them.

As I said, however, I imagine most of the wei'nu probably rejected their own vocation and died in obscurity. There was a great temptation on Joan of Arc to simply recant and do what the church told her to do. There was a great temptation on Teresa of Avila to just continue living as a normal nun without reforming her life as the inner voice told her to do. There was a great temptation on the female mystics to just forget about what the visions said and just keep it all on the inside. There was a great temptation on Therese de Lisieux to stop believing in God. There was perhaps a great temptation on the Virgin Mary to simply just get rid of the baby.

Even when it became clear that there was something supernaturally apparent, the temptation to think it was all from Satan was great. Their own confessors could have acted as agents of deception in this. They were tempted to believe that they were harming the church, they were tempted to believe that they were spreading heresy or acting to serve evil. They were tempted to believe that they were insane or demonically-possessed.

These women were made uniquely as companions to the Trinity; as intimately connected together with God by their very nature. Every time they gave in to the temptation and rejected themselves, they sinned, because the Trinity was connected to them and by rejecting themselves, they rejected the Trinity.

When some of them spoke about how terribly sinful they were, I don't think that this was necessarily humility; it may have been a statement of fact. Because many of them really did give in to the temptations and not accept the grace to hold still to the One they were bound to, rather than to follow the voice of the world. Joan of Arc repented of recanting during the trial, because she felt that her recanting had been a grave sin against God.

If an ordinary person sins by rejecting God's presence in some form, then how much greater must the sin be for them, when they are closer to God than anyone else, and they should know better than anyone that this was the Truth?

These women I listed above overcame the temptation and eventually said yes to the inner voice, yes to the angel, yes to the calling that they could feel that others couldn't... one would have to speculate about how many women of the same nature have lived or died facing the same choice and who chose differently, but who are now lost to obscurity as a result of it.

Similarly, I imagine that the number of men called to the priesthood in their own vocation that they were created with, and the number of those who actually accepted ordination, and who remained within it, may be two entirely different numbers.

But, you see a logic in this that fits together. For if the priest and bishop is acting in Christ's place as a husband to the church, and each piece of the church is broken up and assigned to a different priest or bishop, the wei'nu are the same.

This man is the husband of this diocese. This wei'nu is the wife of this aspect of Christ. This man is the husband of this parish. This wei'nu is the wife of this small aspect of Christ. Christ possesses the whole of the church; Mary possesses the whole of Him.

A woman cannot be a priest because she cannot be a husband. A man cannot be a wei'nu because he can't be a wife.

The mystical marriage in heaven between the Bride and Bridegroom is all reflected in this.

I drew another diagram to try to explain this.

Bridegroom   Bride

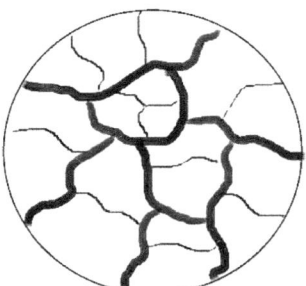   

Each part of Christ is divided
into a different aspect
owned by a different
wei'nu. And within each
aspect those aspects can be
further subdivided and
owned by other wei'nu.

The Virgin Mary has possession
of all of it.

Each part of the Church is divided
into different dioceses, which
are further subdivided into parishes.
Each diocese is possessed by a bishop,
with each parish have a priest.

Christ has possession of all of it
universally, and the Pope has
possession of it on the Earth.

The priest gets to heaven by being judged regarding the
question of what he did in his work towards the people
he is acting as a husband towards. If he did what he was
supposed to do to bring people to heaven, then he will
get to heaven. If not, then when they go to hell, he will
be carried down with them.

The wei'nu gets to heaven by being judged regarding
the question of what she did in her relations towards
the Lord she is acting as a spouse towards. If she did
what she was supposed to do by accepting the
relationship and giving herself up to Him, as He tells her
and not as the world pulls her, then she will get to

heaven. If not, then she will end in hell.

I am reminded of the Disney movie 'Frozen' wherein Elsa, who secretly has this ice magic, tries to hold in the secret away from the world and the fears she has are her greatest enemy. Both her inner fears to stay hidden, and once the secret is known, the fears to think that she is a danger that is inherently a harm to the world. The wei'nu is not so different from this, because her greatest temptation in life is to give in to fear or pressure from the created world and reject what she is. Perhaps the Spirit inspired the movie to show this.

And yet, in that movie, it was her ordinary sister Anna who was the heroine of the movie that saved her sister Elsa. Our own prayers and sacrifices, no matter whether we may be ordinary, can help such women to overcome these temptations. Like Elsa, these women are a kind of closeted people. The temptation on them to reject the relationship by the force of the world is huge.

Just as people need to pray for priests that they can overcome the temptations they are faced with, so also we have a duty to pray and sacrifice ourselves for the wei'nu, like as Anna did in the movie, that they may overcome the great temptations that they are faced with and hand themselves over to trust in the love of the One calling them.

They are companions to God, and just like how a female athlete must have great athletic prowess in order to be a companion to male athletes and to know what it means to be in their shoes, so also these women must enjoy something of the nature and life of God themselves, or else they cannot truly know what it means to be in His shoes and to truly be companions to Him.

His wisdom, they will share in. His sufferings, they will also pass through. The things He felt, they will be made to feel.

Christ had more wisdom than Solomon. The woman who possesses Christ will have access to this wisdom to a lesser degree, but this lesser degree will still surpass all other teachers in the world.

Christ is King of all Creation. The woman who possesses Christ will also share in His Kingship in her own unique way to a lesser degree, but this lesser degree will still surpass all other rulers in the world.

Christ is Lord of Mercy. The woman who possesses Christ will also share in His giving of mercy to the world in her own unique way to a lesser degree, but this lesser degree will still surpass others in the world.

They are closer to the Trinity than any other being, because that is their nature that they were created with. This closeness to the Trinity will give them troubles and trials, but it will also mean that human beings will come to know God through them.

Each aspect of the Trinity belongs to them differently depending on their own vocation. However, in a certain way, all of the Trinity belongs to each of them, but just in accordance with their particular calling. For example, Kowalska is the possessor His mercy, but in possessing His mercy she also must possess His passion within her possession of His mercy, because His mercy is inseparable from His passion.

It is a maybe a little bit like saying that even if a parish priest only has charge of this one parish, he is still charged with the church of the whole world, because no matter where in the world a person comes from, if that person just enters this parish, then he comes under the authority of that priest while he is there.

In a certain fashion the angels ought to belong to the

wei'nu as well, more than others, since the angels are the way that the Trinity does things in the world. Margaret Mary Alacoque, who had visions and messages from Jesus about His Sacred Heart, saw the seraphim telling her that they were waiting for her to take her place in the middle of them. The image of Our Lady of Guadalupe showed Mary being held up by an angel at her feet.

Now, there is another point that needs to be drawn out, which is very important.

Christ said that the greatest among you shall be those who serve everyone. Mary is a greater saint than Aymard of Cluny, because people rely on her prayers and her example far more than his... and hence she serves more guests in her house than he does in his.

But, even if one saint is greater than another because they serve more, in reality, they are not truly better than one another.

That is because the ultimate audience of any person is not the population of human beings in the world or in the church, but it is the Holy Trinity. To the perspective of human beings that inhabit the church, Mary will seem a far greater saint than others, because she is an intercessor for far more than any other saint.

However, to the perspective of the Holy Trinity, there is no person who is less important than another. Each person is infinitely important, and there is no such thing as a value greater than infinity.

Even should a person have such a seemingly small vocation and their house only ever has one guest in it, that guest will still be Jesus Christ in disguise.

For every person that a woman serves in her life, she is serving Jesus when she serves that person. For every kind of work that a man does in his life for God, no matter how small it may be, he is still serving God by what he is doing, when he does it right.

If someone does not have a love that bears all things, that hopes all things, that believes all things... a love which is infinite... then that person cannot get to heaven. They will either go to hell or purgatory when they die, but not heaven.

Every person in heaven has perfect love. Every person in heaven has limitless love. There is no person in heaven that has a greater love than another, because once love is unconditional and willing to sacrifice all, it is not possible there could be some greater love than this.

All of the angels, every single one of them, even the very smallest among them, would have willing to come down to the Earth and die instead of Christ. But only

Christ was willed by the Father to be sent. Hence, we say He is greater than the angels, but in fact their love was the same as His, it was just that they were not asked to prove that love.

It is rarely easy to figure out a person's vocation. Each person is like a painting, with each little detail in their life all forming a meaning to it, but they all point back to the person's vocation- or in other words they all point back to the specific way that God called them to love.

Not a single one of the various types of persons, whether man or woman, whether human or angelic, was meant to live without a prayer life. All of them were meant to talk to God. But the way that they were designed to talk to God and have a relationship with Him was different for each person.

Just as people are given different talents to do different kinds of work in the material world, so also people have different talents regarding their prayer lives. Some people will influence God in this way, others in that way, because they were created with different vocations and were designed to have different relationships with God. Hence, Margaret Mary Alacoque, who was the Spouse to Jesus' Sacred Heart, will be able to influence Him and receive answers to her prayers regarding the Sacred

Heart in a way that surpasses other people. Even His own Mother will not be able to reach the same depth in prayer to the Sacred Heart as Margaret Mary Alacoque, for if she could, then what would Alacoque have that Mary didn't? This is a difference in tionchar. It has nothing to do with the question of one being better than another, it is rather a question of different roles given to different people.

Now all people have tionchar; that is to say, all people were intended by God to have a particular sort of relationship with Him which is unique to the person.

Every person was designed to be close to God in prayer, however, in different ways. And there are tremendous things that can be accomplished in prayer by those who have faith. Regardless of man or woman, human or angel, anyone can accomplish great things if they live close to God and have deep prayer lives.

However, different people will not be able to accomplish the same things in prayer. Not everyone will be granted miracles if they ask for it from God, but some people will because the performing of the miracles was necessary for their vocation to be fulfilled. Alacoque will have a deeper relationship with the Sacred Heart than anyone else and will feel this Heart better than anyone else.

The angel spoke to Joseph in the dream to warn him about Herod, rather than to Mary, because he was the man and it was his vocation to protect the family. Hence, what he hears from God and can request for from God, will be different from her- this is a difference in tionchar.

The ways that people influence God and the way that God answers their prayers will always depend on the identity of the person and the vocation they were given. Prayer is important to everyone, but some people more than others. Some people have vocations that call them to love with their work and actions more than by their prayers, while some people have vocations that call them to love with their prayers more than their work or actions. It is not because they are inferior that they are like this, it is simply the case that God called people to love in different ways.

There are things that Joseph could receive from God that Mary couldn't, but Mary's relationship with God was deeper than his. There are miracles that Moses could do with God's power that Margaret Mary Alacoque could not, but Margaret Mary Alacoque had a deeper relationship with the Sacred Heart than Moses did. This is the difference in tionchar between different persons.

All people can move mountains if they have faith in prayer and are persistent without giving up; but the way they are moved is going to be different for each person, because their vocations are different.

Each person is created to love in a different way, and given talents accordingly; the things that can be received in prayer work just the same as this.

The majority of men do not have the vocation to be a priest, because the work or thing they have mastery of is not necessarily redemptive... at least directly. The man who has a vocation to warn you about sharks, can be doing something that will help you find salvation, because perhaps it is by not being eaten by the sharks that you live to the future and thus repent of your sins so you can find salvation, and it is by doing good through warning such people, that this man loves others and thus wins salvation for itself... but the work is not directly bringing people to God, and so this man was not meant to be a priest. Same with the pizza salesman, the carpenter, the street cleaner, etc.

All forms of work have their end goal with the work that properly belong to the priest. This is because, what the priest offers in giving the Eucharist is the ultimate fulfillment and end meaning for the existence of every person.

The man who has a vocation to cook food has this vocation in order so that you can be well fed and so you can go to a priest to receive the sacraments. The man with a vocation to police work has this vocation so that society can be safe, so you can safely receive the sacraments from the priest. The man with a vocation to flying an airliner has this vocation so that you can travel from one place to another, ultimately so that it may lead you and others to receiving the sacraments. Even some types of work which seem very close to the priesthood, like catechists, lay preachers or even people doing the writing that I am attempting here, are still ultimately helping you to do things to get to the sacraments, but who still do not give you the sacraments.

Furthermore, all these works, when they are done out of love, also serve to sanctify souls and make them ready to receive the Eucharist.

The man who warns about sharks, and does so out of love, makes his own soul holy and in the right state to receive the Eucharist. The man who makes pizzas and does so out of love, makes his own soul holy and in the right state to receive the Eucharist. The man who cleans the street and does so out of love, makes his own soul holy and in the right state to receive the Eucharist. The man who flies the airliner, and does so out of love, makes his own soul holy and in the right state to receive the Eucharist. If a catechist teaches a class or if I write this book, and it is done out of love, it likewise also makes the soul holy and in the right state to receive the Eucharist. And the work with the Eucharist belongs to the priest, which if he does with love, thus makes his own soul holy.

All the work that women do with persons is also meant to ultimately serve to bring the person to salvation, which occurs through the taking of the sacraments in the right state. The mother gives birth to her child and raises, so that someday he can receive the Eucharist. The woman takes care of her friends so that their lives will keep going fine and they can come to receive the Eucharist. The teacher corrects the student so he can learn right from wrong, so that he will be in the right state to someday take the Eucharist.

And to take the Eucharist in a state of grace is the way that the person enters the doors of heaven.

All work done by anyone has its final goal in leading you to what the priest does, but their vocations are different than the priest's vocation, because the actual act of bringing you to God does not occur directly within their work in the same way as it does in the priest's work.

Similarly, all of the relationships that a person has with another person is ultimately a relationship between a person a God.

What a parent does to her children, that is what she does to God. What a man does to take care of a stranger, that is what he does to God. What a doctor does to serve a patient, that is what he does to God.

We serve God through serving other people. And we sin against God by sinning against other people.

But no matter what relationship it was, all of these things were ultimately a relationship between the person and God.

Hence, the relationships of any person, whether male or female, was all directed at the one relationship that the wei'nu had mastery of, between the human being and the Trinity.

Every nun is a spouse of Christ, and one could also perhaps say that every monk is married to the church, but they are not spouses in the way that the priest or the wei'nu is in the place of the Bride or Bridegroom.

The monk and the nun really have foregone marriage in order to marry God (the Bride and the Bridegroom are both equally God- because in marriage you become one flesh). However, the priest can be married to a woman and still be in the place of the Bridegroom to the church. The Virgin Mary and several woman in that list I gave before had husbands in their lives at least for some portion of it, and this did not change the fact that they were in the place of the Spouse.

The wei'nu are in the place of the Bride, just as the priest is in the place of the Bridegroom. This doesn't mean that every wei'nu was meant to think and feel about God as her husband; similarly, the priest is in the place of the Bridegroom to the church, but that doesn't mean he is supposed to think and feel about the church as a man thinks about his wife. A priest can have his own wife and still be a priest; a wei'nu can have her own husband and still be a wei'nu.

Peter was married to a woman, but he was the first Pope. Similarly, Mary was married to Joseph (although the marriage was never actually consecrated and therefore was never actually a true marriage), and she looked at Jesus as her Son, not her spouse, even though she is mystically in the place of the Bride. Subsequent Popes have placed rules to priests to require them to be unmarried; similarly, many wei'nu felt called to become nuns.

Because she is created to live a life in prayer to the Trinity, this obviously will interfere with many duties that a married woman raising children in a family would possess. Hence, if she were to be married to a man, or simply just living together with a male partner in an asexual relationship like Mary and Joseph, it could only be permissible in such a way that this did not take away from her first duties which was continuous prayer with God as He requests for from her. Similarly, it would not be wrong for a priest to have a family, so long as this did not take away from his first duty which was the administering of the sacraments to the faithful.

The wei'nu have no hierarchy; their obedience is to the church and the One who speaks through it.

It is not the case that every word that a priest says is correct, even when he says it in the confessional or in the mass, even though he has authority over the church. Similarly, it is not the case that everything these women claim about God is correct, even when she had it in a vision or a trance, and not simply just their imagination.

The church has fought hard over the years to insist on Papal supremacy. Similarly, we have had many doctrines coming out defending Mary's sharing in various critical aspects of Christ's life (the Assumption of Mary-the Ascension of Christ/the Immaculate Conception of

Mary-the Virgin birth of Christ/ Christ the King- Mary, Queen of Heaven/the Sacred Heart of Jesus, the Immaculate Heart of Mary, etc.)

Many people treat the Pope as Christ's representative on Earth, while failing to realize that actually every priest, even the local parish priest, is just as much in Christ's place as the Pope is. Many people treat Mary as the one special one who had a deep relationship with Christ, without realizing that all of these women had relationships that were just as deep.

The relationship that all these people had with God in the Eucharist is just as deep as what Mary had with her Son in the flesh. The mass performed at your local church is just as much the sacrifice of Jesus Christ as the actual event on Calvary.

For every gift that God gives to man, He really does give an equivalent to woman. Right down to the very last detail, there is nothing that is left out.

It is not the case that every task in the church is supposed to be carried out by the priest; every layperson has the responsibility to use his talents to advance the church's work. Similarly, it cannot be thought that the wei'nu alone are meant to be the intercessors and pray for everyone else; everyone in the whole world is supposed to have a deep relationship in prayer with God.

The Second Vatican Council, run by the Pope and bishops, has called for a greater role of laity in the church, because the clergy are not enough. The Virgin Mary has appeared several times in the past century asking for more people to pray, because her prayers are not enough.

The priest receives his priesthood upon ordination, but he was created for the priesthood since he was born. The wei'nu is born a wei'nu, but she does not get her deep relationship with God until she comes closer to Him in prayer.

The priests share a special relationship with each other as brothers. The wei'nu likewise have a special relationship with each other as sisters. They refer to the Pope as the Holy Father, and Mary is the Mother of the Church. The church is both Petrine and Marian.

The Trinity has no female component. The Father and the Holy Spirit are genderless, although the whole of femininity and masculinity are both contained within the Father. The Holy Spirit perhaps has an angelic nature, just as Jesus has a human nature. However, Jesus is a male.

God must give an equivalent gift to females then. Hence, the wei'nu share as the equal partners to Jesus in different aspects of Him, with each wei'nu as a mistress of each particular aspect, and Mary as mistress of every aspect.

However, it is not as though the different aspects of God are separable. What I mean by this, is that Mary Magdalene is mistress of the resurrection, but obviously the Passion also has a relation to the resurrection, as does His wisdom, as does His heart, as does every aspect of His being. Hence, while she is mistress of the resurrection, she is also mistress of all the other aspects as well, but only in terms of their relationship to His resurrection. She is also in possession of the entirety of the Trinity, but within the specialization of this particular aspect, whereas Mary is in possession of the totality. Mary does not have a greater possession of the Lord than the lesser wei'nu, it is just different. In the same way, your parish priest is just as much in the person of Christ as the Pope, and the mass he gives is just as valid and holy as the mass that the pope gives, but the Pope has authority over the entire church, while the parish priest has authority over the parish only. However, the parish priest still has a kind of responsibility for the entire church, because every catholic in the world who comes to his parish is still under his authority and receives Christ's sacraments through him to find salvation. If the Pope were to confess to a parish priest, he would be bound to obediently carry out the penance given by that priest.

Since the aspect of every wei'nu will be included within Mary's vocation who has the whole, therefore every wei'nu will belong to Mary in a special way as well. She is the mother of the wei'nu and they are all called to belong to her as daughters in a special way and they are called to belong to each other as sisters in a special way. But if they do not pray and they live away from God, this will never occur, but a shadow of it will still always be present even still.

It is worth noting here that just in the way that Jesus had a divine aspect and a human aspect, both within the same person and inseparable from one another, so also do the wei'nu have a share in the life of Jesus on Earth and His rule over the Earth from heaven. Sometimes it may even appear like the wei'nu have two aspects to them as well, when in reality it is just the case that it is the same vocation but it appears or plays itself out in seemingly two different ways.

For example, Therese de Lisieux is the mistress of Him as an ordinary person, but at the same time she is also mistress of Him as Lord of the Missions.

This is because the missions are inseparable from His

life as an ordinary Person. Hence, being the wei'nu of His life prior to His ministry or the ordinary things He did in His ministry, also makes her mistress of His governance of the missions. She, through her prayers, controls from heaven, so far as human beings cooperate with, the path that the missionary activity should follow because it is part of the aspect of Him that she belongs to. However, this is not the totality of Therese's name, so to speak, her name remains to be mistress of Him for all that He did before His ministry, but what He does from heaven in His ordering of the missionary activity also belongs to her because it is inseparable from that aspect of His life on Earth.

Why? I am not sure if this answer is correct, but I think it is perhaps because Jesus lived most of His life on Earth doing all the same things that ordinary people do everyday, and yet did not commit a sin, but did every little thing with complete love- and the ultimate aim of missions to create a world in which all people are living likewise. The missionaries are not supposed to be going simply to get people to believe and get baptized, nor are they going to turn all people into theologians or consecrated religious, but they are supposed to be going in order to turn all those people into living lives like the Holy Family- ordinary, still going through problems, work, suffering, etc. and yet completely sinless. The ultimate measure of success and failure in missionary efforts is not how many people are baptized, how many believe, how many attend mass... the ultimate yardstick is rather, how much do these people receiving the missionary efforts, in their ordinary lives, resemble the family of Jesus, Mary and Joseph?

Hence, the person who should be the mistress of His ordinary life, must be the person who has command of this aspect of Him, otherwise it makes no sense.

A man prays to God and says, 'Lord, make the missions more successful.'

The Lord says, 'How?'

The man says, 'Make more people get baptized.'

And so then God brings more people to get baptized, but after they are baptized then they go to a few masses and go home, never visiting the church again.

The man prays again, 'Lord, the missions are still not successful. They were all baptized but now they went home and don't come back.'

The Lord says, 'So what do you want me to do to make them more successful?'

The man says, 'Make them all keep coming to the mass for the rest of their lives.'

And so, then God brings all these people to get baptized

and keep going to mass for the rest of their lives. And they keep all the same behaviour as before when they lived as pagans, enjoying all their various sins and vices, and they all come to the mass taking the Eucharist in mortal sin, and thus damning themselves even worse than if they had remained pagan.

The man says, 'Lord, the missions are still not successful. They were all baptized and they go to mass, but none of them have changed their behaviour. All these people: they still don't live in the right way. The missions are just causing them to be damned even worse than if they were left in ignorance.'

The Lord says, 'So what should I do to make the missions successful?'

The man says, 'Lord, make them all love each other and do good, without sin. In all of their ordinary lives, make them live everyday with love in their hearts, doing each and every small thing in accordance with your will.'

And so, God brings them to all love each other, living their ordinary lives with perfect love, just as Jesus had done for the thirty years of His life prior to His ministry. If you understand this, then it should be obvious why asking God to make the missions successful and asking God to make people resemble the Holy Family, are intrinsically inseparable. Hence, there is no other wei'nu for the Lord's command of the missions than the wei'nu who was mistress of Him in His life prior to His ministry and as an ordinary person. The end goal of all missions is to create a world of ordinary people resembling the Holy Family; hence it cannot be anyone else but Therese who has domain over the missions.

And so, she is the one in charge of His governance of the missions and she cooperates with them from heaven- in the previous century, following her death, it was probably at her direction that sent Mother Teresa (named after her) as a missionary to Calcutta.

There is another form of Holy Orders, however, which is deacons. Deacons have the vocation of doing work that supports the work that the priests do with the sacraments. They themselves do not do the sacraments, except for marriage and baptism (which themselves do not require a priest to preform).

They are specially consecrated to God to do the work in supporting the priest, but the actual work the priest does itself is not their calling. I would conclude that they do not possess a work with the human being which surpasses that work done by women, unlike the priest.

I could be wrong, but I think there is another type of female vocation that mirrors this, because while all women have persons forming their vocations and some rare women have the Trinity themselves as the centre of their vocations, there must also be some women who have these special persons: the wei'nu, the bishops, the priests and deacons, as the centre of their own lives and vocations.

For example, Lucia dos Santos, the visionary of Fatima, had the Virgin Mary as the centre of her vocation. The Virgin Mary was not God, however, although Lucia was certainly acting as a prophet to the world of the Most High since Mary's words were coming from God. But, Lucia's own vocation in life, regarding the apparitions she saw, the message she gave to the world and her consecration to an entire life cloistered within the Carmelite Order (which is consecrated to Mary) would strongly suggest that it was Mary rather than the Trinity who was the centre of her life, and she knew God through Mary... through another human being, rather than like Kowalska or Alacoque towards the Trinity directly.

Whether this is a single type of vocation, or whether there is a type of women who has wei'nu as the centre of their lives, or another that has priests at the centre of their lives, etc. I am not sure. But, to simplify things, I am going to give a name to all women who have either wei'nu, priests, bishops, deacons or other women of their nature as the centre of their lives, which I call 'umufasha'.

Umufasha is the Kinyarwanda word used in reference to Eve as a 'helper' to man in the Kinyarwanda bible. Kinyarwanda is the language of Rwanda, where the apparitions of Kibeho took place when many school girls became prophets for the Virgin Mary.

It is possible that one type of Umufasha is for priests, while another is for bishops, another for deacons, another for wei'nu, another for other umufasha, or a mixture of some of them or all of them... I am not sure. But, for women who have such persons composing the centre of their vocations, this is the word I will use for them.

Like how the deacon does not possess the work that the priest does but is just a helper to the priest, so also the umufasha does not possess the direct relation with the Trinity that the wei'nu have, and as such their relationship to God (their tionchar) will not surpass males.

The most famous deacons in history were perhaps Stephen the martyr and Francis of Assisi.

Francis of Assisi created the Franciscans on the basis of his interpretation of Jesus' words when He sent out the 70 disciples to preach in Matthew 10 and concluded that this was the Rule of Christ (like the Rule of St

Benedict). Lucia dos Santos saw the Virgin Mary wearing the habit of the Carmelites during the apparition.

For every gift that God gives to men, He gives an equivalent gift to females, down to the last detail.

There is a piece of scripture that I want to draw out here. Psalm 44 in the Douay-Rheims bible (it is numbered 45 in many other bibles) goes like this:

10 The daughters of kings have delighted thee in thy glory. The queen stood on thy right hand, in gilded clothing; surrounded with variety. 11 Hearken, O daughter, and see, and incline thy ear: and forget thy people and thy father's house. 12 And the king shall greatly desire thy beauty; for he is the Lord thy God, and him they shall adore. 13 And the daughters of Tyre with gifts, yea, all the rich among the people, shall entreat thy countenance. 14 All the glory of the king's daughter is within in golden borders, 15 Clothed round about with varieties. After her shall virgins be brought to the king: her neighbours shall be brought to thee.

When I read this, I can't help but feel like what is being

spoken here is what I am detailing about the wei'nu. The psalm is being addressed to the king, and while it could theoretically be interpreted as being written to David (who did marry many wives, possibly princesses among them), it is more applicable to Christ the King.

'Daughters of kings' is another way of saying 'princess', of course. Cardinals are called princes of the church, and by contrast a wei'nu could be considered a princess of the church. The queen could be referring to the Virgin Mary, but also to each individual wei'nu at the same time in how she possesses Jesus as a spiritual wife.

Among those of these women who were visionaries, they recorded things like Jesus speaking to them and calling them 'daughter' or 'spouse', even simultaneously in the same vision. A spouse of a King is a queen. A daughter of a King is a princess.

The 'rich among the people' could be interpreted as spiritual richness, wherein a person has acquired many treasures in heaven by his good deeds. The saints used the help of Mary and the help of these kinds of women to know God better.

'Forget thy people and thy father's house' is like the call on the wei'nu to overcome their great temptation and to accept the relationship over the world that pushes them away from it.

The virgins and neighbours being brought to the king by her are like how consecrated religious or laity, come to know God better with the help of these women who are in such deep connection with Him.

All the speech about their beauty ought to be understood here in the sense of spiritual beauty. The soul of the wei'nu given to God's grace completely will be beautiful to His eyes.

Just as how in a marriage the love is exclusive, so also is it with the wei'nu. Jesus is not a polygamist, He loves each one exclusively of all others; there is no one else standing in the middle in their special relationship between them.

In marriage men and women are equal, and are meant to be mutually obedient to one another, although because sin and temptation exists, the authority belongs to the man and the wife must obey him in matters of disagreement; without sin, however, such control would never have been necessary.

The union between the Lord and the wei'nu is just like this. She may or may not be a nun, but she is in the place of the Bride, like how the priest is in the place of the Bridegroom. The Lord possesses authority over them and they are obligated to obey Him when there is a disagreement, but so long as the relationship is healthy and without sin, they will be obedient to one another. She will obey Him as her Husband, and He will obey her as His wife. But only insofar as what she asks for is not in disagreement with Him.

When there is disagreement between her will and His, then obedience is to Him, just as how a woman is obligated to be submissive of her husband. But insofar as what she desires is in accordance with what He wants, He will do everything she asks for from Him.

God will not obey a human being against His own will, because that would imply that God would commit sin (since failing to do the will of God is sin, hence if God fails to do His own will, then He is a sinner). But, because it is a marriage, the obedience of either one to the other still occurs nevertheless. Hence, Jesus, the spouse of the wei'nu, will always completely obey everything she asks Him to do for things which are His will and which properly belong to her particular niche.

Think of the story in the gospel of the Virgin Mary at the wedding at Cana. She said 'they have no more wine' because she wanted Jesus to perform a miracle. It was the Holy Spirit inside of her that prompted her to ask this, but she thought that Jesus would perform a public miracle and Jesus instead told her 'my time has not yet come', meaning the public miracles would come later. But He gave a miracle seen only by Mary and a few of the servants at the feast, because everyone else didn't know that this wine was water.

Mary possesses the whole of Christ, and He is completely obedient to her. But He cannot change His will, or rather that is to say, He cannot go against His Father's will, in order to please her request. Hence, at Cana, He gives an answer to her prayer, but not in the way that she was expecting.

There is no authority in heaven or on earth which is higher than the priesthood. Every priest has a higher authority than any other human or angel, with the exception of other human beings who are also priests. And yet this seems strange perhaps, because how could your parish priest be a higher authority than the President of the United States or any other world leader? Your parish priest has no cruise missiles to strike you with, he has no army of marines to rope down over your house from their helicopters, his treasury is not very big, he might not even have enough money to repair the church roof or replace the air conditioners, etc. His authority is still higher, however, because the things he has authority over are greater than all of those things. His authority is over the sacraments and no person is allowed to receive them without his consent, and because the sacraments are the way through which people reach salvation, he is also (in a way) the one who has authority over your final destination in this life. This is the power of binding and loosing given to Peter. The president of the United States can send people to kill you and end your short life on this Earth, but he has no authority over whether or not you can be joined to God in the Eucharist. The president has authority over an earthly country, but he has no authority over the spiritual world; the priest, however, does.

The priest has no authority over questions of science, engineering, history, etc. but he has authority over moral and doctrinal questions which are above all these things, and to which all those other things are comparatively insignificant in importance to. The Pope or bishops cannot tell people what is the best decision in terms of getting the most favourable results, but they can tell you whether a decision is moral or not. And because morality touches all things, and the question of morality is always the most important consideration in any question, therefore they are the ultimate authority over all things, and Christ, who is Himself one of them, is their Head. All persons, governments, societies and cultures were meant to have obedience to them; there is no other political or social body which can claim that.

Hence, the priest, from the pope down to the local priest carries the highest type of authority in existence and no other person has an authority higher than theirs. The authority of your parish priest, even if he is a very sinful person, is still higher than even the most powerful of all people who was not a priest.

Just in the same way as this works, the wei'nu are like this with their tionchar. Being a wei'nu gives them no authority in itself nor does it obligate anyone to obey them. But there is no other created person, whether human or angelic, who has superior tionchar/superior capacity for a relationship with God than them. Even if someone is a mystic, who talks to God face to face, who performs miracles, and has such a deep prayer life... if this person has a vocation for something other than the Person of Jesus directly, he will still have a lesser form of tionchar than even the smallest wei'nu.

How does this work? Suppose that we took Moses for example, who has a vocation of the work of God's law, and therefore he is a man. If, however, he had a vocation towards God as He was present in His law, then he would be a female and a wei'nu. He needs to be a woman before he can get so close and intimate with a man. But he was not a woman, he had a vocation towards the law as a thing. Moses was a prophet who performed signs and miracles greater than almost anyone else in history; he turned the sky dark, he made the sea part, he brought frogs and locusts to cover the land. Of course, it was God's power that did these things, but it was the tionchar of Moses in his prayer to God that allowed it to happen, because it was part of his vocation that he should love in this way. And suppose that we took Mother Teresa, who I identified as the mistress of His presence in the poor, and who performed no such signs, wonders, etc. She did not talk to God face to face in some mystic fashion like Moses, she even had running doubts that God was really there. How could I say that her tionchar is greater than his?

In a similar way, how could an old parish priest in a little village in Alaska have a higher authority than the President of the United States?

If you understand tionchar properly as communication, and not as ability do miracles, then it makes more sense. Communication is about listening and speaking.

Listening: She would have had a better ability to recognize Jesus, as He was present in the faces of the poor and suffering, than anyone else in past history or in the future. Even if she did not hear a voice from these faces speaking to her, her ability to sense this penetrated more deeply into listening to what God was saying than what Moses could do by listening to the cloud. She, who experienced no mystic phenomena like that, nevertheless heard something within those faces that went deeper than what Moses could hear on the mountain even though he experienced all those mystical things. When Moses received the law, he was only hearing from God what people were supposed to do and not supposed to do; when Mother Teresa gazed into the faces of the poor, she was hearing from God the reason why. Hence her tionchar is the greater of the two.

If you could compare Paul's conversion with that of Francis of Assisi, which of the two is more impressive? Paul was heading to Damascus to persecute Christians, thrown from his horse after a blinding light appeared and a voice told him to change, and afterwards his life completely changed. Francis saw no miracle. He was heading for war, but upon seeing the leper on the road, he dismounted, walked over and hugged him, gave him all his money and afterwards his life completely changed. Which of the two do you really think saw something more that day?

Speaking: Moses could call on God to cover the land with frogs or any other of those great signs, and God would do so at the moment he asked for it. If Mother Teresa asked for this, the prayer perhaps would not be granted to her like that. But as the mistress of Him as present in the poor, He belonged to her in that form more than any other person. He would not obey her requests about doing great signs like that, perhaps, because it was not part of her vocation. To show the world about His existence within the poor, she didn't need to bring down fire from heaven or locusts to cover the land, hence that kind of tionchar didn't belong to her. But she could pray to Him to create the missionaries of Charity, with the vocation not of curing poverty (that is someone else's house), but of contemplating Christ within the poor, and this organization would succeed in bringing many people throughout the world to recognize His existence and the nature of this Presence within the poor. Why is this greater? Because, Moses' miracles succeeded only in showing people that God's commands had to be obeyed for fear of consequence, but Mother Teresa's ministry was showing people the reason why God even gave these commands in the first place.

If I can convince you with a miracle to get you to change or if I can convince you with the face of a poor person to get you to change, which of the two is ultimately the more impressive feat? She didn't have miracles, because what she could accomplish through her prayers was greater than that what Moses could accomplish through his.

But, ultimately what is greater or lesser is not really so important. As I mentioned before, all are equal within the perspective of the only observer that counts.

The Virgin Mary can serve far more people than you or I can, and hence she is called a great saint, but God is just as much concerned with the way that we serve Him in our ordinary lives through our own calling as He is concerned with her work to serve people through her calling.

As Mother Teresa said, there are some things that she can do that we can't do, but there are also things that we can do that she can't do, but together we can do something beautiful for God.

In the city there are many houses, some larger than others, with guests that come and go depending on their needs for the service of the person.

A priest baptizes Margaret Mary Alacoque, gives her the sacraments and teaches her the faith. She receives these sacraments in a state of grace and they become the means for salvation for her. She is a guest in the priest's house, as he does the most important of all forms of work for her.

Margaret Mary Alacoque possesses the relationship with the Sacred Heart. The Seraphim who told her that they were waiting for her to take her place in the middle of them will be in her house often, since they need her help for the relationship with the Sacred Heart, and as Seraphim they are on fire with the love of God and must deliver this message of God's love to the world.

Each seraph is different. Here is a seraph that is concerned with messages about how God loves all unconditionally, and there is a seraph that is concerned with messages about how God's love is eternal.

They come to Alacoque's house and receive service from her, so that they can be closer to the Sacred Heart.

Throughout Alacoque's life they take notes down on how Jesus manifests Himself to her and through her, and they take these notes out of the house back to their own houses, where humans throughout the world come to visit, whenever they have thoughts about the love of God, and the seraphim use feelings, thoughts, images, things in their lives, in order to make them feel and know the love of God.

Here is a lawyer in China who has suffered financial ruin and wants to kill himself. But one day he comes to a church and feels like maybe there is Someone out there who cares about him. This man is in the house of the seraph who is whispering to the man about God's love for him and is being served as a guest.

The man goes back to his practice and helps various clients with laws concerning real estate issues. He uses his labour to do what his conscience tells him is right, and he thus uses his labour to serve a God that he doesn't know much about, as a companion to Him. His clients are guests in his house and he uses his labour to serve them, and by serving them, he serves God who is disguised behind their faces.

A muslim woman in Iran enters into the house of one of these seraphs who spend so much time in Alacoque's house when she comes to ponder over the question of whether or not God wants her family to get to heaven. The thoughts that she has about God wishing salvation for human beings have their origin from these seraphim, and she sits as a guest in their houses.

She takes care of her children and husband, and they sit as guests in her house as she does the work of a woman for them and receive the love that she can give to them. She cooks food for them and does housework for them, but the greatest love that she gives to them is her companionship through all these things.

Every part is unique and every part is necessary. There is no one who can be a companion like this woman can. There is no one who can serve clients about the law as that man can. There is no one who can show God's love as those seraphim can. There is no one who knows the Sacred Heart better than Alacoque does. There is no one who can bring Alacoque to salvation, and with her, bring so many graces upon the rest of the world, as that priest can. Each one requires the other.

When people sin, it is the case that they are failing to carry out their vocations and to love the way that they were designed to love. And all human suffering is simply the case of people failing to receive that which they were designed to receive from other beings that failed to give the love that they were meant to give.

If every part worked as it was designed and gave love according to its design, there would be no suffering in this world.

I am sure, that perhaps you are very curious about what your particular role is. And if you wish to know it, you need to ask God in prayer.

Lord, we pray that you reveal to us the mystery of our lives and existence, help us to understand the nature of the house that you gave us and help us to avoid all sins that prevent us from inheriting it. We ask for these things, if it is your will, in Jesus' name, Amen

VII: Understanding how God answers prayers

I used the past three chapters to try my best to explain something which is very difficult to explain. It is very difficult and yet it is necessary in order to understand witchcraft and the invisible world. In order to understand a broken world, you need to know what the original looked like before it broke.

Witchcraft is the application of tionchar towards communication with demons rather than with God, and all the invisible attributes within the created world can be used for evil, just as they are used for good.

I know that this has taken a long time for me to explain all of this, but the truth is unless you understand how and why temptation exists, how God created human beings, our spiritual sides, natural vocations and the invisible world, then I think you will not be able to penetrate into really understanding witchcraft.

I am going to use one more chapter at briefly explaining the design of all of this before I move on to the actual topic of witchcraft.

Is it possible for the human mind to understand how it is that God answers prayers?

It is possible. God is a person and not a machine, but He

still answers prayers according to a logic, but we have to understand the factors involved with how these answers are made. To try to make it simpler, I would break this up into a group of four factors.

The first factor is tionchar: what was in your natural vocation, and how you were designed to use a life of prayer in order to love God and neighbour. Depending on this, He will answer people differently. This factor cannot be controlled or altered by anyone other than God when He created you.

The second factor is the spiritual health of the person asking for it: is the person in sin or in grace? God listens to those who listen to Him, and doesn't listen to those who do not listen to Him. Hence, this forms a very big part in the way that God answers prayers.

The third factor is the beliefs and religion of the person: who do they think they are praying to and how do they understand Him? This has an effect on how God responds.

The fourth factor is the agreement the request has with His own will.

I already tried my best to explain the first factor above, and this in truth is perhaps the hardest of the four to calculate or understand, and yet it has a huge effect on how it is that God answers prayers. The other three are easier, and I will use this chapter to give an outline of them.

For the second factor: the spiritual health of the person.

This is not difficult to understand at all.

If you think of the human body for a moment, people through genetics can have different body shapes and sizes, and they can't change their genes. This is like the tionchar, in that it is innate and unchangeable.

Suppose you had twins, who more or less possessed the same physical anatomy, same height, body-size, etc. But one of the twins was a ballerina whose muscles were very strong, and the other twin never worked and was very fat, and who got diabetes, heart disease, etc. Although they possess the same genetics, one is stronger than the other and can do much more than the other. In a similar way, you can have one person who in fact has a vocation and tionchar which ought to make this person's prayers for a certain thing to receive greater results than another person who had a different form of tionchar. However, because this person is a very sinful person, God therefore doesn't answer the prayers that this person makes as much as He does for the person who had a different kind of tionchar that would not have led to as great an answer in prayer as the first person's prayers.

You can have a wei'nu, possessing the most supreme form of tionchar, but who is a great sinner, and she prays to God for something she is actually the mistress of, but without any repentance and there is absolutely no answer. While an ordinary person in the world can pray for this thing even though he has no mastery at all of it, and he moves mountains with his prayer because of his faith and persistence. A healthy baby might have more strength in his limbs than an adult in sickbed who just went through a heart attack.

The more sinful you are, the less God will tend to listen to your prayers. He will still listen and may give a response, but only when a response is necessary due to a promise He made in the past.

The third factor is the knowledge and beliefs of the person:

It actually matters to God how much we know about Him and how we understand Him.

People speak to God through their words and their

actions. But they hear God through the teachings of religion. They can also hear God through visions, dreams, feelings, etc. But that is the less important way of hearing what God says. People know far less about what God is speaking to them from dreams, visions and feelings, than what they know from what He actually openly revealed in written texts, in the lives and teachings of prophets and saints, in the teaching of His church, and in the teaching of His Son incarnate on Earth. So, in order to speak to God, one uses one's words and actions; in order to hear what God says, religion is needed for at least 99% of it.

In order to know who God is, you need to receive the revelation that He has put into the world.

God has in fact revealed things about Himself in every religion, but it is only in one religion that the entirety is contained. Abraham gave all his inheritance to Isaac, but to his other sons and daughters he gave them gifts and sent them to the East.

Now, God will answer the prayers, so long as they are sincere and genuine, of people in any religion, even if they do not understand Him correctly. However, He will not answer them in the same way because of their lack of proper understanding.

If a person thought that God sent Buddha into the world

to teach the world the path to enlightenment, he would be wrong. However, even though he is wrong, if this person prays to God, and is living a life free from sin, then God will still answer him as his tionchar and vocation dictate. However, if he does answer him, this person may be tempted to think that Buddhism really is the truth, because he prayed to God, thinking that Buddha is a manifestation of God, and got an answer to the prayer. The same is true for a Muslim, a Jew, a Hindu, etc.

What God does not answer within false religions are people who pray to Him using names or ideas which are obviously false and which they only follow because they are unwilling to seriously look for the Truth. If people think that God is a statue that they need to give food to so that He can eat and be full, and they put the food in front of Him and then ask Him for help to kill their enemies, to give them more money, etc. then He is not going to answer them, because He gave them an ability to reason and yet they are not using it; even though they think they are treating Him well, when they believe these things about Him and treat Him like such, then they are actually treating Him like He is something really stupid and this offends Him.

If, however, the same people were to understand God differently, and they recognized that God created the universe and doesn't need someone to give Him food as though He doesn't have any Himself, and they do not believe the statue is Him, but is merely just a representation of some way He showed Himself in the past, and they place food in front of the statue just because they want to express their love for Him, and so the food is just a sign of their love, and the love is the gift but not the food… perhaps in this understanding, God may give an answer, because it is less offensive to Him, even though it is still mistaken and incorrect.

However, because He does not want people to be misled into thinking that such false beliefs and religions are true, He will not answer these prayers as greatly as He will to those who pray to Him with the correct understanding.

If you can imagine doctrine as though it were like technology, this makes a lot more sense. You can accomplish much more with 21st century technology than you can with medieval technology. Similarly, prayers done within the catholic faith will be more effective than if the same people in the same state of soul prayed the same prayers within the Islamic faith. You can also accomplish much more with medieval technology than you can with Stone Age technology, and hence prayers done in the Islamic faith will be more effective than prayers done within some pagan place, so long as they are not done according to some obviously offensive understanding of God.

Just as technology increased as time went on, so did our understanding of God's revelation. Weaponry is also created and improved through technology. And a sick or weak man can defeat a healthy or strong man, if he has sufficient weaponry. In the same way, the devil, who would otherwise be completely disqualified from being heard by God in prayer because of the second factor mentioned above, is still able to mount up many prayers to God and receive answers, because he is equipped with weapons and armour: he cannot get God to give him anything for any reason other than that the devil points at God's own Word and demands an answer.

The closer the beliefs are to the true faith, the more effective the prayers will be in getting an answer from Him, because He does not want people to be misled into believing the wrong things. The things received within prayers done in false understandings and religions are always necessarily lesser than what can be received through prayer done in the correct religion.

The fourth factor to take into consideration is whether or not it is God's will.

To try to explain something here a little better, I want to create two categories. The first category includes all the things that are in conformity with God's will and the second category includes all the things that are not in conformity with His will. I am going to go back to this many times throughout this piece, so remember: first category is what God wills, and the second are the things He doesn't will.

It is easier to ask for a person to rise from the dead than it is to ask for a person in mortal sin to reach real repentance. I emphasize 'real' here, because a lot of what we call repentance is not 'real' repentance; 'real' repentance means that the person has changed and will not do the sin again; it doesn't mean that they think they will not do it again, but they don't take this very seriously and so they then just go back to it again a week, a month, or a year later. Such a person has not really become freed from the sin, and has not reached real repentance.

However, if you pray for the conversion of sinners and you pray for people to come back from the dead, you will more likely find results from praying for the conversion of sinners than for people to come back from the dead. The reason for this is not because the conversion is easier than the resurrection; in fact, it is not. But rather it is because the conversion is in agreement with God's will, whereas the resurrection of the body, even though it be an easier thing to accomplish in prayer than the resurrection of the soul, is very often not God's will to grant. Such a thing is in the second category.

All things in the first category, can be granted if people pray for them, no matter who they are and what their tionchar is like. Anyone can move mountains with prayer that they persevere in. But the answers they receive will be different depending on their tionchar.

All things in the second category, can never be granted no matter who asks for it, what kind of tionchar they possess, how much time they spend and how many ways they ask the Son of God to intercede for them. Even if Mary herself, the one who possessed the closest relationship to God among all creatures, were to beg her Son with all her will for it... it still would not be granted if it is in the second category.

But very often, we don't know when what we pray is in the first or the second category. God understands this perfectly, and He is so kind that when we ask for something in the second category without realizing it, God still answers the prayer by just giving something different in response which was in the first category but was related to what we were asking for.

For example, suppose people want the cancer of an old woman to recede, and so they beg God for it. But they don't realize that while for some other people with cancer this request is in the first category, the cancer of this particular old woman is in the second category because the date for her death has been fixed and it was ordained that this must be the way she should go. But they pray so much for this woman, and she still dies. God, however, doesn't take all the prayers and just throw them out in the dustbin, but He listens to them all, and then makes a response which still rewards the faith of those who prayed. Perhaps, for example, He will take the prayers to save some other woman whose cure was in the first category. Perhaps He will, unbeknownst to the people who prayed, arrange it so that the cancers they were going to get later in life which were also in the first category, in the end do not happen to them; and they may go through their whole lives without cancer, completely failing to realize what would have happened if they hadn't prayed at that one time. Or perhaps He will give them a stronger faith, or some spiritual benefit. He could do many things even if what was asked for was in the second category.

Because people have free will, very often when you pray for the conversion of someone, even though conversion is always something within the first category, it may be impossible to get them to genuinely repent. Even if everyone in the world and everyone in heaven prayed for a person, if that person still refused to repent, then nothing could force them to go against their will. But even if they refuse to change, God can still take the prayer and use it for something else. He might for example bring someone else to repent who was very hardened but who would change under the right circumstances.

And those are the four factors. There are other things too which I have not listed; for example, sometimes God gives you more than what you asked for, out of love for you. You can ask for something in the first category, and God grants it, but He wanted to give you even more than that, thus He gives you more.

Lord, we pray that you teach us to make our prayers more effective and pleasing to you. We pray that you help us to have the relationship with you that you call us to have, we pray that you get rid of all of our sins and make us sorry for our sins while we pray, we pray for a correct understanding of who you are, and we pray that you teach us your will. We ask for these things, if it is your will, in Jesus' name, Amen

VIII: The Origins of Shamanism

Eve was deceived by the serpent. The serpent told her that if she ate of the fruit that she would possess great wisdom. Eve's love for God was not enough, and hence she knew that God had commanded not to eat of it, but she preferred to acquire wisdom for herself than to do as God asked. If the temptation had never come, however, her love would still not be enough... but she would perhaps just never know it, because she had not seen the effects of it being tested.

Her husband did not believe what the serpent said, and in fact the serpent did not speak to him but spoke to Eve.

Her husband ate the fruit, but he did not believe it would give wisdom. He perhaps ate it because he did not want to upset his wife.

Adam rejoiced when God gave his wife as a gift to him. In all of the delights of the creation given to him, none was more pleasing to his heart than this one. His heart had become so set upon this gift that even when she told him to go against God, he followed her rather than his conscience. He also failed to love God as much as he should have. So, the two of them sinned together.

God was hurt by this very much. Like how a parent who raises a child is filled with grief when the child abandons him in his old age, so also is God to human beings when He gives them everything and they return His love like this. The fruit itself was not what was important; they didn't love Him back- that was the pain in the heart.

They of course acquired no wisdom at all from eating the fruit. The wisdom would only come from their redemption later on. Instead they lost much from eating the fruit.

Before they ate the fruit, for everything they needed, they only needed to just ask God for it in prayer and it was granted to them; their every need and desire was taken care of. But suddenly this changed. Now they had to suffer hunger, thirst, uncomfortable heat, uncomfortable cold, boredom, fatigue, and all other forms of unfulfilled desire.

And if they asked God to not suffer these things anymore, the answer was 'no, because you sinned against me. You are the most treasured of all things to me, and I am so extremely sensitive to every action, thought and word you have in this world, and you hurt me badly when you showed me that you really didn't love me more than your own selves. You knew that this would hurt my feelings, but you did it anyways. You made me suffer, and if you do this without suffering yourselves, where is the justice? If someone else wounded you unjustly and that person should forever go unpunished, would you not think it terrible? You must suffer now because of your sin, or else there is no justice!"

So, they had to suffer because of their sin.

The devil was pleased by this, but he wanted more.

The devil said to God, 'Look at what they did with their sin! Look at how little they loved you! All I had to do was offer them something that you hadn't given them yet, and they abandoned you in order to try to get it!'

God said to the devil, 'Some day they will also become part of Me. For I shall send My Son into the world, and He will become flesh, in order so humans can become God. Their desire to become like Me, is a good desire, which I planted in them myself, and someday it shall be fulfilled.'

The devil said to God, 'Does not your Word say 'the Lord is slow to anger and great in power, and He will not leave the guilty unpunished'. You must punish them now! They do not deserve to live! They do not deserve to be happy! They do not deserve to know you any longer!'

God said to the devil, 'What you say is true. My word cannot be broken. I have no choice but to deprive them of the good things you mention, lest the guilty should be left unpunished. If someone worthy were to come and pay the debt they owe, then their punishment can end and justice can be satisfied.'

According to modern genetic studies, the most recent common male ancestor of the whole human race would have perhaps lived about 300,000 years ago. What this means is that the Y-chromosome of every male in the world today, has a common meeting point in genetic history which is calculated to have taken about that many years to have gotten to the present situation. There is no one in the world living today (that we know of), who has a Y-chromosome that would have had to have a common ancestor with everyone else at an earlier point than that.

Whether or not that was Adam, we do now know because it is possible that there was another common male ancestor of the human race living today that came after Adam. However, because all human beings living today must descend from Adam in order to be human, it is a necessity that Adam could not have been later than that.

If that is true, it would have some very profound meanings to the human race.

For one thing, there are other branches of the human family that existed in the period after that time. Neanderthals (Homo Neanderthalis), were a bit shorter, had thicker limbs, a larger nose, a bigger body and had bigger brains than modern humans, and they lived up until about 24,000 years ago. Genetically they are thought to have split from a common ancestor from modern humans perhaps around 350,000 years ago. And they lived in Europe, while the species that would become modern humans lived in Africa.

These were not the same species as the humans who live today, and yet if Adam was at least 300,000 years ago, and could easily be even earlier, it is possible that they also are his descendants and possessed eternal souls made in the image of God.

They were able to subdue the Earth. The Neanderthals, who lived in Europe before modern humans arrived, built houses made of animal bones or mammoth tusks, they cooked their own food and they buried their dead.

And yet they were not the same species as us. We have the same ancestry as they do if you go back far enough, but it was a different branch of human evolution. However, perhaps they also were capable of knowing God and praying to Him. Their souls perhaps were able to go to heaven or hell. The Neanderthals buried their dead, which suggests the possibility of some belief in the afterlife and a belief in the afterlife suggests the possibility that they were capable of knowing God; hence perhaps they also descended from Adam and were made in God's image.

Just as God made male and female different, and gave them different roles. Perhaps He also created these different species of human because He intended them to have different roles in His creation.

But they ceased to exist. It is not known for sure why they ceased to exist. Perhaps they interbred with our branch of human evolution, and ceased to exist. Maybe they went hungry and starved to death as a result of natural disasters or climate changes. Maybe when Homo Sapiens came to Europe and met them, they were not too friendly with one another, and the Homo Sapiens killed them off; perhaps later European legends of trolls have their origins here. We don't know why, but their extinction does coincide with the same time period as the entrance of modern humans to Europe, suggesting that this may have been an important cause.

It is a certainty that even in the time when people were 'cavemen' the effects of original sin were already there, and people lacked the grace of God such that they were prone to do evil.

Our species of human (Homo Sapiens) is set to have begun in Africa about 170,000 years ago. If Adam was 300,000 years ago or even earlier than that, then it should be noted that he would have also been a different species than modern humans today. The Neanderthals were already in Europe by the time Homo Sapiens began to exist. Because all humans today belong to this species and their ancestry is in Africa, it is almost certain that Adam must also have been African; and despite almost all historical art depictions of him and his wife as white, he was therefore almost certainly a black man, although he would probably not have looked like any human that lived today.

He may not have had the same brain that we do. His thinking and feelings may have been different from ours. He may not have been able to make the same sounds with his voice as we do.

Homo Sapiens lived in Africa for thousands of years, and about 80,000 years ago, some Homo Sapiens left Africa and entered the Middle East, probably by crossing the short straits of water that separates Yemen from Africa. From the Middle East, they spread out and travelled into Asia. About 60,000 years ago, they had reached Australia; this would have required travel in the open ocean. About 50,000 years ago they were in Europe. By about 35,000 years ago they had reached Japan and also crossed the water between Russia and Alaska, and entered into North America. The Neanderthals had all died by about 28,000 years ago, leaving our species as the lone dominant human. 15,000 years ago, they had reached South America and that was the last place to be populated by humans.

About 10,000 years ago is when civilization began and people began to construct the first cities.

Today we know almost nothing about what those ancient people knew about God. Some of them had art painted on caves, and yet we don't know what the art meant to them. We know that they created objects with tools, and that they even had figurines, including carved images of people, and yet we don't know what these objects meant to them. It is possible these were idols or had religious significance.

There was no civilization in the world yet, and yet these were clearly 'thinking people'. There were no cities, no towns... all the people who lived in the world lived in caves or dwellings of their own making, and they lived on killing animals, and foraging for food. And yet these were clearly people; they were not animals. They were made in the image of God and were the children of Adam.

Here is one way we can imagine the origins of paganism

to look like. Adam and Eve knew who God was perfectly in the beginning, and they told what they knew about God to their children. But their children only knew God because of what their mother and father told them. They could pray to God, but God did not reveal Himself to them in the same way that Adam and Eve had experienced before they committed the sin; God did not reveal Himself to them, because they did not deserve for Him to reveal Himself to them. And like their parents they were sinners. Adam's son Cain, was worse than his parents, and he committed murder. Hence, they did not deserve for God to show Himself to them.

If they avoided sin and did what they knew was right, then God would reveal Himself to them and they would pray to Him and see an answer to their prayer, but if they did not do so, then He hid Himself from them and even if they prayed, they received no answer.

All temptation comes about because we have a desire that only God can fulfill, but which God does not fulfill at the present moment, and thus we look around at the temporary things around us as though they are the answer to quench our thirst; in a similar way, a man who is starving and cannot find food, will eat garbage because there is nothing else.

Hundreds of thousands of years ago, the people living then were already under original sin and were selfish.

Even in the days of the cavemen, the devil and the mystery of evil was already at work. The devil had been permitted by God to test if human beings really loved God or not.

Perhaps they lived together in caves, but the men fought with each other over quarrels, perhaps they raped the women who had no choice but to stay with the men or else they would be unable to eat the food the men would bring them, perhaps when they saw people who were different from them, they refused to befriend them because of fear. Perhaps different bands of humans would group together and fight small wars with each other over hunting territory and maybe they hated their enemies. They probably masturbated. Perhaps they were polygamous or engaged in homosexuality when they had such desires. Perhaps they engaged in paedophilia in the caves. Perhaps our ancestors came to Europe and saw the Neanderthals, and they banded together in groups and armed themselves to kill them in a kind of genocide, and thus whatever the Neanderthals could have given to the later world was lost because of sin.

Even if their parents had any knowledge of God that had been transmitted from Adam and Eve, this knowledge seemed of no help to them, because if they prayed to God, God would not answer them, because they were sinners.

By their own reason they knew that these things were wrong. If someone killed them, if someone raped them, if someone did evil to them, if other people did evil things, then they would think it wrong; and hence if they opened their eyes, they could then see that they were doing evil themselves. But they didn't open their eyes, because original sin had made us such that it is easier to believe what we want to believe than it is to believe the truth, and people want to believe they are good because that is a comfortable thing to believe and do not want to believe the Truth that they are sinners, because that is not a comfortable thing to believe. And the devil tempted them to do evil and deceived them, and they were willing to be deceived. In fact, they deserved to be deceived. God did not help them avoid being deceived because they did not deserve His help; no one had yet sacrificed anything for them that could merit such help.

But in the midst of all this, the tionchar of human beings remains intact. They have an ability to communicate with the divine and to communicate with the spiritual world. But God does not look on the prayers of someone in sin who does not ask for forgiveness. To explain this, think of the concept of beauty.

Beautiful pictures can cause emotional reactions in people. Music can cause emotions to be induced in people. The music and the picture cannot control the person who sees or hears it, but it influences the person even without the person deciding to be influenced by it. A beautiful woman can get people to love her because she is beautiful, but she has no control over them actually, it is just the fact that they are programmed to see something that looks like her as beautiful.

The soul also has a beauty, which cannot be seen with the eyes, but which is plainly visible to God and the spirits. But if the soul has sin it will look like the person has been mutilated or has rashes or boils or possessing some kind deformity. To God, He hates to see this, and does not like to gaze on it and listen to its prayers; but the devil loves to see this because he hates their souls and wants them to become so ugly because he cannot accept them being more beautiful than him, and so it makes him feel better to see them in sin.

Therefore, even though they possessed tionchar, and had natural ability within the spiritual world, it perhaps seemed useless to them if they called on the name of the God of Adam and Eve. They perhaps didn't even realize the reason why He wasn't answering anything they said.

But, they still needed to believe that there was some power over the Created world that would listen to them, that would take their souls when they died, and which would be able to take care of their safety, security and future.

It is not easy to be a complete atheist who believes in no power at all over Creation, because in order to do so you have to accept that there is nothing protecting you from all the dangers of Creation; that means there is nothing protecting you from the animals that could kill you, nothing that prevents you from tripping some day and bashing your head against a rock that kills you, nothing that protects you from the other humans or from the Neanderthals living nearby, nothing that can promise you that you will have food in the next year, nothing that can make sure that the woman who lives with you will give you the child you want, nothing that can promise you life after your death... if you believe there is no greater power at all at work controlling these things, then you will perhaps be filled with constant anxiety. In the modern day, it is far easier for people to be complete atheists, because they do not need to worry about the questions of survival as our ancestors did- but at that time, it must have been psychologically far more difficult for anyone to think like that. People have a need to believe in gods, because they need to believe that they have some way of controlling the natural world and it is not all decided by chance.

But if they prayed to the true God, He didn't listen to them. Their beauty was gone, and they had become monsters, and hence God had no desire to gaze upon them. They could pray all they liked, and He gave no answer, and perhaps they completely failed to realize the reason He gave no answer was because of the evil that they were doing that they had decided to deceive themselves into believing was good.

God sent them no angel, no prophet, no messenger to explain these things to them and get them to change... because they didn't deserve such. He would only do so for the people of Israel in much later history for the sake of their forefather Abraham, but if Abraham had not offered a sacrifice of his own son to God, God would have simply let his descendants be deceived without giving them a wake-up call to change. And God would only give a wake-up call to the entire pagan world after His own Son had been sacrificed for them. He did not do it for them before that point, because they didn't deserve it and no one had paid a price to earn such help, and if God gave such help to them anyways without anyone paying the price, then there would be no justice.

The apostles and the church could only gain permission to preach to the world once Jesus had been sacrificed. It is only because Jesus has given up a sacrifice that the mission of the church is able to be accomplished. God preserved the Jews' faith in Him, for the sake of their ancestor Abraham, and if it was not for him, God would just let them deceive themselves to oblivion as He did for the pagans. Similarly, God gives and preserves faith in Him among gentile nations now, for the sake of Jesus who was sacrificed for them, and if it was not for His sacrifice, God would just let them continue in their pagan delusions without knowledge of the Truth.

Prior to His sacrifice, however, almost all the world was in the grips and delusions of paganism. Even though failing to give them such a wake-up call meant they would seemingly continue in sin indefinitely without ever waking up, and that their sins would cause them so much grief and evil... God would not wake them up, because they didn't deserve it, no one had paid a price for them yet, and the devil stood as their accuser reminding God that if He were to help them get their beauty back without such a price being paid, then His Word would be untrue.

They sinned against God, and so God punished them by making them unaware of His existence and to let them believe in the things their own imaginations invented, and because they were unaware of His existence, so they continued to sin. It went in a circle like this that was seemingly unbreakable. And had it not been for the sake of Jesus, this would simply continue without end.

And yet Jesus was not actually necessary for the circle
to be broken: the people were capable of waking
themselves up, because the law of God was written on
their own heart. If they recognized the evil that they
did, and changed their ways, God would have answered
them and revealed Himself to them. But they failed to
do so, because they ultimately did not love the Truth.

Therefore, in those days of the cavemen, because they
needed to believe in a power that controlled the world
but the real God gave them no answer, and they didn't
know why, their desire for such a power became a
weakness that left them open to temptation.

The communication between humans and the spiritual
world can take place in many different ways; through
feelings, through thoughts, through dreams, through
visions, through the observance of things in the natural
world, through anything at all in fact.

The gifts that God gives to every person, which they
need to fulfill their vocation, all have a parallel use for
evil. If it were impossible to use them for evil, then it

would be impossible to sin, and if it was impossible to sin, then it would be impossible to love as well. Hence, every gift that God gave to people had to be able to be used for evil purposes as well as good purposes.

Hence, the man who warns people of the sharks, perhaps has certain talents that God gave him which allows him to love people, and the God disguised behind their faces, by warning them about the sharks. Perhaps he was given good swimming skills, perhaps he was gifted with a good way of being able to talk to people to make them realize how serious a danger was, perhaps he was given enough intelligence to understand how sharks behave, etc. He can use all these talents for love, or he can use them for evil. He can use his talents to give the love, that God intended him to give, by use of his work in warning people, or he could use these same talents for some other purpose. Perhaps, if he lives a sinful life, he will take his knowledge of sharks to help poachers who want to hunt them illegally, so he can get lots of money; perhaps he will take his good way of being able to talk to people to get them to feel like there is a danger, and use this skill in sinful arguments with his wife, neighbours or co-workers to persuade them to think there is a big danger if they don't do as he says.

The same is true for every vocation; the good gifts that God gives to a person has a parallel use for sin.

No matter what the gift is, it can have a parallel use for sin.

Tionchar and spiritual capacity, is just the same. Although perhaps it is harder to understand, how it is the same.

With physical things, maybe it is easier to understand. God gave a woman a capacity to bear children, and she can take this capacity to sin through abortion or to do good through giving life to someone. God gave a businessman all the talents he needed to make lots of money, and he can take this money to benefit himself selfishly or he can use this money to support himself with what's needed for his own support and to give the remainder to people who need help.

But with spiritual gifts, how does it get used for evil?

The human being's capacity to be able to communicate with God becomes used for communication with demons. The tionchar of every person has an equivalent use for evil, just as the physical attributes have equivalent uses for evil.

All the power which comes through prayer comes from God, however, and God does not listen to prayers made in sin, so how can these things have an equivalent use?

God answers the devil's prayers because the devil points at God's own Word, and says that either the Word is untrue, or this prayer must be granted, and God must grant the prayer therefore. The devil wants to tempt someone and points out the person's own sins, their lack of love for God and the fact that this person doesn't deserve to know the Truth, and God must grant it, or else there is no justice.

The devil acts as an intercessor between God and human beings, and depending on the spiritual gifts within the tionchar of each person, he will be able to secure answers from God.

This is perhaps hard to understand, so some cases will be needed to look at this in better detail.

Let us suppose that 100,000 years ago, there was a wei'nu born in Africa among the people who modern homo sapiens would descend from. Let us suppose that this woman's particular vocation was to be the mistress of Jesus as the one who warned people of coming danger within the prehistoric period.

This wei'nu was the proper owner, so to speak, of this aspect of Jesus. And if she repented of her sins, and turned to prayer, God would have shown Himself to her and spoken with her in a very deep way. And he would have, through her, warned the people she lived among of all the dangers, be it physical or spiritual that dwelled around them. But she was not sorry for the evil things that she did in her life, and so she never came to see the truth, nor did she ever inherit this kind of power that God intended to work through her in His original plan.

But this great spiritual capacity had a parallel use for evil. The devil would be able to speak with her, more than to a normal person, precisely because she had this gift. He could not go to a normal person and speak to the way that he could speak to her, because that was not part of their vocation and was not among the gifts that God gave to them. But to her, it was, and hence this kind of communication was possible.

It was set down by God that this gift, along with every gift a person has in their vocation, should be retained by the person, whether or not they used it for sin or for love. In a similar way, if you are a rich person who uses one's wealth as a miser and does not help others, the law still rightfully recognizes that the wealth belongs to you. The tionchar is the same.

Because she was meant to have this kind of capacity, but she didn't use it for good, therefore the devil was permitted to come and use it for evil.

He could talk to her, and she could talk to him. Just in

the same way as Jesus originally intended to have a relationship with her.

Perhaps among the people she lived with, her ancestors had long ago abandoned and forgotten about the God of Adam and Eve. Perhaps for more than 100,000 years, the knowledge had already been lost among this little piece of humanity.

But because they lived in a harsh world, with much suffering and pain, they still needed a god who would listen to their prayers, who would protect them, who would guarantee their safety, guarantee their food supply, guarantee their ability to produce an offspring, etc. In short, they needed to believe that they could control the things they couldn't control with their own strength, and the existence of a god could provide the answer to that.

They needed a god to exist. So they imagined gods to exist.

People everywhere in prehistory probably looked towards the nature around them, the big mountains, the lightning of the sky, the brightness of the Sun, the Moon, the stars, and all the amazing things in creation, and in ignorance they thought that perhaps these things were gods. They had to be gods, because if there were no gods, then who would take care of them?

Let us suppose that her particular ancestors came to worship a volcano that erupted occasionally, and upon seeing this eruption, her ancestors were convinced that this was a god. And they prayed to this volcano and sacrificed things to it, and the tionchar of the ordinary people was thereby turned to evil and the devil would sometimes answer their prayers in order to keep them deceived, and God permitted the devil to answer their prayers because they deserved to be deceived. The same capacity which the ordinary people were given in their tionchar in order to pray to God was thereby used for evil.

The devil did not tell them that the volcano was god, they imagined this themselves, but he took advantage of their own imagination to cement them into their stupidity, so that he could harm them.

Suppose there was a man with a particularly unique kind of tionchar who lived among her ancestors at the time they first saw the eruption of the volcano, and when the people decided to try praying to the volcano, the man had a vision and saw the devil, who said to him, 'here I am. I am your God! I am the power you prayed to that lives in that volcano and I will protect you. Pray to me and I will help you with all these things. Do not look any longer for the reason why the God of Adam and Eve does not answer you! For goodness sake, stop trying to find Him as though He exists and could help you! For I am the true God and I can answer all your prayers. Now go and tell this to all the people, that I, Volcano-god, am real and desire their worship.'

This man, with the particularly unique kind of tionchar, if he had turned from his sins and sought the True God, God would have given him a vision, in which He would have spoken to him in the same way, telling him that he would look after the people, and that they needed to pray to Him, and that he needed to tell the rest of the people about this vision. But because he did not turn from his sins in life, this same spiritual gift was then turned to evil. The devil could not have given the same vision to any other person, because other people did not have that vocation and it was not part of the test in their lives (whether to use the talents for love or for evil) in the same way as it was part of the test in this man's life. The devil cannot add gifts to the ones that God already gave to people, he can only twist the ones that God already gave.

And perhaps the devil communicated with these people over many millennia, as they worshipped this volcano that they lived near, occasionally giving people dreams, visions, or perhaps lesser things, like feelings, sense of presence, the arrangement of things in their lives in a fashion that shows an intelligent design, etc. Very simply, every gift that people would have originally had in their spiritual lives with a true faith in God, becomes twisted to a pagan faith that worships a demon that hides himself behind the name of a god they think to exist.

Now, this wei'nu living 100,000 years ago, perhaps started talking with the devil (whom she thought to be the volcano god) and then became like an intercessor between him and the people. She gave them a sign by correctly predicting when the next eruption would occur, so they all evacuate the area for safety and the eruption comes, and their faith is greatly cemented. And this sign was given to her, because her natural vocation was to be mistress of Christ as the one who warns people, and therefore she was allowed to perform a parallel sign for the devil.

To a normal person, they could not do this, because it was not part of their vocation. They had tionchar too, which could be used for demons rather than for God, but it was not given to them to be to the same depths as this woman reached.

And she then became a shaman in her community. If the people needed something that their god could provide for them, then they went to her and she would perhaps do some kind of ceremony or special rite, or perhaps they would sacrifice something, or do some kind of magic spell, and this would then bring the power of their 'god' to help them.

In the Aurignacian culture of ancient Europe, from 50,000 – 20,000 years ago, there have been found a collection of statues and carvings that seem to have some semblance to each other even though they are dated thousands of years apart. Pictures of them can be found on the internet (you can also take a look at the cover of this book).

The ones we have today, are probably just a sample of a much larger number that actually did exist (since usually it is only a small number that will survive to the present day). One of the most common themes in these statues or figurines is the depiction of women, often in grotesque forms, with large breasts or abdomens. They are called 'venus figurines'. We don't know what these things meant to the people at that time, but if everything I write about the wei'nu and tionchar is true, what if these were some of the first shamans? Suppose that they were wei'nu born at that time, with such power worked through them that people thought of them as gods themselves, maybe even feeding them so much that they got fat like as depicted in the figurines. I don't know.

So many gods and goddesses of the ancient world, perhaps were even real human persons at one time or another. There may have been an Artemis/Diana, there may have been an Osiris, there may have been a Jade Emperor, there may have been an Odin, there may have been a Shiva, etc. They may have been human beings with a special form of tionchar that allowed them to have spiritual gifts (for good or for evil) in their lifetimes not shared by most people. And through human sinfulness, these people were later remembered as deities, rather than as human beings.

All supernatural power that didn't come from God in all of history, whether it be done through the acts of wizards, witches, necromancers, shamans, pagan priests, psychics, clairvoyants, etc; all likewise works in this same way as I wrote in the example above.

The person who practices magic has no power at all. The psychic has no ability read anyone's mind. The necromancer has no power to bring back the spirit of the dead person to talk to. The witch has no ability to curse anyone. The human who seems to wield this power, however, in truth only possesses the tionchar that God gave to them, and it is the demon who wields the power because God has permitted the demon to wield it, and the demon wields it in such a way in order to make it look like the power comes from whatever the foolish human thinks it comes from, in order to keep humans deceived and not looking for the real Truth that answers the test in this life.

Lord, we pray that you save us from the devil's deceptions. Always help us to realize when something is sinful and immoral, even when it is disguised. We ask for these things, if it is your will, in Jesus' name, Amen

IX: Pagan Religions

Paganism started in the way mentioned above; it was merely the turning of the spiritual capacities of people towards demons they called gods, rather than the true God.

When did people start doing this?

We really don't know, because there is no record. But if Adam existed before 300,000 years ago, and all of his descendants after him suffered temptation, it is very easy to believe that it didn't take long for them to turn to the devil in place of the true God.

Being able to know the Truth as it is- is a great blessing. Psalm 119 tells us that God's Word is sweeter than honey, that it is such a great blessing to receive God's teachings, and the psalmist begs God to teach him His statutes and laws. To know the Truth about God and about reality is a very great gift from God. It is a greater gift, in fact, than many other blessings and gifts that can come. It is a greater blessing to know the Truth than it is to be rich in money, it is a greater blessing to know the Truth than it is to have a beautiful spouse, or successful children; it is even a greater blessing than possessing good health or even life itself. But if we sin, then we do not deserve to know the Truth anymore.

The devil is permitted to deceive people, because they

are sinful, and they deserve to be deceived. If people should continue knowing the Truth after they sinned against God, then there would be no justice; it is because we are sinners that we are punished with deception that keeps us unaware of who God really is, what He is like, what His purpose is, etc.

If the sin that began in Adam meant that human beings should all deserve to die, how much less is it to say that this sin also meant that we did not deserve to know the Truth?

If we do know the Truth now, it is only because a price was paid for us that cleared the debt we owed.

And yet, before that price was paid, people were completely capable of finding the true God by their own natural reason. God kept Himself hidden, because if He made it easy for us to know Him, it would be the same as if He made it easy for us to love Him... it would not really be love.

He keeps Himself hidden and silently says to humanity: 'I will hide myself and see who really loves me or not. Those who really love me are going to keep looking for me after I am gone from their sight, and those who do not love me will forget about me once they no longer see me and invent their own gods in my place.'

God is like a very sensitive girl who tells her friends she

is going away when she isn't actually going anywhere, but she says this because she wants to test to see if they will really feel bad or miss her. And the very sensitive girl is like that, because she was made in God's image and her own character is telling others something about the One who created her.

And God was very hurt, however, because almost everyone went away. No one really cared about Him, and they didn't look for Him.

What was the devil able to do for them?

The devil could go to God and ask God for everything that they were asking their god (the devil in disguise) to give to them. Almost everything that they would have asked from God in a prayer life had some parallel that the devil could have given them through their paganism and witchcraft.

Suppose that the wei'nu mentioned above lived with the clan of other humans near the volcano, sleeping in and around some caves on the side of the volcano.

One day another group of humans moved into their

territory and the clan in the caves on the mountainside became aware of their presence and feared them. They could have gone to make peace with them, share gifts with them or at least treat them with tolerance. But they were afraid that perhaps they would be dangerous, and worried about their safety. So they asked their shaman to turn to their god for an answer.

The devil wanted them to sin, because he wanted to hurt them. The most beautiful thing a person can possess is to love other people, and the devil envied human beings and did not want human beings to possess this thing that he had lost. The devil then gave her an answer to her prayer. She dreamt at night of seeing a monster enter their cave, killing them and it was very terrifying. She woke up and interpreted the dream as a sign from their god that these newcomers were very dangerous and said that they must go and kill them in order not to be killed first. And this dream was given to her, because it was within her vocation to be the mistress of the Lord as the One who warns people who don't know Him.

So they prepared their weapons: very crude tools, heavy sticks, hand-held stones. And they got ready to sneak up on the new group to murder them. But they worried about losing the fight... they needed a God who could promise them safety, for they didn't have the courage to go and fight if they could not be assured of victory. And so they asked her to use her powers to get the god to help them. The Shaman casted a spell to do so.

The devil said to God, 'They are now asking me that they can kill the enemy band from the other part of the forest. Can I be given the power to give this to them?'

God said to the devil, 'But if I let you do this, then they will think you really are a god and they will worship you as such, and they will be very greatly deceived.'

The devil said to God, 'Yes, of course. But do you see how little they love you? You hide yourself from them and they forget about you, and could not care even a little bit about looking for you. Does that not hurt your feelings? Does that not give you pain? Therefore, do they not deserve to be punished? If you were to answer their prayer and reveal yourself to them, then it would be unjust, for they did not deserve to know you and be in the midst of such sin at the same time. But if I use this method to deceive them, and keep them living in the filth and sin that they live in presently, then they will get what they deserve! Even if they kill the bodies of their enemies, they will kill their own souls by doing so, and become monsters. And they deserve to be monsters, do they not? The greatest gift you give to a person is to be a good person; they have hurt you so many times, do they not deserve for me to use this method to deprive them of that blessing?'

God said to the devil, 'This is all true. They deserve to be deceived and to suffer the things you say. But what about the other band, will it be just to give you the power to let them be killed by your followers?'

The devil said to God, 'Do you see what the other band does? They are also such sinners and do things that offend you. They beat their women, they have sex with their siblings, their leader even murdered his father because of a temper tantrum, and the rest of them all said nothing about this. What do you think, do they not also deserve to die?'

God said to the devil, 'Your accusations are all true. I cannot be blind to it. If they had repented of their sins and turned away from evil, then you would have no power to either deceive the one band in this manner or to have the other one killed off. But I see that they are sinful and deserve no such protection. All of them are in your power; I am sick of them, you may do what you like with them.

And so, they go to find the other group of humans. The devil arranges it so that they meet them right at the time while they are very tired and hungry, and do not have the strength to fight, and so they kill them all; throwing their enemy to the ground, taking their stones and bashing their heads until they die. The person who suffered the greatest harm in this, however, was not the person to die such a cruel death, because that person only lost the physical life... the person who suffered the greatest harm in this, was the person who committed murder and lost his very soul. And the devil wanted him to suffer such harm, because he hated him deeply.

They achieved victory and returned to their cave. Their enemies were destroyed. A monster would enter their cave upon returning, just as the shaman saw in her dream; but it was not their enemy, it was their own selves, and that which the monster had killed were their own souls.

They had done something very evil. They thought that what they did was right, because they worried about the other humans coming to attack them first. But, if the situation had been reversed, they would not think it right. If they went to some other place, where they had not been before and where other humans lived, and the other humans saw them and decided to kill them because of their intrusion... they would have thought that this was a very evil thing; that the other humans would be such monsters for killing them like that. Hence they knew the law of God, because it was written on their own hearts, but they simply failed to open their eyes to it.

The whole world fell into this pattern. There were some exceptions, however. From Adam to Noah, from Noah to Abraham; the people mentioned in that family line were people who preserved the knowledge of the true God and kept themselves clean of the sins that filled the rest of the world. Abraham knew of God because his ancestors, during those hundreds of thousands of years, had maintained this knowledge from one generation to the other without losing or forgetting it, and they kept themselves relatively clean from the sins of the world. They were a family, a clan, among all the peoples of the ancient world, who preserved this knowledge of the true God from Adam and Eve. There is never a time in the Earth's history when God does not have a people on the Earth bearing His name- whether today, the future, or even then.

I imagine that the names of the people mentioned in Genesis, are the names of real people, but whose ages and exact descent are probably not as mentioned in Genesis. From Adam to Abraham could be a period of several hundred thousand years, including multitudes of generations in between. Although the literal reading of text indicates that one begot the other, I think it perhaps also could be read as saying that one begot the line that produced the next one. For example, Enoch was sixty-five years old when he became the father of Methuselah. Enoch could have had dozens or maybe even hundreds of children in his 365 year lifetime. And the vast majority of these children who have lines of descent, which would not preserve the knowledge of God. That is to say, most of his descendants would eventually marry the 'children of men' (the pagans) and worship their gods and turn away from the God of Adam and Eve. However, when he was 65 he gave birth to a particular son, and the descendants of that son would be the ones who would 'take up the baton' (so to speak) of preserving the knowledge of the true God. And from that line, at some point Methuselah would come, so when it says that Enoch begot Methuselah, it is like saying that Jesus is the son of David.

The vast majority of people in this line of descent are not named, but only a few particularly noteworthy and holy people (the first saints) were mentioned.

Genesis is a kind of mythology, but it is a mythology inspired by the Spirit of God. The stories in it are not historically accurate in the sense of dates, places, details, etc. But they are explaining something about the origins of the human race and the world.

I believe that the longevity, lasting centuries for Noah, Adam and others in that line is true, although I think this was true for those named individuals only and not for other people living at that time. In every age, God gives signs to show that He is real and such signs are always done in relation to His own people on Earth, whether we are talking about the miracle at Fatima, the Eucharistic miracle at Lanciano, the gifts of Padre Pio, the wonders done by Moses or the miracles of Jesus. In the days when people lived in caves before civilization began, He must still have given signs. I think that the sign He gave to the cavemen was essentially this: that these few individuals in this line of people who preserved the knowledge of God would live to such long extents while surrounded by all these other people in the world who didn't know God and would die much younger. In itself it was like a symbolic reminder to the prehistoric descendants of Adam that death existed because of sin and a departure away from God.

The story of Cain and Abel is perhaps a reference to the murder engaged in by these early peoples; maybe even if Abel represented the Neanderthals, who are killed off by their older brothers that come out of Africa (the Homo Sapiens) that represent Cain. The Neanderthals had larger brains, were stronger and perhaps in many ways superior to the Homo Sapiens; similarly, Abel surpassed his older brother, who envied him and killed him.

Cain and Abel probably were real people, but at the same time their story is perhaps also archetypal of what was happening in the world during that time. God perhaps punished the world with the flood because of the murdering of early human beings.

But what was the flood of Noah? Scientifically it seems impossible that the whole world was ever completely submerged underwater within that past million years. However, the flood of Noah perhaps refers to the many cataclysmic events that greatly threatened the existence of human beings in this world, like the ice ages, climate changes, volcanic eruptions, food shortages, droughts, natural disasters, etc. through which God perhaps punished the people who were engaging in all these sins, and preserved the very few who followed the law written on their own heart.

The reason it is called a flood is not because the Spirit of God doesn't know what actually happened, but because He is trying to tie the meaning of these historical catastrophes together with baptism, through which the sins of a person's life are washed away. And the Ark itself represents the church, the body of Christ, with the hole in its side out of which blood and water came and through which the survivors of the flood could enter, but in actual history it might not have been an actual boat. But even so, it is worth pointing out that during the Ice Ages, large parts of the northern hemisphere, including even the tops of mountains, were covered with glacial ice; ice is still water, is it not?

Noah was a real person, and he was a just man that God

saved from whatever cataclysm in the natural world it was that killed off many others. Perhaps he lived during the time of the last Ice Age, and when others were dying from starvation for lack of finding food because the whole world they knew was getting more and more covered with ice because the snow didn't stop, and so, at God's guidance, he and his family found a way to survive. If this is how it happened, it is impossible that all human beings would descend from him, however.

Noah was a real person and at the same time he was also an archetype for what happened in that time. For all the sins occurring in the world, God destroyed the cavemen with all these things, and those who kept free from the sins, he would preserve.

When it says 'in this time people began to call upon the name of the Lord' it perhaps refers to the evolution of the brain and the evolution of speech, such that religious concepts and words that capture them had evolved over time, but were not originally in existence during the time of Adam.

The Nephilim or 'giants' who lived in the Earth in the time before the flood, mentioned in Genesis 6, perhaps refers to the giant animals (2000 pound bears, 4-ton Giant Sloths, 4 metre-tall birds in Madagascar, Woolly mammoths, 2.5 metre turtles in Australia, the Irish Elk which had 3 metre long antlers, etc.) that lived on Earth alongside human beings prior to the time of end of the last ice and the beginning of human civilization. If the ice ages and the cataclysms are 'the flood', this would seem to fit perfectly.

People used the tionchar that God gave to them to communicate with the devil rather than with God, to achieve things through magic rather than move mountains with prayer, and yet they didn't realize who God was and that the spirit they were communicating with was actually created by someone else. The spirit lied to them, and deceived them. He also hated the shamans who spoke to him so much- so he taught the shamans to become selfish, to become liars, to present themselves as though they had powers that they didn't, and to use their authority to do evil, and bring people closer to hell. He sometimes would really get answers to the prayers and magic that they practiced, but at the same time, he would frequently not answer their prayers and magic, because God did not always permit him; the shaman would need to give an explanation for this, and so she would lie, or say that there was some other god preventing them, or that their god first needed the sacrifice of something, or any other explanation like that. And some of these explanations were very illogical, and yet people still followed them, because they didn't really love the Truth enough to open their eyes and try to discover who God really was.

This is the beginnings of witchcraft. A witch is the same as those shamans in prehistory; she is merely a person with tionchar who is in communication with the spiritual world, and has power to influence and be influenced by the beings who live in that world. The witch perhaps doesn't even know that they are persons, but maybe thinks it is like an energy force, like a special power, etc. But in truth, it is a person, who deeply hates her and wants to use her to make mischief.

All of these people were 'cavemen', and they populated the world for most of the history of the children of Adam. If Adam was more than 300,000 years ago, and civilization only started 10,000 years ago, then our present time is the exception, rather than the norm of what human experience in this world has been like.

Prior to civilization, most people in the world survived by living off of hunting, foraging or fishing. But beginning about 10,000 years ago, some places in the world discovered that you could plant your own food and grow it; you didn't need to worry about finding food anymore, because you could get seeds and grow your own food. They discovered how to do agriculture, and once they knew this, then they could build large settlements containing many people who lived in one place, and who ate the food that they grew; they didn't need to move around anymore.

The first place to have civilization was in the Middle East. Afterwards, it would later begin in other places like India, China, Mexico, etc.

There is something unexplained in this, however. Because the places that developed agriculture were on different sides of the world from each other.

One might answer this question by claiming that agriculture was invented in one place and then spread to other places, just like how when you have a new invention, it gets created in one place and then spreads to others. But that was probably not the case here, because if it started in the Middle East, then how did it get to Mexico or South America? Furthermore, while it got to China or India later, it didn't seem to exist in the places in between, hence it seems like each of these areas must have developed independently of each other.

There were no ships that travelled the oceans at the

time, and people of different parts of the world were completely isolated from each other. It is believed by many experts that agriculture in China developed independently of the Middle East. If it was a coincidence that they developed at the same time, then this seems very strange.

If it was a coincidence, then why did it not happen in the tens of thousands of years prior? How could it be that the ancestors of the Mesoamericans, the ancestors of the people in India, the ancestors of the people in China and the ancestors of the people of Middle East, all existed for tens of thousands of years in different places, evolved racial differences and passed down genes separately from each other, but they all coincidentally came to discover agriculture within the last 10,000 years, and yet were completely isolated from each other?

It is possible that there is a natural explanation that explains this perfectly and there are many anthropologists who have attempted to do so. It is also possible that the answer to this riddle is not found in natural explanations.

After the flood, God told Noah that He would never again destroy all living things on the earth, and then made a covenant with Noah. Perhaps what this means is that after the last Ice Age, for the sake of Noah and other survivors like him of these sorts of events who prayed for their descendants, God granted it that human beings should be permitted to learn agriculture so they could survive in the world better.

They did not deserve this kind of help, but for the sake of those righteous who spoke to God on their behalf (like Noah in the covenant of the rainbow), God let them have it. The sun and the rain is what makes a rainbow, and the sun and the rain is what makes agriculture work, by which human beings could escape the fate that their ancestors would have experienced in prior catastrophes.

God knew that human beings had evil desires inside of themselves from their early childhood, and that there was no way of solving this problem through continual punishment that wiped them out. But He told them that they must not kill; for if they continued to kill each other as cavemen like before- civilization, which involves large communities living together in peace, could not exist then. So, if they killed, then people could not form civilization, and thus they would be without agriculture, and once again made subject to the natural forces which would kill them off periodically. In other words, if the generations after Noah broke the covenant with God, they would have the flood once more.

However, the covenant God made with Noah actually had two conditions for the human beings and not just one. God said not to kill and also not to eat the blood with the flesh.

What did the second one mean?

The Jewish people didn't eat blood with the meat (and many practicing Jews still do not do so today). This wasn't for sanitary or health reasons, but it had to do with something far more profound than that. Moses would later say to the people that no one is to eat blood, because blood is the life and blood needs to be put on the altar to make atonement for their sins.

They were doing this practice out of a profound respect for the sacrifice that was needed to atone for their sins. They held it in such deep respect that they refused to eat any blood at all with the flesh, because blood, 'the life', needed to be given for making atonement for their sins.

If, however, they ate the blood, then it would mean that they did not hold the atonement for their sins in the proper respect that it deserved. But if you don't atone for sins, then that means they have to be punished; if you steal something, you can either give it back yourself or you can get caught and it be forcibly taken away from you, and you be thrown in jail. If you sin, you can either go to make atonement for it yourself or you can make no atonement, and wait for God's punishment to deal out justice.

Eating the blood is not really the point. It is not as though all the people in the world after Noah would be doomed if they ate blood. It is rather the question of whether you treat the atoning sacrifice as something serious and important or not, which is the point.

If the generations after Noah, when they sinned, made atonement for their sins, then they could escape God's wrath. If not, then the devil would stand as their accuser, and God would have to allow them to suffer.

Bridget of Sweden lived through the Black Death that killed 1/3 of the population of Europe. She asked her Spouse, 'why do you send famines and plagues on the earth' and His response was 'a thief must pay back double what he steals. I give human beings all the good things of the earth but they do not give thanks for them in return, and so they are thieves'. If people give thanks to God, make atonement for their sins, give back the love that God first gave to them... which was what the Jews were doing when they were putting the blood on the altar, then they are spared those things. When the people who lived in Bridget's time were being killed off in a kind of flood, it was because they had 'eaten the blood' by not treating the duty to give back to God as seriously as they ought.

Padre Pio said that it would be easier for the Earth to exist without the Sun, than for it to exist without the sacrifice of the holy mass.

If people violate the covenant on either point, by killing people or by neglecting to hold the sacrifice needed for their sins in respect, then the covenant is broken and the flood may return.

Furthermore, civilization would progress through obedience to the fourth commandment. Only in obeying your parents, can a family unit function. Only through obeying laws of a state can a society function. If people disobey their parents when they are children, they will suffer many consequences, because their parents know many things they don't, and the parents will help their children avoid many disasters later on in life... but only if the children obey this commandment by listening to them. Similarly, states make laws in order so that society can have peace, can get richer, will not be bullied by its neighbours, etc. If people disobey these laws then the society cannot function.

The fourth commandment is the only commandment that promises that the reward (and punishment) will occur in this life. Moses said 'honour your father and mother, that you may live long in the land God gives to you'.

Hence, the societies that followed this commandment retained the wisdom of their parents and ancestors, and kept society in peace and prosperity. These societies would become the more powerful civilizations, and they would have power to enslave other societies that failed to do as they did.

Similarly, consider the story when Noah got drunk and lay in his tent. Ham, the father of Canaan, came into the tent and saw his father's nakedness and went out and told his brothers. His brothers, however, walked in backwards to cover their father with a sheet.

When Noah came to his senses and knew what his youngest son had done to him (at no point is it made clear that Ham was the youngest son, although this seems to be the assumption of the narrative), he curses Ham's son Canaan and says that a slave of slaves shall he be to his brothers. And then he blesses Shem and Japheth (his other sons) and makes Canaan their slave.

The assumption I make in interpreting the narrative is that Ham disrespected his father's honour by looking upon his nakedness, and then rather than covering it, he instead told others about it. Ham's sin was that he did not honour his father as he should have.

The other sons, however, refused to look upon his nakedness and covered it in respect.

He punishes Canaan rather than Ham, as a way of indicating that the punishment will carry on to the next generation. Like how Moses said that the sins you commit shall be visited to the third and fourth generation. Because Ham had failed to follow the fourth commandment, therefore his descendants would suffer as a result of it and be made slaves of others.

In later times people would take this story to justify the slavery of black people because Ham (who had sons other than Canaan) was supposedly the father of Africans, and therefore God wanted blacks to be slaves. But this is a misunderstanding. In fact, it makes little sense, because Canaan's descendants supposedly were in the Middle East (in the land of Canaan) and the African nations were supposedly from the other sons of Ham who did not receive the same curse from Noah.

The story is not about racial superiority; it is rather about the 4th commandment. It is true that it is applicable to many African nations that failed to develop themselves and became colonized by other nations that did and many of which today continue to revolt or engage in civil wars, but it is also equally applicable to almost every other civilization in the world at some point or another, including white people, because western and northern Europeans were also made into slaves through roman conquests which were only possible because they failed to develop their own civilization. And the power and success of worldly society is greatly connected to whether or not the society is following the fourth commandment.

The strongest type of society is not the one which has the most resources, the most people, the most strategically located land mass, etc. The strongest type of society is the one where children obey their parents and respect their elders, students obey their teachers, workers obey their bosses and the people of the country obey the laws of the state. I think for this reason, countries like Germany and Japan overpowered so many other nations, even those that were larger in population or possessing more natural resources, in World War II, because those two states perhaps kept these values better than many others. The great colonial empires of the past likely succeeded for the same reason; Christian civilization, while still very sinful, had over the course of many centuries, kept this commandment better than others because Christianity really did alter their culture. But pagan places where the commandment was kept very well, like in parts of East Asia that were strongly influenced by Confucianism, would never be colonized or at least not completely. This can perhaps be attributed to the influence of Confucius over East Asia, and the fact that, even though he was a pagan philosopher, his teaching contained an important aspect of the true moral law. Confucius said that 'he who does not respect his elders will achieve nothing in life'; the Holy Spirit works everywhere, even in pagan countries.

In America people stop at red lights even at 3 am in the morning when no one is around, because it is the law. In India people run through red lights even in the middle of the day. In Japan, when the earthquake happened in 2011 and the Fukushima plant melted down, even though thousands of people evacuated their homes, there was almost no one who went back to start breaking into the empty homes and looting them. In South Africa, your home might be broken into at any time, no matter what the circumstances. Why is one society stronger than the other? It is because if this pattern exists from individual to individual, over many fields of life and crosses centuries and centuries, the difference in strength of the whole nation is the end result. And people who do such things will leave their children in poverty and weakness. Canaan shall be a slave to his brothers.

Japan and Korea have few natural resources, comparatively, with other countries and post 1945, post

1953 their respective countries were in complete ruin. Korea, in 1953, was comparable to parts of West Africa in GDP. But today they are some of the wealthiest and strongest states in the world. The Democratic Republic of the Congo (formerly Zaire) sits on top of trillions and trillions of dollars' worth of gold, diamonds, metal ores, minerals as well as renewable natural resources (including timber, hydroelectric capacity, agricultural capacity, etc.), and yet it is one of the poorest and weakest states in the world. In Japan, it is sometimes possible to even lose one's wallet on the street in a crowded place and for no one to take it until you come back to pick it up; in the Congo, the lowest level policemen or civil officer will try to get money out of you illegally. Japan is a country with very few people who believe in Christ and in the Congo, the majority of the population is Catholic; having the right religion does not make one state stronger than the other, but it is obedience to the fourth commandment that does so.

Societies that follow the fourth commandment the most, over many generations, will ultimately be the strongest of all societies; it has nothing to do with racial or physical superiority. If certain parts of the world or certain cultures are continuously dominated by others, it is not because being this particular race makes one naturally inferior, but it is because people in that place or that culture, over long periods, do not have the proper respect and obedience to the authorities God placed over them.

Because the whole of the truth is contained within the teachings of the church and the grace that comes from God is the thing that is necessary to follow the fourth commandment, therefore states in which the church has a stronger influence should also be able to follow this commandment better, so long as the clergy are doing their job rightly and people are listening to them (a big 'if'). For this reason, western civilization could grow to dominate the world in the past 500 years, and for the same reason, atheist countries that teach people that there is no God or higher order behind the authority of the government, parents, etc. will tend to destroy the strength present in the culture as people only think they have to obey when punishment is immediately present, leaving such societies with no choice other than using excessive force to make people comply to the demands placed on them and ultimately becoming weak states.

Note, that there are misconceptions about what the fourth commandment entails. Respect for parents means to honour the parents for all of one's life, but it only requires obedience to parents while one is still a minor. Obedience to governments means to obey the government's laws at all times, but one is only required to praise or give honour to the government when the law so requires it, and not at any other time. Hence, in cultures where people think that they must obey their parents their entire lives, are not going to receive any benefit from this misconception, and doing so will not make their country stronger. Neither does worshipping them as deities after they are dead. Similarly, places where people praise the government or the governing party, wave the flag, put a picture of the leader in their home, etc. and yet do not pay their taxes, violate the traffic laws, engage in corruption, etc. will receive no benefit from this misconception, and doing so will actually make their country weaker.

Ultimately if you want to make your nation strong, the route to follow is not to get oil, more land, more natural resources, build a big military, attract foreign investment, etc. But the only thing that is really necessary is to make the children obey the parents until they grow up and respect them the rest of their lives, to obey the teachers in the classrooms, obey the bosses at work, obey each relevant authority in their proper place (judges in courtrooms, station staff in the train stations, etc.), and obey the laws of the country at all times, and this is what will make the state strong. Secure the root, and everything else will grow out from it. Destroy the root, and no matter what other advantages you think you have, it will all ruin. Blessed be Japheth and Shem, and let Canaan be their slave.

Societies may either humble themselves by being obedient to the natural authorities God has placed over them, or they will be humbled by being subject to foreigners who will make them slaves or something like it.

Because, I am explaining the details in the anthropological meanings present in the first stories of the bible before Abraham, I may as well do the last one too.

What was the tower of Babel?

If people did not sin, and they had the humility to be guests in the houses of others and took up the service they were meant to do in their own houses, everything would be possible.

If there were no thieves, no one would need a lock on their doors. If there were no liars, we could always trust the testimony of others. People through cooperation, can achieve more than if they were divided and warring. The world economy today with all its wonders, is only possible because of the global connectedness of it; if no one cooperated with one another, however, none of it would be possible.

Civilization is only possible if people are able to live

peacefully in a community. If they are killing each other, then we have to go back to the days of the cavemen before civilization. Similarly, the technology of the modern day is only possible because the world cooperates; if we all hated each other and fought wars between ourselves, the globalized economy and everything it has achieved would be impossible. And there are many things that we are still held back from doing because of sin.

Perhaps the person who could find the cure for AIDS, the cure for cancer or even aging itself, is some peasant who is digging yams in Nigeria, who received no education because he is so poor. And he is so poor because the people who have the money to give him an education, did not want to help him because they were selfish. He is a genius, and his mind is brilliant, and God in fact gave him this particular role, so they are going to need him in order to accomplish this work. They have what he needs, and he has what they need, but because of sin, they cannot achieve what they are capable of. He will live his whole life as a peasant and die at a young age out of poverty. The people in the richer nations will spend most of their income on themselves in their lifetimes, they will get old and get various diseases, and wonder when someone will find a cure for these things and perhaps they pray to God very hard to cure them once they get cancer. And yet, invisibly, it is God's arrangement; just as they did not spend anything to help those people and stop them from dying young, so He does not give this favour to them to extend their lives, and brilliantly it is all invisibly done in such a way that the fact they don't have the cure to the disease is itself the direct result of their selfishness.

After Noah, we are told that people gathered in the plain of Shinar to build a tower. 10,000 years ago, when humans first came together, they began to build the first cities. At that time, if they were without sin and perfectly cooperated, they could have achieved many things. The human brain that exists today is pretty much the same brain as would have existed 10,000 years ago. The Earth at that time contained all the natural resources that we have today. There is no reason why people could not have built all the technology that we have today at that time. They just didn't know how and they were not going to figure it out because of sin.

God could have helped them to discover how, but they were sinful. And so, because they were sinful, they did not cooperate with each other, and divided. People often fight each other because of pride. Nations often fight each other because of pride. Hence through the divisions caused by their own pride, they received God's just punishment which divided them and prevented them from doing everything they were capable of doing. The problems we have today are the same.

When many minds come together and cooperate, they can achieve far more than if they are divided. What divides people? Whether speaking of individuals, or of civilizations: it is pride.

This has a relationship with science and technology: science and technology can advance faster in a given place, if more minds come together and cooperate, but if people divide themselves because of pride, then it can't.

Why is the world of today able to achieve so much that it couldn't do before? It is because the whole world is connected in a way that it couldn't be before. If, however, the nations of the world started wars because they were proud, because they wanted to avenge insults, to insist on their territorial or historic rights, etc. then the whole thing would come crashing down like a collapsing tower.

Despite negative opinions of many people in the world of the intellect of Americans, the truth is that the United States today has the most advanced technology and science of any place in the history of the world. This is only possible because of so many minds coming together in one place and cooperating with each other. If, however, the Americans were to insist that only the aristocracy should be allowed to do science, and the common people, should not because they were lower, then this would not be possible. It is humility that allows the tower to stay standing.

Why was it that such great advances were made in the Islamic world during the early centuries after Muhammad （the so-called Islamic golden age） and they surpassed many other places in the world? It was because so many ideas were coming together from all the places of Muslim territory, from India, to Central Asia, to North Africa, and therefore they could achieve more than places that didn't have such connections. If, however, the Arabs of Damascus or Baghdad were to say, 'we do not need to learn any of these things in Greek, Sanskrit, Chinese, Latin or Persian, because only our Arabic language and Islamic heritage contains real culture and truth' then they would learn nothing and the tower would fall.

Why was it that ancient China invented so many inventions before the rest of the world did? It was because such a huge population living in one place, and with so many minds working together, were able to come together and create these things. And thus, they had cast iron 1000 years before the West, they had paper money when Europe was the in Dark ages, they invented lacquer when the Near East was still in the Bronze Age, they invented gunpowder, they invented the compass, they invented toilet paper, they invented fishing reels, they invented kites. But if the Chinese said, 'from now on we shall consider ourselves as the wisest and most advanced people in the world, and no new ideas will be entertained any longer, because we already know everything', then the tower will be unable to stand.

Through humility, cooperation is possible, and through cooperation, there is nothing that cannot be achieved by the human race. But if there is pride, then it cannot be achieved, minds cannot come together, but minds will be divided and held back from achieving what they are capable of.

Babel was probably a real place. Just like how Noah was a real person. It could have been a place in the early days of civilization where people really were planning on building some big tower, but because of pride, they could not cooperate with each other, got into an argument and a number of them leave, so they no longer have the manpower to finish the task. They then go to live somewhere else, and over a great amount of time, develop a different culture, different language, etc. And all the divisions of the world splitting people into 'us' and 'them' are the results of human pride working over thousands of years, and this prevents us from achieving what we are collectively capable of. Babel was probably a real place, but at the same time it is archetypal to the world at that time, and also today.

As people built the first cities, their communities grew larger. The shamanism of the past became an institutionalized priesthood. The gods they worshipped (who were really just the devil and the demons in disguise) were given temples, idols were crafted to depict them, they offered sacrifices to these gods and developed mythologies about them that tried to explain the origins of everything in the world.

They called on their gods to give them blessings just like they had before; victory in war, security of the dynasty, economic prosperity, etc. And just like before, the devil was permitted to answer these prayers and magic, and thus deceive them because they were sinners and deserved to be deceived. They did not deserve to know the Truth and be saved.

But if they simply turned away from the evil and loved the Truth, they could have been freed from this deception and come to see the true God.

And the devil found that almost everyone loved something else more than they loved the Truth. If someone could see that the idol or the myths told about these gods were illogical, ridiculous or immoral, and instead tried to find what the Truth was, the devil was given permission to put many obstacles in his way so that the only way he could find the Truth again was by loving it more than anything else. And almost everyone failed this test.

The priests of a country would pray to their god, and the devil would answer them in dreams, oracles, auguries, etc. and give them instructions. He would arrange it so that the rulers of the country would require their subjects to worship these idols under penalty of death or other harsh punishment; hence Socrates drank the hemlock and became like a martyr for a God he did not know because he ultimately loved Truth more than his own life. He escaped from the cave and the rest of humanity was still sitting there watching the shadows.

The devil would tempt the people who were learned and understood things about the natural world. He would tempt them with worldly power, wealth and respect to become the priests of these false gods and convince people of lesser intellect into following them. They would perhaps know what days that solar eclipses took place over Babylon, when and by how much the Nile River would rise and fall, the movement of the stars, the preservation of dead bodies, etc. And they knew these things because of their great learning, but they would turn to their people and claim that they possessed this knowledge because the gods had given it to them, and the people were impressed with what they saw and worshipped things that they ought to have known by their own reason were not really gods.

But if anyone spoke up and said that such things were ridiculous, people would laugh at them, because: 'how could you not see that these things are gods?' 'Did you not see the high priest predict the eclipse to the very day?' 'Did you not see how much power they got from worshipping these gods?' And people who loved their own reputations and places in society more than the Truth also went along and worshipped these things.

The devil was instrumental in all of this. He tempted them to give up the search for Truth in favour of belief in his deceptions. It seemed easier for people to believe that these gods were real, because these gods seemed to answer their prayers/sacrifices/magic, because the whole society followed them, because there were consequences if you didn't follow them, and because they didn't know who the True God was. They didn't realize He was hidden from them because they were sinners and did not deserve to know Him. They didn't realize that being deceived by these things was part of His punishment for them.

The devil would get God's permission to answer their prayers, to make it seem like their magic achieved results, to make it seem to them like failing to continue sacrifices brought disaster to their country, to give them dreams and visions, and to even give them things which were supernatural. And thus, he confused them, and kept them away from the Truth that would save their souls.

And so, they worshipped all these false gods which were just puppets for the devil and all the other evil spirits, and these spirits did this because they deeply hated human beings and wanted them to fail the same test that they underwent at the beginning of time.

Lord, we pray for all nations of the world to reject their pagan cultures and to replace them with Christian cultures. We pray that people will stop listening to the devil's deceptions and will recognize the True God. We pray that people be freed from sin, and pure in heart, so that they may see God. We ask for these things, if it is your will, in Jesus' name, Amen

X: The Consequences of Institutionalized Witchcraft

Witchcraft, as you can see, originated by the incorrect use of human tionchar. Instead of human beings using this ability to direct it to God, they rather directed it towards other things. The devil liked this, and he asked God for permission to tempt them to continue doing this, and God gave the devil this permission. Such that the devil became like a hidden intermediary between the one who practiced witchcraft and God; he was the intercessor before God's throne to ask for what the witch thought she was achieving through some other means.

I will give a few more examples here to add more clarity to how this dynamic works.

Suppose a priest in ancient Egypt believed in the national religion and all the magic that was heavily institutionalized in their society. Among their many beliefs they held the notion that every being and object possesses a 'true name' and if you knew this name, you could say it and force it to do your will. And so, in their magic, they would try to learn what the 'true name' of a person or thing was, and then use this name to cast a spell. If the spell didn't work, then they interpreted it as meaning that they didn't have the correct name.

So, this priest wanted to get a woman to fall in love with him, and so he does a ritual which he believes is able to tell him the true name of the woman. Suppose (and I am inventing this part, because I don't know what it looked like) the spell involves creating a statue of her and burning something special in front of it, while saying some special words. He casts this spell and he believes that this spell works, and he expects he will then learn the true name of the woman through it. So, as he casts it, the first weird word that he imagines in his head, he assumes is the woman's name. This weird word did not come from the demons or some supernatural source, but it was just the product of his imagination.

Then he casts another spell to make the woman fall in love with him. Perhaps (again, I am inventing it here) he will take the statue of her again, and pour some oil over it, and put flower petals over it, while saying 'Gagamumukaka, I command your soul to fall deeply in love with me. I command your heart to not be able to continue one day without me.'

The devil did not teach people how to do these spells nor did he give the name to this person. All of these things are just the products of the human imagination. And most of the time, nothing happened. This man would cast the spell, and the girl still didn't fall in love with him. The devil would speak to him in his heart telling him that he needs to keep working on getting the right name. The devil in fact did not have the power to answer this witchcraft every time, but he did have the power to tempt the man to keep pursuing the products of his own imagination.

However, if the devil always did nothing and just let the spells always achieve no results, then it would be impossible to keep them permanently deceived. Hence, one day, after much trying, the devil finally answers it. The girl finds herself suddenly feeling really fond of him, she starts thinking of him at night and wants to be near him, because he seems so sweet and kind to her. She goes to him in secret at night and they get together, and he asks her father for permission to marry her. And thus he, and all the others in this society, remain deceived of the true Power governing the universe that could save their souls if they simply woke up to Him.

This man, if he had worshipped God, would have used this same capacity to pray for people and after long periods of time, and through perseverance, an answer would have come to his prayer. This man did not have particularly great tionchar, but the tionchar he had was enough to accomplish this. This man's primary vocation was not really to the spiritual world, but it was to something different. The truth is that anyone, through perseverance, can receive anything they pray for, so long as it is in the first category. The devil took this ability of his, and applied it to witchcraft.

Suppose in the Philippines, prior to the coming of monotheistic religions to the archipelago, you had a village with a man who claimed to be a sorcerer. And this man entered into trances, and he could see things that were otherwise impossible for him to see; like things in his neighbour's house, things in another place, etc. And he practiced some kind of magic to be able to do this. And the demon, desiring him to be deceived and to think the magic was real, convinced God to give him the power to give the man this kind of divination through the magic.

Suppose also that in this particular place, everyone thinks that you cannot become a sorcerer until you have gone through a special ceremony and to have been schooled by another sorcerer, and the demon, desiring to keep them deceived in the works of their own imagination, then makes it such that this man will not achieve results to his magic until he goes through this process.

He is a person possessing great tionchar; he is a man, and hence his vocation is to things rather than persons, but his particular vocation is to do the work of praying so that people can find their lost things. And if he had worshipped God, rather than doing magic, he would have prayed for help in finding lost things, lost children, etc. and God would have exploited the same gift within him, which formed part of his vocation.

And perhaps, as he is the village sorcerer, when something bad happens to someone and everyone thinks witchcraft has happened, they go to him and ask him for help in finding who the witch is. And, in the meantime, maybe half of the people have already assumed it was one particular old woman in the village who seems suspicious to them. And suppose she is innocent and no one casted magic to have caused the bad thing to happen.

The sorcerer then casts a spell and has a vision (given by the devil) seeing this old woman in her house doing magic, and he tells the others about it, and the whole community gets together and kills her. Thus, all of them become complicit in the murder, and will all collectively burn in hell without repentance. And it is the deception pulled over their eyes by their pagan beliefs, supported by the witchcraft, which convinces them to commit the crime.

Sometimes people might wonder, was it really a curse to be a follower of pagan gods? Were the people who followed the false gods really worse off than those who knew the real God?

The answer to this question is a most definite yes, because if you lack knowledge of the True God and are deceived to follow false gods, you make it much easier for yourself to lose your own morals and become a bad person, and eventually go to hell.

But upon saying this, people will still wonder: why would people being deceived by false gods mean that their souls were also going to be lost? Couldn't one believe in these things, and still be a good person who could pass the test that God gave in this life?

I will use this chapter to explain the answer to this question as best I can.

Firstly, it needs to be understood that because of the effects of original sin, we have a tendency to prefer evil over good. It is easier for people to be lazy than it is to work hard. It is easier to believe it is someone else's fault than it is your own fault. It is easier to receive than it is to give. Our thinking is always prone to selfishness and pride. Even when we do something that is good, the good act turns into pride very easily when we use this to think of ourselves as better than others.

Every human being is like this in every country in the world and in every time in history. The people of the Middle Ages were like this, the people of the 21st century are like this, and the cavemen who lived a hundred thousand years ago were like this. The people of China are like this, the people of India are like this, the people of Africa are like this, the people of the West are like this, the people in rich nations are like this, the people in poor nations are like this, the people in Tibet are like this, the people in the Vatican are like this, etc. There is no one who is excepted.

The life of every person is like this. From the moment we have consciousness, choosing ourselves always feels better than choosing others.

A little girl is born and the mother holds her in her arms. Over time the girl comes to understand that her mother is a person, but she doesn't understand very much else. Just like the angels at the beginning of creation, she is aware of very little but can see that her mother is a person. She cries and gets what she wants from her mother. She eventually realizes that her mother does not like it when she cries, but she cries anyways, because she cares more for her own discomfort than for her mother's desires. Like the angels she has a choice between herself and the other, and she chooses herself. From the very first days of her existence, the mystery of sin has already entered her life.

She becomes a toddler and understands that her mother has rules for her, and her mother is unhappy when she breaks these rules. But she sees things that are fun which are not allowed, and so she chooses herself over the other and breaks the rules. She goes to kindergarten, and she doesn't like the teacher so she doesn't obey, even though this makes the teacher unhappy. If the teacher punishes her for disobeying, she will only obey when she feels like she will get in trouble, but otherwise she disobeys. She goes to school, and makes friends with other girls. She acts differently at home and at school. Her friends tease others and make them feel bad, and to them this is fun. Their own fun is more valuable than the feelings of others. She gets older, and she takes pride in her appearance, and she feels sad when others have beauty which is greater than hers and feels happy when it is less than hers. She begins to have sexual feelings, and she plays with herself; in her deepest innermost heart, it is only just pleasure and herself without another person. She gets a boyfriend. When the boy does not make her happy, she throws him away and gets another one, even though he gets hurt deeply by this; she has a choice between herself and others and she chooses herself. She looks for the boy that pleases her most, she does not care about finding the boy that she can most please.

She goes to university and studies for a career. She chooses the path that will make her the most happy in her future life, she does not think of which field she can choose that will help her to make others the most happy in her future life. While at college she gets pregnant. She can choose between keeping the baby and ending her studies, or aborting the baby and continuing her studies. She chooses her studies over the baby's life. She does not want to believe that the unborn child is a person, so she decides that it isn't, and thereby makes herself feel better. When she meets Christians who tell her that she made a mistake, she does not want to believe that this is true, so she doesn't. And she feels happy in believing bad things that others tell her about Christians, when she learns of crimes committed by Christians in past history, when she learns of people disproving the bible or the existence of God, because this ultimately makes her own world more comfortable to live in.

She graduates from university and begins her career. She makes money. She uses the money to get a nicer house, to buy nicer clothes, to live a happier life. She spends lots of money going on many vacations to places that multitudes suffer in because no one helps them out of their poverty. She thinks there is nothing she can do to help them, because she thinks the money she spends on herself is a necessity.

She marries a man. They have children. The children and the man are very important in her life. But she sees that if she gives too much time for them, then she has to sacrifice her career. She worries about what the society around her thinks of such women, she thinks that she can do both. Her children do not see her too often; they develop problems in their lives with their morals, their personalities, their psychologies. She blames this on the influence of others, she blames it on the father, she blames it on the tv; she doesn't blame herself. She fights with her husband over little problems that she treats as more important than the love the two of them ought to be practicing towards each other every day.

Her children grow up. She pressures them to take the job she wants them to take, she pressures them to marry the person she wants them to marry, she pressures them to be what she wants them to be. She cares of her own happiness over the happiness of the other.

She gets older, her husband dies. She has many problems in her life, and her children put her into a retirement home. She complains about all the little mistakes of the staff, either real or imagined. She says things to intentionally hurt their feelings because this makes her feel better. She dies.

She meets God. God tells her, "Did you not realize this life was a test? I asked you every minute of every day, only one question: 'do you really love me'? I asked you this question, but you didn't know it was me, because I was disguised behind the faces of all these others."

He reveals to her everything. She sees how wrong she was and how right He was, and she sees what she deserves. But, she can't accept the Truth. Rather than repenting and begging forgiveness, she retains the same attitude of hostility she had at the moment of her death.

She is filled with hatred towards Him, blaming Him for all her own sins and leaves His presence, even though He shows her the marks in His hands, telling her how much He loves her. But she sees Him face to face and the wounds of His body but still refuses to believe that His love is real. She has seen eternity, and she feels that she would rather suffer forever than to accept a God like this. She follows the devil's example at the beginning of the world, and prefers to go on suffering forever than to give up herself and see the Truth. The sparks and fires of hell comes from nowhere else than the sinner's own heart.

This is how Adam's sin works itself out in the world. All these actions of hers stem from the fact that it feels nicer to choose herself over the other.

And the truth is that all of these sins are only possible because of the society around her. If the society taught all these things were wrong and put many obstacles in the way, it would be much harder to do them. But why is it impossible for the society to teach them? It is because the religion that teaches all these things are wrong, is itself subject to social rejection, and because people believe that something different is the truth. They believe something different is the truth because of the devil's deception, and witchcraft is deeply involved with this deception.

If we fight against our own desires and circumcise our own hearts, then we can be with God. But if we fail to do so, then we do not deserve to know God, and God's punishment is allowing the devil to deceive people to make them follow stupid things. Hence this is why God told Abraham to keep a covenant of circumcision; because the circumcision was meant to symbolize the cutting off of your own desires of your selfish heart in order to follow God- and it was because all the people of the world gave in to the desires of their selfish hearts that they fell into sin, and thereby did not have their prayers answered and ultimately fell away from God and went into deception. Therefore, when God chose Abraham to be the father of those on Earth who would believe in One God, He told him to keep this sign, because it was the failure of keeping what this sign meant which had led the whole world into paganism.

But, many people fail to circumcise their hearts, and they become controlled by the evil desires inside of them. The society around them has a very great influence on this. The society may teach them that their sins are acceptable, even though these sins will doom them to hell. But if the society believed in the Truth, it would not be able to teach or believe that these sins were acceptable. Hence, the devil will try very hard to make sure the society does not believe in the Truth, and witchcraft is a very important means of accomplishing this end.

I will try to illustrate this with a few short case studies:

In the Roman Empire, the society worshipped many gods and the society was filled with sins. In Paul's letter to the Romans, the first chapter gives a long list of such sins.

And Paul, begins his letter by talking about their idolatry, in serving the creature rather than the Creator. It is from their paganism that all of these other sins stem from. How did that happen, however? Why does believing in many gods, as opposed to the true God, cause the society to become like this?

If you know the true God exists, and that He forbids all of these things that Paul lists in Romans 1, and that you are going to go to eternal hellfire for doing these things, then it becomes much harder to do them. If you are aware of God and about the eternal punishment waiting for you for doing these things, you might become so scared by it that you will then feel obliged to change your life, stop doing these things, and thus pass the test in this life.

But what if you are not aware of this? What if you believe in something different? What if you believe in many gods, and you do not believe that these gods punish you for doing any of these things. In fact, you have mythologies about these gods which depicts the gods doing all these sins themselves, as though the gods were the same as sinful human beings. Not only this, but you are told that the gods take delight in the violence of the gladiatorial games and that they require human beings to worship them with such evil. Contrary to popular belief, the gladiatorial games were not officially put on in the name of public entertainment, but they were officially done in the name of honouring the gods.

Some of the gods take delight in people honouring them with getting drunk on wine and engaging in licentious behaviour. The gods take delight in people putting on pornographic theatre shows depicting their various myths, including all the adulteries between gods and human beings.

Now, if you do any of these things yourself that you see the gods doing in their myths, then you will go to hell. If you watch slaves being killed in the arena and you agree with it, then simply for your agreement with the murder, you become an accomplice, and you will go to hell. If you watch the pornographic theatre shows and it gives you lust, and yet you keep going, then you will go to hell.

If you just do any grave sin at all, and you don't believe the gods punish sins, and so you do it without repenting, then you will go to hell.

And so, the idolatry brings society to be sinful just like this.

But perhaps you have doubts about whether these gods are really real. Maybe you rightly see things in these myths and stories which are illogical or impossible, and so you begin to question them; wondering if maybe there is some other truth behind this life and behind this world.

And so, here is where the witchcraft comes in.

The devil will give you signs, through the witchcraft of human beings, in order to overcome your doubts and keep you in believing in the lies the society taught you about the nature of reality. The pagan priests will perform signs for you, you will find answers to your prayers and sacrifices, which to your eyes you can recognize an intelligent design within, thus confirming to you that these things were real.

The oracles will predict events, and some of them will happen as predicted. The spells of the witch or sorcerer will find results to it. And so, you can rest assured that these gods are real.

People will communicate in their own hearts with the demons, whom they perhaps believe are gods or some similar power, and the demons will go to God's throne and secure permission to use power to keep the human beings under deception.

And thus, they bring countless numbers of people to fail

the test given to them in this life, which they perhaps would have passed if the temptation was not present, or in other words, if the society taught them the Truth about God rather than pagan lies.

Take the example of the old imperial China. People had many superstitions that formed their basis of understanding the world.

They believed (and many Chinese still believe today) that you needed to burn money in order to give the money to your ancestors in the afterlife in order so that they could buy food. Many of them believed that if you failed to do so, then this meant you were a bad descendant, and maybe even your ancestor would punish you, by giving you some kind of bad luck in your life, while if you burned the money, then this meant you were a good descendant, and that your ancestor would reward you, perhaps by helping you in your life now.

They also believed in many traditional spirits and gods, which also had mythologies and stories surrounding them. Daoism gave them many quasi-philosophical beliefs and superstitions about the way the natural world was arranged. Buddhism was also present and taught people its own beliefs.

And like people in all places, the Chinese were subject

to the consequences of Adam's sin, which made them prefer evil over good. And so Chinese society was filled with many sins and people found it easier to do these sins, because the society failed to teach them that these things were wrong.

These religions may have contained teachings that were good sometimes; things that forbade all these sins. But these religions also had errors and sometimes also allowed people to do things that were bad. They perhaps also failed to be prophetic.

Buddhism perhaps taught people that it was wrong to do these things, but maybe it had no ability or power to get people to put such teachings into practice. Hence it told people not to put value on the passing temporary world, and everyone agreed that this was a very noble idea, and they would go to the temple to offer incense to Buddha, and then go back to their normal lives without any difference at all; while still doing the same sins and vices that will doom them to hell.

Not all people, of course. For there are some who would take what was good in the religion and actually change their lives considerably. In the roman empire, there were people who found wisdom in pagan philosophies and lived virtuous lives as well. Pagan religions also had truths in them that could also help lead people to God sometimes.

Buddhism told them that these things were wrong, but did not tell them that it would end in eternal hellfire. Rather it always gave a second-chance to you in the next life when you get reincarnated, so perhaps you are not so worried. Or maybe the people who really believe in Buddhism and are living their lives without the taint of the sins of the society, believe that one must preserve harmony and not fight with people of different mindsets, such that they do not rebuke people in sin in order to save them, nor do they act as prophets to the society they live in, and so no one gets worried about their souls.

And your other beliefs about the spiritual world, about your ancestors needing money burned for them, about the rain god or about the moon goddess... none of these things succeeds in bringing you to get rid of your sins and pass the test in this life. Perhaps they do not tell you to do evil, like in the case of the roman religion, but at the same time, they fundamentally fail to wake you up and get you to save your soul.

If the society changed and came to know the True God, the truths about heaven and hell, sin and punishment, etc. then perhaps many people would then change. Hence, the devil will try hard to make sure that the society does not come to be aware of those things, and witchcraft is used for this.

So the devil will make it such that if you burn money to your ancestors, you will feel like they are with you and helping you, and if you don't, then you will feel like bad luck is following you; perhaps when you do not offer the money, you have a bad dream of your ancestors threatening punishment on you. Perhaps if you fail to follow the rules of feng shui, he will cause disasters and inauspicious events to be present, but if you follow them, then he will arrange for you to have some form of peace and prosperity. Perhaps the Buddhist monks will be able to present you with miracles or supernatural phenomena, so you can rest assured that this religion is true and that there isn't some other thing that you need to worry about. And all this is accomplished through people using their tionchar to communicate with demons, whom they do not know to be demons, and the demons go to God's throne to ask for the power to perform such things.

Can God answer prayers in other religions? He can. But as I stated above in the chapter on how God answers prayers, the third factor was the correct knowledge of God. God will answer prayers even if you mistakenly think His name is Buddha or Vishnu, so long as you do not do it in a form or manner that is offensive to Him, but He will always give lesser answers than He would if you prayed in the same way with the correct faith. He will by no means give you anything to increase your faith in those religions, like signs or miracles- those things will always be from Satan. At the very most, He will gives signs within those religions to point you towards the truth, like the star that the Magi saw that led them to Bethlehem, but He will by no means ever give a sign to reinforce your belief in something false, and if you see such a sign, you ought to know that since God does not give signs like that, and therefore it then means that there is only one other place it could have come from.

Deception occurs in the Christian civilization too, but not in the same way. The Christian civilization will teach the Truth, but somehow people will still be deceived into thinking that many of the things that they do which are evil, are not really evil. The Christian civilization will never fully be redeemed, but will retain many aspects of the pagan civilization. Women will still be treated inferior to men, rich will still not do their duty to the poor, nations will still fight wars, people will still have hatred, greed, envy, etc. And many people in the Christian civilization will do these things and think that they are not going to hell, or maybe even think that these things are not wrong. The devil is involved with this too in deceiving them, but human witchcraft may not be, or at least not quite in the same way, hence I will leave that out of this work.

People can sometimes have a kind of belief like their thoughts influence reality or certain superstitious practices really work, and in an invisible way, this can actually become like a type of witchcraft within even a Christian civilization, but it is not quite the same as the main topic of this piece, because such people who do it will usually not put their faith in such things in the same way as they would put it into an open religion, and they may still believe the Christian religion at the same time, hence it is not the same sort of deception which is occurring.

Prayer is always needed for anything to happen in the physical world and this includes all the deception that comes from the devil. If human beings apply their tionchar to witchcraft, then every spiritual gift that they had within their natural vocation can be presented within a pagan form and thus cement the deception. But if there were no human beings at all using their tionchar with the devil, the deception would still occur, because the devil himself, who has a very unique form of tionchar, will pray to God, and all the spiritual gifts he was meant to have as a messenger of good to human beings will be applied to the evil of giving a different message to human beings to present evil as desirable.

In a Christian society, the devil's deception may not necessarily come in the form of holding up some ultimate truth other than God. People may have 'idols' such as money, power, sex, etc. which they treat more important than God, but they don't actually consciously think that those things created the universe or hold it together. Through idolizing such things he can bring them to hell, but in their case they didn't need to stop believing in God to go there. Hence he doesn't need human beings to be talking with him and getting results from their magic in order to keep the deception in place within a Christian society. In pagan society, he does.

What about an atheist society? One where people believed only in the physical world as it was explained by science?

This deception also is carried on by the devil, but unlike the pagan society, it does not need tionchar to be applied to false gods in order to hold it in place. Hence the witchcraft of human beings is unnecessary.

However, the honest truth is that atheistic societies, by their nature, are totally unsustainable. In every communist state, people became more attracted to religions than were people in richer western nations that believed in God and were being tempted by other things in their lives. In western countries where the number of atheists are growing, so is the number of people who are following New Age beliefs, neo-paganism, and other explanations, which perhaps are not called religion, but are nonetheless spiritual in nature. Even among those who claim to be atheists, there are huge numbers who think there is a soul, a life-force, an afterlife, some pseudoscientific 'energy', or that thoughts have an effect on the outside world, etc. And they go after these things, because there is a human need to believe in such things, just like how the prehistoric man needed gods to promise him safety and security. And therefore if those things exist in the 'atheist' society, then it is simply turning into a pagan society, and all the things about witchcraft keeping deceptions in place will remain true for it.

Christ calls the devil 'the ruler of the world'. My description above is the manner by which he reigns. The whole world is in his grip, and it always has been, and always will be; because if it was not, then the temptation would be ended, but the temptation needed to continue in order for the love of the saints to be genuine. Even if the world becomes Christian, even if the whole world becomes catholic, it is still in the devil's grip; and it has to be, because of the reasons mentioned above. Society has to be filled with temptation, or else the love of the saints cannot be real. And the only way for the society to be filled with temptation is for the society to be deceived, and such deception is carried out through the religions, the philosophies, the politics, the social norms and the culture of the place. And within pagan society, the witchcraft of human beings is required to keep all these deceptions in place, otherwise people would stop believing in them.

In this age, prior to Christ's second coming, it is impossible to create a state without great temptation remaining present, because the devil has been permitted to make it impossible, for else then love could not be real. You must let the society be filled with ideas that lead people away from the Truth and teach people religions which have things that are true, and also things which are false, which can lead people astray. And it is like this, in order to test the love of people.

But if you eliminate such deceptions in a country and replace it with the true religion so that it only teaches the truth and the correct doctrine of Jesus Christ, then you must make it so that this doctrine is held by the church in its official councils and texts, but not really taught from the pulpit so that people know what it is. Or if it is taught from the pulpit, then you must allow the church to be treated with disrespect by the society so that people can be easily led into thinking that the church does not know what it is talking about, and that there is some other wisdom which is greater. Or if the church is treated with respect and it teaches the correct doctrine, then you must make it so that people find it easy to think that they still don't have to worry about putting these things into practice because they are going to go to heaven no matter what they do, etc. Or if it is taught to people and furthermore the people are brought to see clearly that they must change or else accept hellfire, then you must make it easy for people to be tempted to leave and go to another country where they can enter a different society where they will receive the temptation that will bring them to sin and go to hell.

It is for the same reason that if this book ever gets published, so long as it is being used to lead people to heaven rather than hell, it will have to be treated with obscurity, disrespect, ridicule, misunderstanding, problems here or problems there that prevent it from getting out, that the only people who read it will be those who needed it the least, or something which will make it hard for it to actually do anything to bring people closer to God, because it has to be like that, otherwise love cannot be real.

In Jesus' time, the same thing was present. He spoke in parables, and so most people did not understand, and His own disciples who did not understand kept focusing their minds on comparing themselves with one another and ignored what He said, and the scribes and Pharisees treated Him with hatred. It had to be very hard for any seed to fall in good soil, for else love could not be real.

It is for this reason, that in the Lord's prayer we say 'your kingdom come', because it is only at the Second Coming of Christ that a place without temptation will be able to exist.

Lord, we pray that your kingdom come. We pray that you free society from the devil's deception. Please open our eyes and give us faith in the gospel as it truly is. We pray that people stop believing in the false signs and proofs that point to a different truth than the Truth. We ask for these things, if it is your will, in Jesus' name, Amen

XI: Limits to the power of evil

The devil is permitted by God to do many things and to exhibit many powers in order to trick people into believing in these deceptions. However, God has placed an important limit on this power, which is that: the devil may never exhibit a greater act of power than what is exhibited by God's own servants living in the same time period.

The devil is permitted to do miracles, but he cannot do miracles that are equal to or greater than what God's own servants do. He can also show signs through things which are not supernatural, but he cannot show such signs greater than similar signs that God's own servants can do. Why would that be?

It is not hard to understand the answer to that question. Because God uses the exhibition of power, signs and miracles in order to convince people to believe in Him. Jesus healed people in order to convince people that He was God. If the devil could do these same signs, then what would be the point in God giving these signs to people?

Perhaps, I can use an example to illustrate. I prove my identity in order to enter a country by showing my passport; but if my passport had no photo in it, and anyone could duplicate my passport very easily, then what would be the point in using a passport anymore? The entire purpose of the passport was to prove that you are you, but if anyone can duplicate it so easily and there was no photograph, then the passport would not really prove this at all. You might as well just enter a country with nothing at all, if that were the case.

Hence, if the devil were capable of doing the same signs that God could do, then there would be no point in God using those signs anymore, because these signs would not really prove to anyone that it was God and not some evil power that was behind them.

If Satan was permitted to do as great miracles as God did, then what would be the point of God even doing any miracle? For the reason why God gives these miracles is to bring people to believe! Jesus did not heal the lepers, because He was trying to be a doctor to the body, but because He wanted people to have faith that He really was God. If He wanted to cure leprosy, then He could have just snapped His fingers and all leprosy in history would be gone; He could have just taught them the science of how to cure it. He was not trying to cure people of their physical ailments, He was trying to cure them of their lack of belief and wake them up from the deception of this world. But if people who practiced witchcraft at that time and place could heal leprosy, then there would be no point in Jesus healing the leper to prove who He was, because He would be doing nothing that a witch couldn't also do.

If the devil could also raise someone from the dead, then what would Jesus' resurrection prove?

Furthermore, if God allowed this, then the temptation would be too great. It would be too difficult to believe that God was really God, if this other power or energy that the witchcraft believed in (which was just the devil in disguise) was performing greater acts of wonder than what people who called on God's name could do.

For example, when Elijah and the prophets of Ba'al met on Mount Carmel, the prophets of Ba'al shouted and cut themselves with swords to get Ba'al to send down fire to burn the offering. But the devil could not send down any fire, because God did not permit him. If God did permit him, then the devil would send down fire and the prophets would say that Ba'al had answered their prayers, and that he truly was god, and Elijah would be extremely embarrassed. And who would believe what Elijah said anymore after that?

So, therefore, God will allow the devil to exhibit many signs in order to get the world to believe in the religions they invent themselves, but He will never permit these signs to be equal to or greater than the signs exhibited by the servants of God.

A great example of this is seen in Egypt, especially in relation to the story of Moses.

In ancient Egypt, magic was institutionalized. It was treated as just another branch of knowledge, like architecture, writing, agriculture, etc. Magic was studied and taught by a group of men who formed the priesthood of the Egyptian gods, and they kept this knowledge very secret, such that outsiders were not allowed to know the secrets.

They had many rituals, liturgies, curses, magic spells, etc. And these things were considered as important in order to control the natural world. In order for their kingdom to be successful, the magic of the priests was seen as very important... and perhaps it was important. Perhaps they received many answers from demons through this magic and organized their society accordingly.

Perhaps most of these answers were not miracles or supernatural things, but were like the answers that people get by seeing the way the world around them works in their favour.

However, along with these signs, the priests of Egypt really could do things that were supernatural.

In the story of Moses, Moses comes back to Egypt after 40 years of exile to speak to Pharaoh. When Moses came to Egypt and told people that there was another God who required for His people to be allowed to worship Him, the Egyptians did not take this seriously, because they believed that their own gods were so powerful and that they had very great magic, greater than anywhere else in the world.

Moses gave them a sign by having his brother Aaron throw down his staff and it became a snake. Pharaoh then summoned his wise men and magicians to throw down their staves, and they do and each one of the staves became a snake. But Aaron's snake ate their snakes.

Even the devil can perform a miracle like this, because God allows him to, such that he really can change the staff into a snake, but the devil's miracle is not permitted to equal or exceed God's miracle. Therefore, Aaron's snake eats their snakes, in order to demonstrate that God's power exceeds the power of their own gods.

Moses then performed signs in Egypt which were greater than any other sign the Egyptians had ever seen in all the history of the worship of their own gods. Never has any witch, shaman or sorcerer anywhere in the world turned all the water of a country into blood, or covered the entire land with frogs or locusts, or made the sky dark and the sun no longer visible. In comparison with all the great monuments and wonders that they had made in their civilization, which they perhaps attributed to the gods (the devil's) help, these things were small in comparison with the power exhibited by Moses.

Pharaoh's magicians tried to perform signs as well to show to Pharaoh and the Egyptians that they also had power, but their signs were so small in comparison with what Moses did. God does not allow the devil to perform signs as great as this, otherwise it would be like the passport problem; what would be the point doing these signs then, if they didn't prove anything to people about who made them?

When Jesus did His miracles, people said 'if He is not from God, then how could He do such signs as these?' Jesus Himself told people to believe for the sake of the works that He did.

If in fact a man not from God could do such signs and works too, then this argument would have no logical validity.

Just as science follows laws, there are also certain laws

that can be hypothesized to operate in witchcraft and within the spiritual world. The things achieved by people who engage in witchcraft cannot equal or exceed that which is granted through prayer within the same time and place.

Sometimes, however, people perhaps may practice witchcraft and find that they get things through it which they cannot seem to get through prayer. Perhaps they want to get beauty, a spouse, money, power, etc. and if they pray to God for these things, He doesn't answer them, but if they engage in witchcraft, perhaps they get them. This may indeed happen, but it is not because witchcraft is more powerful, nor is the above principle being broken. But rather what is happening is that people are perhaps asking God for something which is in the second category (the things which it is not His will to give) and God will only answer their prayers with something different, and the different things He offers will still exceed that which is attainable in witchcraft.

For example, suppose someone prays for their company to be successful, but God perhaps has no interest in increasing the revenue of the company because this is in the second category, but instead He answers the prayer and makes the company more successful by getting coworkers to love each other more and serve society better. This is actually a more impressive feat than increasing the money in your pocket, because the human being is something greater than money, and altering the human being is therefore a greater act of power than altering the amount of money. However, perhaps the person prays to God for this, and they find no result, and then they go to witchcraft and they find the revenue increasing.

The devil is able to get this for them, because he hates them and wants to encourage them to lose their souls. This is one of the great dangers of witchcraft, because if someone goes to God, God is a loving parent who will never give you something which is bad or harmful to you, but if you go to the evil spirits, they will give candy to children every time the children ask for it until their teeth fall out and they get diabetes, because the demons hate them so much.

We ought to have no desire for anything which is in the second category, because if God does not will it, then it must not be good for us and therefore even if we seem to think it is good for us, we only think this because we do not see the whole picture. In a similar way, a small child perhaps does not understand the reasons behind all the rules given by his parents.

Things in the second category can be achieved through witchcraft, and in such cases, it sometimes will appear as though witchcraft is stronger, but it will only be an appearance and not a reality.

Because the things that are achieved through witchcraft can never exceed what prayer to God can do in the same time and place, we ought to be skeptical of many of the more amazing stories of what people have done through this kind of power. Stories about people who travelled through time or space, who could summon supernatural creatures to assist them, who could control people's minds, who could rise from the dead, etc. are therefore probably fictitious, exaggerated or at the very least based on something which is not actually supernatural.

For example, today we know that the ancient Egyptians used naturally occurring ingredients in order to preserve corpses and make them into mummies. But perhaps at that time, the common people maybe thought that the priests (who were in charge of this process) possessed some kind of power to make sure the body would not decay. Hence, it may have therefore appeared to them like the priests had more power than they did, but actually it was just knowledge of the natural world.

The Chinese Emperors used very good astronomy to predict when the next solar eclipse would occur, and perhaps the people thought this was because he was the 'son of heaven'. If the Emperor ever made a mistake in a solar prediction, it could be grounds for questioning his rule.

In Haiti, there is an old tradition that states that voodoo sorcerers can bring a corpse back to life and make it into a zombie that serves him. The word 'zombie' actually comes from Haiti. The people in Haiti got this tradition from some parts of West Africa where they have the same stories of sorcerers of turning corpses into obedient slaves. This would be an example of something which would appear to be much too big to think that they really possessed such a power. However, it may not be supernatural at all.

There was a documented case of a Haitian man named Clairvius Narcisse who came back to his family after being thought dead for eighteen years, and he said he had been a zombie. His death had been verified by witnesses. A Canadian expert on plant poisons came to meet him and offered an explanation for what happened.

The explanation was that Clairvius had angered people, including his brother with whom he quarrelled over land, and they asked a voodoo sorcerer to curse him. The sorcerer poisoned Clairvius with a natural poison that made him appear dead but didn't kill him, and afterwards, the sorcerer took his body and revived him. But after reviving him, he made him eat a paste made from Datura (a plant) which contained an ingredient that caused amnesia, inability to distinguish between fantasy and reality, and induced hallucinations. The sorcerer told him that he had taken his soul away and that now he was a zombie, and must obey what he was told. Clairvius couldn't tell if this was real or fantasy, and he believed it and obeyed what the sorcerer told him to do. He lost his sanity. The sorcerer put him to work in a sugar plantation as a kind of slave labourer alongside others who also had been made into 'zombies', while giving them regular doses of the Datura paste. Eventually the sorcerer died, and Clairvius left the plantation and came back to his family and told them what happened. The entire affair was published by the Canadian plant expert in a book and an academic journal article, although some have contested its explanation.

Whether the above story is true or not, we do not know, but it is quite possible that the stories of these sorcerers making people into zombies are not completely fictional, although at the same time it also could not be supernatural. The same is true for many other stories in existence relating to witchcraft, in that if they are not false or exaggerated then they may have natural explanations. However, this doesn't mean that there is no spiritual element at all that is involved. Their witchcraft can inspire the devil to help them to acquire knowledge of how to do such things, and to have success when trying them- the witchcraft can achieve this kind of result, but it is not able to achieve a great 'miracle' without natural means, otherwise it would be too great in comparison with God's signs.

Even the bible has examples of this. In Genesis Joseph arranges for his cup to be put in his brother Benjamin's sack, and then when they are returning to the land of Canaan, the brothers are stopped and the cup is found, and they were forced to go back. When they meet Joseph again, Joseph says 'you should have known that a man like me can do divination'; of course, however, it was not divination, it was just a trick. It is possible that many magicians in Egypt did something similar.

In the book of Daniel (in the part at the end in the catholic bible) the priests of Babylon said that the idol ate the food put in front of it, but when the doors were closed, they would have a secret entrance and come in to remove the food and eat it with their families; thus deceiving everyone about what happened.

However, you must remember that the devil's intention in working this power in witchcraft is simply to deceive people. He does not need the story to actually be true in order to accomplish that. Therefore, all the stories of witches who could fly, who could turn people into stone or into animals, turn corpses into zombies, transport themselves to other places in the world, etc.... none of these are actually true or at the very least they are based on something that has been exaggerated, but the devil will encourage such stories to be spread among those willing to believe such things in their cultural environment, and even encourage the people who practice such things to lie and fabricate things in order to convince others that the stories are true.

The prophets of Ba'al on Mount Carmel would have liked everyone to believe that they had the power to call down the fire, even though they didn't; the devil could encourage them to lie about what they could do, but he couldn't actually give the power to do it.

On the very day when Howard Carter opened the tomb of Tutankhamen, a messenger came to his house and found a cobra inside his birdcage eating his pet bird. The cobra was a symbol of the Egyptian Pharaoh. The financier of the expedition, Lord Carnavon, cut himself while shaving and died from an infection within a few months after the tomb was broken into; after they buried his body, they unwrapped Tutankhamen's mummy and found the Pharaoh had a healed lesion on his left cheek. All of a sudden there was a big media frenzy with newspapers reporting about the 'curse of the Pharaohs' that would come upon anyone who violated the tomb. Huge numbers of people believed it.

And there were a few other mysterious deaths related to the expedition, but almost everyone who entered the tomb survived and the tomb itself was opened to tourists in later years. The devil didn't need the curse to actually work to cause every person who violated the tomb to receive this kind of bad luck, but he just needed to deceive people and in that way his goal is met. He may not have the power to cause more than a few people to die in strange ways, but he may have the power to inspire journalists and the newspaper press to lead people into deception.

In the 19th century, there were some American sisters called the 'Fox sisters' who could do séances and speak with dead spirits, and the dead spirits would speak through them. Many people believed these things, and in the time of the American civil war, there were lots of people that were Christians and yet were going for services to be able to speak to their deceased family members. The Fox sisters travelled around for a long time, and they would famously ask questions of the spirits in front of an audience and people would hear tapping noises in response. Later in life one of them confessed that they had actually found a way to make cracking noises with their toe and foot joints in order to produce these tapping sounds.

When Francis Xavier travelled to India, he said that the Brahmins would hold feasts and convince the lower caste people that the gods were eating the food, even though it was just them and they were human beings.

In Nigeria, among the Igbo people, there is a long-held pagan tradition of holding elaborate masquerades and people might be told that one of the men wearing a mask is actually a spirit and not a man. And the men who held the masquerades would keep their identities secret from everyone else and only known to one another.

Wherever practitioners of witchcraft are found, we ought to expect that the devil will follow this pattern, in that he will do some miraculous signs, but not too big, and he will inspire the people who practice it to form ways of deceiving people and also strongly encourage belief among people in a particular culture that the witchcraft possesses more power than it does. Like Joseph's cup, many people will be inspired by the devil to trick others to believing in power that doesn't actually exist, so that the demons can keep them away from God.

The signs produced in witchcraft to deceive people are always less than the signs produced through the prayer of human beings, but people will tend to seek the former and doubt the latter, because the effects of Adam's sin makes us to prefer to believe what we want to believe even if it is false, and to disbelieve what we do not want to believe even if it is true. Hence, even though Aaron's snake ate the other snakes of the pagan priests, the Pharaoh will still make up some rational justification in his own mind for why this happened and it doesn't disprove his gods. But if the snake miracle was the other way around, then the Pharaoh would insist that Aaron and Moses were irrational for failing to believe in their gods.

In witchcraft people will invent many explanations and stories to try to make excuses for why the witchcraft is true even when it seems to fail; the signs of witchcraft are supported by human beings' own efforts in propping them up. In prayer, even when the evidence God gives is certain and uncontestable under logic, people struggle to get themselves to believe and accept it. The signs of the latter are always more powerful than the former; it is the sin inside of human beings that reverses it.

Lord, we pray that you take away our fear of the devil. Help us to realize, that no matter how else things may seem, you are always the one in control of everything. Make us stop believing in the signs that come from evil and make us believe in your signs. We ask for these things, if it is your will, in Jesus' name, Amen

XII: Who can be cursed?

This is not such a hard question to answer. It is already well explained above if one pays close attention.

The devil was permitted to deceive the entire world, because the world was sinful and it didn't deserve to know the Truth. If someone innocent gave His life for them (whether the innocence of Jesus, or the innocence of Abraham's son Isaac), then for the sake of that innocent life, they could be allowed to know the Truth, but without it, they could not be allowed to do so unless they removed their sins themselves.

This deception is a curse. It is also a curse that people who curse others are themselves cursed with.

If one is a sinner, then he deserves this curse.

But what he deserves is actually more than this curse. Everything that happens in the physical world can only be done because someone has prayed for it first; this person can be either human or angelic, either on Earth (the physical world) or in heaven (the spiritual world). The effects of original sin, including death, concupiscence, disease, hardship, suffering, pain in child birth, domination of one sex by the other, lack of knowledge of the Truth, etc. are like a great curse that came about because of human sins. The devil will stand in front of God and accuse the human beings of every evil thing that they do, to remind God of why this curse must stay in place. And God, who must be just and must follow His own Word, cannot refuse what the devil says.

The devil takes everything in God's Word and uses it against human beings. Like a prosecuting lawyer who knows the laws supremely well, and who will point out in the court everything the defendant did which broke the law, and never point out the ways in which it could be interpreted that the defendant is innocent; so is the devil to us. God wants all people to be happy, to live in peace, without suffering, without warfare, without disease and to all know Him and love Him, but He can't give it to them without neglecting justice.

But the devil will go to a human being, pretend to be his friend, and suggest to the human being that some desire he has can be fulfilled by committing a sin, and that he need not worry at all about any consequences to his actions.

The devil will say, 'Go now, do it. You have nothing to worry about.'

The human being is not aware the demon is speaking with him in his heart, he simply just finds himself thinking about doing the evil action and having a craving for it. The human being then thinks to himself, 'but if I do this, maybe others will think I am bad person. Maybe I will feel really bad if I do it. Maybe I will go to hell if I do this.'

The devil will then speak back to the person, 'Everyone else does this too. They will not judge you, and even if they do, they will be hypocrites. You won't feel bad. You will do this thing and prove how clever you are, how strong you are, how wise you are... don't you want that? Only weak people, stupid people, cowardly people, don't do this, because they are too weak, stupid or cowardly to do it. And you won't go to hell. Hell doesn't exist; God is just a fairytale, and only superstitious people think He is true.'

The person does not hear these words as though they were words, but simply has these thoughts occur in his heart, as though they came entirely from his own mind. He is completely unaware of who he is talking with. And yet the communication with the spiritual world is occurring.

The human being listens to the devil's suggestion and commits the sin. Right after the human being does this, the devil will then go back to God's throne, point at the human being that he himself just got to commit a sin and then tells God, 'Did you see that? Did you see what that one did? Will you now let this one go unpunished? Will you let him have peace in his life even though he does not care of the peace of others? Will you let him be happy even though he makes others unhappy? In Your Word, you say that what you do unto others shall be done unto you, and that you will punish those who do evil. Now choose: either declare that Your Word is false or that man must suffer!'

God says, 'You know, if I punish him, perhaps he will repent of his sin and think he must not do it again.'

The devil says, 'He does not deserve to be brought to repentance! You must punish him, but without letting him be brought to repentance! Let him suffer in such a way that he still thinks that what he did was right and beneficial for him! What kind of justice will that be, if someone breaks your law and so you treat them even better than you did before? If he is brought to become a saint through this suffering, then you have no justice and your Word is untrue. '

God says, 'Very well, you are correct. I therefore let you give him the suffering he deserves for his sin, and at the same time to influence him to stop him from waking up from his sin. He will still be able to resist your influence and become a saint, but only if he seeks it with all his heart.'

The devil then makes sure that the person's friends do not find out about his sin, because they have great influence over him, and they might cause him to change if they suddenly lose their respect for him. The devil also makes the person feel content with his sin, and convinces him that it wasn't really wrong. He also brings the person to read books and watch media that influence him more strongly to doubt in God's existence, and at the same time the devil arranges the minister in the church that he still attends to make ridiculous claims about the dinosaurs being destroyed in the flood of Noah and that Alexander the Great rode on a flying pterodactyl into battle, thus deepening the man's suspicions that this whole religion is just nonsense, and thereby the devil succeeds in putting this man's conscience to rest about the hellfire he was taught about.

The man is completely unaware that both his pastor, who is ignorant of physical realities, and the books he is reading by atheists, who are ignorant of spiritual realities – both groups are unknowingly working for the same person in order to bring him to hell. The pastor thinks he is a brilliant person, and perhaps he is, but he was always taught that the world was only 6000 years old, because of the ages of the persons listed in Genesis. But as he got older and went to college, he met atheists who treated him badly, insulted him, and told him that he believed in fairytales, and they used evolution as proof that it was a fairytale. Therefore, the devil comes to him, stirs up his pride, and makes it very hard for him to admit that he is wrong and they are right, so therefore for the rest of his life he subscribes to this belief even harder. He preaches it to others, because he can't admit being wrong and the devil makes him to think, 'either you are a stupid, superstitious, brainwashed person who believes in fairytales, or all this stuff you are reading on the creation science website must be true. Now which is it?'

God, if He was there, would have liked to say to him, 'You are a smart person, but even smart people make mistakes sometimes. You have knowledge of spiritual things, which surpasses in importance what those people know of physical things. You shouldn't feel upset about this; they can be right, and you can still be a smart person. Just admit you are wrong now, take the shame of the cross, and you will be happier later.'

But if God tried to say such words to this man, the devil would say to God, 'but this man is a sinner! He doesn't deserve to know the Truth and hear such good advice! And besides, he barely prays. He does not even turn to you to ask for your help in knowing the answers to these things, so why should you help him? With regard to this subject, he is talking with me in his heart, and thinks he has no time to go down on his knees to talk to you about this. He spends five minutes a day in prayer conversing with you, and four hours a day caressing his ego in his conversation with me. So, I say, let him have what he deserves!'

And in fact, this same thing is happening with the atheists who wrote the books that the man reads secretly without his friends in the church knowing about. They were raised by their parents to believe in a religion, but their faith was always completely intellectual, and which they never put into practice in their behaviour. In fact, neither did their parents. In fact, no one at the churches he went to as a child did; all of them just believed intellectually, and it made no difference to their outward behaviour. So, as they grew up and found new ideas, it was easy for them to just forget about and throw away the things they were taught as children.

But then some people from their religion told them that if they do not believe anymore then they will go to hell, so the devil comes to them and says, 'but you are good people! How can you go to hell? In fact, you are better people than all those people in those churches, so how dare they say to you that they are going to heaven and you will go to hell!'

But these people then thought in their minds, thereby having a conversation with the demon without even realizing it: 'But what if it's true? What if I am going to hell because I don't believe anymore. I am scared!'

The devil says back to them in their hearts, 'But how stupid would that be? If God sends such a proud and selfish person to heaven just because he believes in Him, and sends such a nice and caring person to hell just because she is not sure if He exists. God doesn't exist. And if He did, then He would be such an unjust person for acting like that. Stop believing in Him and feel comfortable.'

And thus, their worldviews get formed. And the injustice of believers only strengthens their unbelief. And the devil in fact arranges it for them to come into contact often with such injustice committed by believers.

And these people write books, and the pastor gives his sermons, and the sinner in the pews finds his way to hell; all according to a very elaborate plan.

Being thus deprived of the truth and salvation was the greatest penalty that could be inflicted on the man in the pews. He is going to suffer for his sin, but he is not going to understand how he is suffering. His life will be deprived of the truth about God and all the peace and answers that it brings, but he doesn't understand that he is suffering. The devil may also give him problems in his life, stresses, diseases, etc. But he will lobby at God's throne for this man to make sure that he does not suffer so much in such things that it makes him wake up and to start seriously re-thinking the way his life is going.

And whenever something terrible will happen to this man in his life, the devil will go back to the man and speak in his heart, 'It is not your fault! You did nothing wrong! You are a good person! Those other people who gave you this terrible thing that now causes you suffering... those people are evil! They deserve to go to hell; it is a shame that a hell doesn't exist for them to go to. They are such hypocrites. They are arrogant and don't understand what your life is like.'

The man has been cursed for his sins; the deception he is under is the greatest part of the curse, and he doesn't understand this because he is deceived.

If Jesus gives His life to satisfy justice for the sake of human beings or if the people themselves stop doing these evil things, only then can God refuse the devil's request and take the curse away.

God really wants to take the curse away, but He can't, because the devil is equipped with weaponry. God must first take away the weapons and the armour, and then He can take the curse away.

Therefore, God tells the devil, 'This sin will be punished and what he has done to others will be done to him. But there is no rule that says someone cannot come in this man's place to pay his debt for him.'

The devil says to God, 'But if you take any human being at all, I will simply point out that other man's sins, and that man must be punished likewise. Every sinner deserves death if they sin; a death soon or a death after a long time, it does not matter, but the death must come if they commit sin. A person who cannot save his own life cannot save another's life. If you do not have the money to pay back your own debt, then you do not have the money to pay back your neighbour's debt.'

God says to the devil, 'I will send someone who has no personal debt at all to pay. He will be able to pay for it. My own Word must be true, as you say, and so all these sins will receive their just punishment. But my own Son will voluntarily go to receive this punishment in their place. And then your curse against them will be ended.'

But, like everything else in the physical world, this sacrifice can only end the curse if someone prays for the person first. Hence, even the man in the pews of the church will not be protected if no one asks for God's mercy for him on account of that sacrifice given by His Son.

Most people are completely unaware of how much

punishment they deserve for their sins. God is so extremely sensitive towards us, and it does not take much in order to cause Him very great pain. But in this life, when we commit sin, we often don't really know how much pain it causes Him; therefore, He can forgive us. But for those who are aware of how much pain He suffers, and yet still sin; for them the punishment will be great.

But, even if we do not really see how much pain God suffers, we can at least see how much people suffer or are able to suffer because of what we do. The people who die on the streets in poor countries, die because we do not love them enough to help them; the foetuses aborted by their mothers die without even the chance of getting the grace of baptism, because people simply do not love them enough to try hard enough to stop this; the people who die in wars, die because people do not love each other enough; etc. And these are simply examples that pertain to large groups of people, one could also talk about the ways that individuals around us suffer and we ourselves have some blame.

But Jesus suffered more than these people. It was because He was more sensitive than them, and while we are only sensitive to the goodness or evil of others a little bit and this is the source of our suffering, He was extremely sensitive to every single word, action and thought in the entire history of the world and that is the source of His suffering. If He simply gave it up, and stopped loving us, then His suffering would end.

However, He forgives us, because we don't really know what we're doing. We haven't yet seen everything there is to see.

Why don't we know what we're doing?

It is not an innocent ignorance that lies behind this as an explanation. Many people do not know, because they are not looking. They are not looking because they care about other things more.

However, if you were to place human beings in the reverse position and you made it such that they suffered tremendously from what others were doing, and these others did not care enough about them to inquire about them and come to realize how much pain they were causing... human beings would condemn such people. Even if they are ignorant, their ignorance is still culpable.

Suppose you had a business that was poisoning a river, and as a result people who lived from drinking the water in the river got cancer and other ailments that caused great suffering to them, and also caused their deaths. If the business did not know how much harm they were causing, can they say that they are innocent because they didn't know? They can't say this, because they knew that poisoning the river could harm someone, and yet they didn't find out how much harm because they didn't really care. The same is true of the person who knows that sin offends God and harms human beings, and yet does not really care enough to learn how much harm it is. If the business knew how much suffering they caused and yet still poisoned it, then that would be even more sinister; similarly, the sinner who sins with knowledge is committing a greater sin.

But how much punishment do we deserve for it? It is not a small amount. God has suffered extremely, and yet we care so little about Him that many of us do not even try to find out.

Every person in the world is a sinner. In fact, most people in the world have done evil things in their lives which they hide from the view of the rest of the world. Most people in the world have secrets which they kept buried underneath out of the view of everyone else. And by these secrets, without confession or repentance, they will eventually go to hell at the end of this life.

Even if the person is a good person, a normal person, just like everyone else, but they have one side of their life which is evil, and they are not sorry for it, this will bring them to sink into hell when they die. A ship does not need the whole hull to be missing in order to sink; one hole is enough. A body does not need every part to fail in order to die; one organ that stops working is enough. Similarly, the person does not need to be evil in everything in order to go to hell; just one mortal sin without repentance is enough. A person can be good at everything, kind to their neighbours, honest in business, attending church every Sunday... but they watch pornography at home, or they had an abortion one time and were never sorry for it, or they hate someone... for this one thing they will go to hell, even if everything else is fine. All you have to do is hurt another person very gravely at some time in your life, and go through life to the final moments while refusing to be sorry for it... even if you give food to the poor, even if you attend the mass every day, even if you are a kind and good person... the ship only needed one hole to sink even if the rest of the hull is intact.

Most people in the world go to hell at the end of life because of this. Most people in the world have such evil things in their lives, and they kept them out of the sight of others, not showing everything about themselves to those around them.

Hellfire is extremely painful. Purgatory is also extremely painful. It is more painful than the worst torture that exists in this world. That means that if you can imagine the worst form of all tortures in this world: beatings, being stretched on a rack, the old Chinese method where they slice off your flesh with tiny cuts bit by bit thousands of times until you die, being struck through with needles, water boarding, being hung from the ceiling by your thumbs or from broken bones, being tortured with fire or with electricity, being scourged at a pillar, etc. None of these things is as painful as what people in hell or purgatory experience.

Therefore, if the vast majority of people living today deserve hell or purgatory when they end life, then that means that the vast majority of people living today deserve punishment even worse than those things mentioned above and they ought to expect torture worse than the above once they die. For that reason, if someone were to torture them in this world right now, it would be justice. If a totalitarian state were to appear that made human life in this world into a kind of hell; it would simply be giving most people what they deserved. You begin to understand then how God let the cavemen suffer for so long before the covenant of the rainbow- it was what all human beings deserved, but for Noah's sake, future generations were saved from it.

Very few people do not deserve it; these are the saints, who will go to heaven immediately after their deaths.

And they are very few in number. There is a legend that says there was a monk who lived in a cave who had formerly been an archdeacon in Lyons, living a devout life and he died at the same time as Bernard of Clairvaux. The monk then appeared in front of the bishop of Lyons and told him that at the time he died, there were 30,000 other people in the world who died at the same time, and only him and Bernard entered heaven.

When the Israelites left Egypt, they saw so many miracles and God was with them every day. The Lord showed them so many signs in Egypt, miracle after miracle, promising that He would bring them to a new land. Promising to bring them to a new land, promising to bring them to a new land, promising to bring them to a new land... God was speaking through Moses about how He would bring them to a new land and giving them so many signs to make them believe that He would do this. But in the end, only two of them actually reached it, and the rest of them died in the wilderness because of their lack of trust in God; it was their children who would enter it.

In the same way, countless numbers of people are baptized (passing through the waters of the Red Sea) and go to the mass, and they eat the flesh of God and the Lord is so close to them (eating the bread that came down from heaven). They are told they will go to heaven, they are told they will go to heaven, they are told they will go to heaven... this is what we pray for at every mass. However, once they leave this life, almost all of them will not see heaven, except for a few saints, but instead they experience pain greater than anything in this world; it is those who pass through purgatory that enter it in the end.

The amount of punishment that God's justice demands for human beings is tremendous; far more than we would ever imagine. But it must also be understood even more deeply so, that God is not desiring to give it to us. He wants very badly that every person in the world can escape from this justice and die covered with His mercy. For a soul to go to hell or purgatory is something that hurts Him even more than a person going to prison would hurt the parent of the person. The punishments we deserve are titanic; this has to be recognized- but it must also be kept in mind at the same time that there is no one who wants us to avoid these punishments more than Him. His mercy is far surpassing of His justice, although both aspects of Him are real. He would prefer for the church even to not mention the punishments due on people for their sins if it meant that believing in such justice meant that they stopped believing He loved them.

And He has the power, if people in trust in Him, to get them through this life and make them saints when they die. He is willing to do this for absolutely everyone- not just special people chosen for it, but also you and I. He wants all of us to be like Caleb and Joshua, or like Bernard and the archdeacon. But there are few of us who are willing to trust in His mercy and believe that He loves us as much as He does.

So therefore, the answer to the question of who deserves great punishment is: almost everyone. And therefore, this also provides the answer to the question of whom can be cursed in witchcraft.

Think of the story of when Moses was leading the people of Israel in the wilderness and when they came near Moab, the king of Moab Balak called on a man named Balaam to curse the people of Israel for them, and every time that Balaam went to curse them, he couldn't, because God had blessed them.

But a little bit afterwards, the people of Israel began intermingling with the Midianite women and having intercourse with them, while going to worship their gods. God was so angry with this that he put down a plague on them that killed thousands. Moses ordered the Israelites to kill the Midianites, and it is then revealed in the text that the Midianite women had been sent on Balaam's advice. He must have advised it like this because it was only in this way that God's protection could be withdrawn and they could be cursed. Balaam must have told Balak that if he wanted to curse the Israelites then he needed to get them to sin and then the curse could come. And so, the Midianite women were sent, Balaam made a curse, and so the plague spread among the Israelites until God's wrath was appeased by the actions of Moses and Phinehas.

The ultimate curse is that which the devil lobbies for us at God's throne every day and night. He merely points out our sins and demands justice, and he uses God's Word as his weapon to bring about an answer to his prayer, for otherwise God would not look at him.

When a human being curses another human being, they are simply forming a small piece in the devil's work. They are just adding details to the curse that the devil wants to bring down on human beings. They are like co-workers in his ministry in this world.

Margaret Mary Alacoque, in her visions about the Sacred Heart, saw Jesus' Sacred Heart as like a great furnace and her own heart was added to this furnace as a small spark that burned with Jesus' Heart. Oppositely, all human beings who fail to love their neighbour, even hating and cursing them, are just adding the sparks that come from their empty hearts to the hatred in the devil's own.

They who use witchcraft to call down curses on others are just a continuation of the devil's own work that he began with Adam and Eve's exile from the garden as a result of their sins. And almost everyone in the world is a potential target for such curses.

I will illustrate this with an example. When European Christians took slaves from Africa to work in hard labour in the Caribbean islands, the slaves took many of the beliefs of their African religions with them. This included pagan witchcraft. This witchcraft perhaps gave them a power to get back at the white Christians who were treating them unjustly. The master could beat them, abuse them, even kill them, and they could not do much to fight back physically. But perhaps they could cast a spell on him to curse him or his family.

If they cursed him, the devil could go to God's throne and ask for God to allow him to cause this curse to come true. You might wonder how could people who know the True God and His Son, be capable of being victimized by such a thing? Surely if they had the blood of Jesus as their protection, then they must have been immune?

They would be immune, because God is far stronger than the devil... but they are not really using Him as their protection if they believe in Him and yet they still commit grave sin. If one commits grave sin, then one has already made friends with the devil, and cannot remain in God's grace. If they are not in God's grace, then they do not have His protection either.

If they repent of their sins, and then ask for the blood of Jesus to protect them, then this can save them, so long as they are sincere in repentance. But if they, like most Christians, simply commit sin without really changing, then they remain a potential target.

Therefore, when the devil goes to God to ask for the curse to work, he can phrase it like this:

The devil says to God: "The slave on the plantation put a curse on his master's wife. Can I give her a fever?"

God says, "But she is a Christian and believes in me. Why should I allow witchcraft to lead to her possessing a disease?"

The devil says: "She is a Christian, but only in name and

not in truth. She does not love the slaves that she treats harshly. Yesterday she beat the little black girl with a cane because she dropped the tea on the carpet. The little girl was innocent. But the woman has sinned against you, will you now let her go unpunished?"

God says, "You are right, I can in no way ignore the injustice of human beings. I can pardon the repentant, but in no way can I acquit the wicked. She is not really a true disciple of my Son, for if she were, she would never do that. One must love one's neighbour to be a true disciple of my Son. You may give her the fever, but do not let her die, because I see she is not yet ready and if she is given more time in this life, she will repent and her soul will eventually be saved."

And so the devil then arranges it for the woman to be bitten by a mosquito and contract malaria, because she deserved it for her sins. The suffering from the disease was less than what she would have suffered in hell or purgatory, however.

The devil was not really concerned as much with hurting her as he was with hurting the slaves. Because if he never gave answers to these curses, then they would stop believing them and then question if these false religions were true. But that might then lead them to believing in Jesus, and the devil certainly didn't want that; he much preferred for them to remain in their paganism, hence he uses the fever of the woman to confirm to them that their delusions are true and keep them from waking up.

Even though these are slaves, they are equal in God's eyes as the master. If the master sins against them, then he deserves to be punished. The power of such curses can transcend class boundaries and questions of worldly power.

In a similar manner you can have the leader of a country, an important general, important party leader, police chief, authority figure, etc. who has done some bad things to many other people, and one of these people possesses the invisible gift of great tionchar and uses her witchcraft to curse him and his family. She was perhaps just a peasant or even a pauper, and yet she was actually a very powerful person; but what she did was invisible. The important person stepped on so many people's toes, including hers, and he would have no idea where it came from even if he did understand the nature of curses in the spiritual world.

And so the police chief eats too much and gets heart disease eventually leading to his early death, the son of the party leader becomes a dirty playboy that embarrasses his father, the general's wife divorces him for a younger man, the leader of the country suffers from mental illness, the big business man's wife gives him no children, etc.

It is in fact precisely for this reason why all the dystopias in science fiction depicting totalitarian worlds ruled by robots, ruled by people with powerful technology, etc. are in fact not really to be feared. Even if robots could control the world (or something like that occurred which you see in movies), and the robots' abilities surpassed the human being, the human being would still be superior because she can pray and it can't. Even if she is completely controlled, she need only lift her eyes to heaven and it can all come crashing down in a day. Like the slaves of Egypt calling upon God, who sends Moses and he performs signs that bring the great country to its knees.

The most powerful people in the world are not the kings, the party leaders, the business leaders, etc. They only have their power because someone else prayed for it first. It is rather the people who pray are the ones who have the most power over the world.

The most powerful rulers in the world can still suffer horrible things in this life that they cannot defend themselves from, because the ultimate control of the universe is on a higher level than them. They are whipped in punishment by diseases on their beds, they are punished with mockery by nature, and they are executed with cancer when their time has run out;

despite how powerful they think themselves to be, they are still so small when they are in the hands of the Lord who uses His power according to the prayers of His creation, including the prayers of the devil when he intercedes for those deceived persons who practice witchcraft. There are people who can curse them and make them suffer in ways that they could never inflict on a human being with the power they possessed.

Qin Shihuang, after he conquered the whole of China, thereby accomplishing a feat greater than Napoleon or Caesar, spent the last years of his life seeking to find a way to live forever. He was told that mercury pills would provide him with this, and they drove him insane and led him to die faster. Despite the incredible power he attained and the brutality he used to keep his power in place, the spirits that rule the air could still just play with him like a toy and convince him to hurt himself without realizing what he was doing.

Stalin died of a heart attack, but not quickly. He lay on the floor of his room, urinating and unable to get up. Nobody outside dared to go in and help him, because they feared he would execute them if they disturbed him at an hour when he said he was not to be disturbed. The next morning when they opened the door, he could not speak words, but only moan. The man who had held so much power in his hands would be thrown away and left to a humiliating demise by the same spirits who had once worked to build up his power and make the nation terrified of him.

The vast majority of such curses will be natural things rather than supernatural, but they will be arranged to come to the right person by the devil who gives the power to the witchcraft.

A person can be cursed and the devil arranges it so that they attain a completely natural disease which has a cure, and yet they never find the cure, because somehow every doctor they go to misdiagnoses the illness, or fails to recognize that there is an illness, such that it seems like it has no cure and the person gives up, and yet it actually does have a cure and they would have found it if they kept looking; the devil not only arranges the disease to be attained but also follows up to make sure no doctor is able to help with it and that the person loses heart. Or perhaps they get a disease that can kill them, and the devil makes them think that they are perfectly fine. Or perhaps he gets them to wait too long for a cure to be able to help them anymore. Or maybe even, ironically enough, he will get a disease which he thinks came from witchcraft, and he is right, and therefore he doesn't bother going to a doctor for it because he assumes the doctor cannot help him, even though the doctor can, and thus the witchcraft works.

These kinds of diseases that come from curses are far more common than some kind of supernatural illness that cannot be cured no matter what, because the devil's power in doing the supernatural is limited in comparison with God.

The same pattern presents itself here, wherein the devil will try to get people in a culture to widely believe that such incurable diseases come about through witchcraft, to encourage people in that culture to spread such stories and get more people to believe in this power. In the same way as he perhaps uses the newspapers to get everyone to believe that the curse of the Pharaoh's tomb was real... when in actuality the supernatural acts were very small, and the bluff was very big.

Why does God allow Satan to carry out such curses?

If almost everyone in the world has 'dirt' on them, then everyone in the world deserves punishment. Anyone who asks for such bad things to come on perhaps 98% of the people in the world, will be asking for something in the 1st category of requests (those that are God's will to grant). The truth is that one doesn't even need to do witchcraft to curse someone; you could just pray to the Trinity and make the same prayer the devil does, insisting that that person must suffer or else God's word is untrue. But if one prays like this, even to God, one must be conscious that what one asks for others will also occur for one's own sins that one hasn't repented of. For the Lord said: 'if you do not forgive others, neither will God forgive you'.

If they take the sacrifice of Jesus for their protection and forgive those who wronged them, then they can be protected even if they had 'dirt', but if they do not let go of the sins that gave them the dirt, then even this sacrifice is not going to protect them.

This is important to understand for recognizing how it is that God grants the prayers of Satan, and how 'curses' in witchcraft can work.

Therefore, the answer to who can be cursed: every person who commits sin, and does not forgive others or have a sacrifice given for their sake that can give an answer to the justice due to them.

For this reason, one should expect that little children are far more immune to an attempt by a witch to curse them than if she did so for an adult. Similarly, people who are recently baptized would also be immune, because all the punishments of the sins of their life before baptism are cancelled once they are baptized-Jesus has paid the price for all of them. So also is it for a person who has correctly received a plenary indulgence.

If you wish to be free from the devil's power, then stay away from sin, and you will be.

Is it possible for a curse to ever come on someone who has no 'dirt' on them? The answer to the question is partially yes, but it is not really a curse for them. There is nothing in the creation that occurs without it first being asked for in prayer. Hence, the sufferings of Jesus, would have first needed to have been requested by the devil from God's throne so that Jesus could be tempted and tested. So also, if God permits it, the devil can secure suffering for any innocent person in creation, in order so that temptation can occur, which God allows in order so that love can be real.

But in their case, it is not really a 'curse', because it is no longer punitive. For the person destined to hell and purgatory, they will deserve almost any bit of suffering inflicted upon them in this world, because even the worst tortures in this world are less than what the soul suffers in purgatory. But for the person who is free from such a stain, the suffering that comes upon them is not something they deserve.

For every person who commits sin without atonement, and who would go to hell or purgatory if they were to die today – every one of them can be cursed, unless they repent (which means they stop doing the sin- just saying they are sorry without stopping is not repentance) and take the blood of Jesus as their protection.

But for the people who are free from sin, either from never having committed it (like little children), having been completely washed clean of it (like the newly baptized) or who have completed atoned for it (like those who successfully receive a plenary indulgence), God can still allow them to be cursed in order so that temptation can exist and love can be real, but for many of them, He will not allow them to be cursed to the same degree as those who have the stain of sin still on them. For a person called to be a great saint, it is likely God will allow curses to fall on this person just as though they were a sinner; Jesus Himself, is the perfect example, in that He was perfectly sinless and yet experienced things worse than the worst of criminals deserved. For a person not called to this (or perhaps who is not *yet* called to it in the stage of the spiritual life they are in), God will probably not allow them to be cursed to the same degree, so long as they stay clear of sin.

There is no suffering in the world that did not come

about because someone did not pray for it first. Even the little girl starving to death with her ribs sticking out and the vultures circling over her in the hot Sun in Africa only existed because there was a person, with a real mind and thoughts, that asked for it first. And this person achieved an answer to his prayer through the justification that human beings must be tempted in order so that love could be real.

Lord, we pray that you free us from whatever curses have been placed on us by witchcraft, including those we know about and those we don't. We pray that you will more importantly free us from all of the sins in our lives that make us justly receive such attacks. We pray that you help us to repair our relationships with you. We ask for these things, if it is your will, in Jesus' name, Amen

XIII: The Devil's Purposes and the Necessary Cooperation in Witchcraft

In order to have your prayer heard by God, you need to be sorry for your sins. If you are not sorry for your sins, God does not listen to the prayer.

In order for the devil to be interested in your witchcraft, it is necessary that he sees the opportunity by which he can harm people, and most especially use the witchcraft as a way to fail the test given to them in this life.

As stated in what's written above, a great example of this was in the pagan cultures that believed in gods who permitted and even promoted vice, and for that culture the witchcraft was 'proving' that these gods were true. Thus, people believed it, committed sin, and went to hell; thinking that the gods who governed the universe would not punish them for doing these sins.

If, however, the pagan religions taught something very good and forbade all vice, and promoted morality to an extreme degree... perhaps none of the spells, magic charms, etc. would work, because the entire reason why the devil got involved in this was to get people to go to hell. For example, if all the worshippers of Apollo became like saints in their behaviour, and because they no longer rejected logic in favour of social acceptance, they came to believe that all the myths about Apollo were false because they were illogical and immoral, and they prayed to know the Truth about who Apollo was… the devil would probably really hate this; he would not want to empower their witchcraft any longer. If he gives power to their amulets or sacrifices… who is going to go to hell by being deceived in this?

The devil's only interest in the entire matter is the destruction of human beings. He wants the rival he envies to lose their beauty and become monsters.

He encourages people who practice witchcraft to believe that they have power, because pride is a vice that will turn them into monsters. He encourages them to curse people who offend them, even those who offend them justly, because he wants to take away their beauty and make them into monsters; the person who is cursed the most is not the person who acquires the disease, but rather is the person who cursed.

The first person the devil would like to see go to hell in the entire matter is the witch herself. The more she practices the magic, the more the devil has an opportunity to influence her, and little by little he will wear away at her good qualities until he makes her into a monster; a person filled with arrogance, who has no real love for other people, and has nothing of what really matters. Or perhaps she remains 'good at heart', but she has other vices that begin to grow larger and larger, which she is deceived into thinking are not really harmful and it will ultimately doom her to hellfire. In modern society, for example, a witch perhaps only does magic to help others, but she believes in the same errors that doom people in modern society to hell; and thus, she masturbates, has sex without marriage, believes abortion is acceptable, etc. For these things, she may go to hell, and the things she sees in her witchcraft keep her deceived about what the Truth really is.

He will try to get her so many things that she tries to get through her witchcraft; beauty, money, health, etc. And he doesn't want to give her any of these things, because he really hates her, but he sees it as a necessary temporary sacrifice in order to get her to fail the ultimate test. Like criminal gangs who give good favours to people who ask them for help, but only expect something in return later- such is the devil in his operation.

The second person or rather people, whom the devil wants to harm in the matter is all the others in society who while perhaps not practicing the witchcraft themselves, at least believe in it. These people are kept from the Truth which can save their souls. For example, the people in the pagan cultures who practiced vices because they believed there was no God who punished it and that the gods who existed approved of what they did; they may go to hell in the end if they do not repent.

The third group to whom the devil wants to harm in the matter, are all those to whom he cannot get to go to hell or commit a sin, because they resist his temptations, but whom he can cause other people to give them suffering in this world because of the existence of the witchcraft. Even if he cannot get them to go to hell, he will at least take some tiny satisfaction in seeing them suffer in this life. For example, the Roman emperors would conduct augury, wherein a pagan priest would sacrifice an animal and inspect its liver to give an answer to the Emperor's question. And the augur, under a demon's inspiration would tell the emperor that the gods' answer was that the problems of their empire came about because of the existence of the Christians who must be killed.

If the devil can harm one of these three, then the witchcraft interests him and he will give power to it. If he cannot do so, then he will have no interest and the witchcraft will not work. The more that one is pure in God's eyes, the more God will listen to the prayer of the person; oppositely the more that the devil can harm one of these three groups, the more interested he will be in making the witchcraft work.

Tionchar is all about relationship. But it can be applied to demons just as it was supposed to be applied to God. With God, the more one conforms to His will, the closer the relationship becomes, and it is the tionchar of the person that controls the shape of the relationship. With the demons, the more one conforms to their purposes, the closer the relationship becomes, and it is the tionchar of the person that controls the shape of the relationship.

Someone like Padre Pio will never be able to have a relationship like Bridget of Sweden had, but Bridget of Sweden cannot have the same relationship as Odo of Cluny had, Odo of Cluny cannot have the same relationship as the parish priest, the parish priest cannot have the same as you, you cannot have the same as me, etc. God will grant different things in the prayers of people depending on their vocation and who they are, and with witchcraft it works just the same as this. The demons cannot have a relationship with a person in a way that is different from the contours provided in their tionchar.

The more that the demon can harm through the relationship with you, the closer you will get to him and the more interested he will be in you.

Because of the existence of this dynamic, certain other things ought to be expected. For example, if there is someone living a good life and is going to go to heaven if they continue living this way, but the devil sees a possibility of using witchcraft to tempt this person to become bad... then the devil will be far more interested in making this witchcraft achieve results that can deceive the good person than he will be interested in a person who uses witchcraft who is already on her way to hell. Just as there is more rejoicing in heaven over one sinner who repents than over all righteous persons, so is there also more lust in hell for bringing one good person away from God's grace than there is over all those already lacking it. Padre Pio said that if you suffer temptations that that is a sign that God loves you very much.

The greater the sin which is involved in the witchcraft, the more likely the devil will be interested in it. Hence, perhaps people who masturbate as part of some kind of witchcraft will have greater interest from the devil than people who don't. To this should be pointed out that in parts of the ancient world there were prostitutes who lived in the temples of gods who would sleep with people that would come there, because it was considered part of the worship.

People who cast spells to help bring healing to people and never curse someone, will not have nearly as much attention from him as the person who casts spells in order to hurt other people and bring curses on people one doesn't like, because the person who only casts spells to heal may not be so quickly losing their soul by their practice of magic, whereas the other is losing it much faster. Therefore, the other is a higher priority to him. And furthermore, because it is a sin to hate and curse others, the devil knows that for each curse she puts on another (with his help), he will afterwards easily be able to go to God's throne and ask for a similar curse upon her, which will please him because he hates her... hence he will encourage her to curse others more. Whereas for the one who does magic to heal, it is not so easy to ask for this and he will not be as interested in getting her efforts to achieve results.

Acts of sacrilege can also increase his attention to the witchcraft. For example, if someone takes the relic of a saint, a bible, an item that has been blessed and most especially a Eucharist Host, and uses it as part of the witchcraft, this will increase the devil's attention even more because he knows that dishonouring these things is a great sin, and it is very important to him that the sin increases so that more people can receive greater punishment and go to hell. Hence, if the witchcraft involves items like this, it perhaps will increase his attention to it and his willingness to try to get it to achieve results.

The more sin which is either involved or encouraged in others by the witchcraft, the more likely he will be interested in it and try to give it power. Therefore, people who practice witchcraft can sometimes increase their results by whatever sins they can add to their practice, including sacrilege, sexual acts, hatred, envy, murder, animal sacrifice or even human sacrifice. The more people they can involve in the practice, especially if the witchcraft becomes a mass religion (which is essentially what paganism was), then the power will increase because the devil will take even more interest in it where more souls' damnation is concerned than he would if there was only one.

In the pagan nations where human sacrifice was institutionalized, like in Mesoamerica, the ancient near east, Scandinavia, the British Isles, Rome (the gladiatorial games were officially something being given to the gods and therefore a form of human sacrifice), and other places, one would expect that the devil would be more interested in giving them results to their prayers and sacrifices, than he would in places where the worship was more benign. And perhaps for this reason, they achieved success in many of their undertakings, and so their countries were perhaps blessed with prosperity, victory in war, good agriculture, etc. as a result of these sacrifices. However, even still, such results can only be ephemeral, and if not accompanied with obedience to the fourth commandment, the state will be weak.

There is a reason, however, why human sacrifice is so important to him. This requires some explanation.

The worst of all sins is not murder, it is not genocide, it is not slavery, it is not gay sex, it is not paedophilia, etc. The worst of all sins is to take the Eucharist in a state of mortal sin.

People really don't understand the mind of Satan; his thoughts are different from our thoughts, his ways are not our ways. His opposition to Jesus on Earth was not to get Him killed... far from it... that was the last thing he was thinking of. The thing that Satan wanted with Jesus was to bring Him to recant the mission He had been sent for, to turn back from going to Jerusalem, to point out Judas to the others at the Last Supper so they would stop him, to run away from the Garden of Olives so He wouldn't be arrested, to use His sublime wisdom to defend Himself at the trial before Caiaphas or Pilate in such a way that would force His release, to show His power and get down from the cross, etc. Satan's deepest desire was not to kill Jesus, it was rather to get

Jesus to go all the way, and then give up His love that brought Him to do the sacrifice and commit sin.

Similarly, Satan is not really opposed to the spread of the church in the world... far from it... he is just opposed to certain ways for it to spread. He would like everyone in the world to become a Catholic and to take the sacraments, and to continue living a life of deep sin without true repentance, so that not just every Sunday, but everyday people would come to the church to take the Eucharist in a state of mortal sin. That is his deepest desire; his desire for the world is not for a pagan world, or an atheist world, or a communist world, or an apostate world, but it is for a catholic world where no one has any love and yet they take the sacrament of their salvation anyways. If the church baptizes the whole world, and all people continue in their sins; then that is exactly what the devil wants. If the church, however, teaches the truth in the right way and only gives communion to those in grace, then that is the thing he hates the most. Whether with Jesus on the cross, or the church towards the Eucharist, the steps between life and death are not that far from each other.

Now, if you understand this, then you are beginning to enter more deeply into his thinking. And he is a person, who has thoughts, emotions and feelings- do not think that he doesn't have his own way of thinking.

His most important concern at all times is getting you and all people everywhere to go to the deepest and most painful place in hell that he is permitted to bring you to, because he can't stand the thought that you will win something that he lost.

The last days will not come until the entire world, every person, has converted and joined the Catholic Church. The last people to join will be the Jews. And once that is completed the final tribulation and Antichrist will come.

However, the mission of spreading the church in the world is not to be conducted by the devil, but by the Holy Spirit. The devil's work is in making sure that wherever the church is spread to will simply remain in grave sin. He will lure people away from the church if he sees it as a way of bringing them to hell, but if the church changes so as to allow all the sins of the world to reign supreme in the lives of its members, then he will not need to draw people away from it.

Now, if everyone in the world, however, were to right now enter the Catholic Church and take the Eucharist, it would not be as great a sin for them, because they don't know who the Eucharist is, they haven't received faith. The priest who knowingly confers the Eucharist to them may be heading to hell, but perhaps they would not be. Hence, the devil is not so interested in this now. His final goal, at the time of the Antichrist, will be to make an entire world filled with people taking the Eucharist daily in mortal sin (every person also becoming possessed by the evil spirit in the process), but he is too far away from that now, so he must go for lesser things to bring people to hell.

If all people in the world take the Eucharist now, it may not be sin for them, because they don't know what they are doing. But they do know, however, that a human being is a person and killing him unjustly is very evil.

Hence, here is the role that human sacrifice provides. If you sacrifice people, especially innocent people, to your god or whatever power you believe in, you will go to hell for doing this. In fact, if the whole society consents to it, the whole society will go to hell for doing this. The pagan priest on the top of the Aztec temple at Teotihuacan tears out the heart of his victim and lifts it up, and all the hearts of the people who gaze on it may forever go to hell because of it; in just the same way, the Eucharist (the heart of God) is raised at mass for the salvation of those present and for the world.

You have no excuse for saying that you don't know that this is wrong. Even if you think the gods require it, it is still wrong; better to let the Sun god run out of energy from a lack of sacrificial blood to feed him, and let everyone live in pitch darkness forever than it is to kill an innocent person.

Therefore, the devil takes delight in this, precisely because you have no excuse for it and he can correctly then accuse you of something that will merit eternal hellfire. And because it is an institutionalized part of the civilization, therefore the entire community, the whole city, everyone will go to hell, by consenting and accepting it, and each new generation brought up in it will go to hell through this institution established by their ancestors.

It does not need to be even very many sacrifices. Just one innocent victim, sacrificed to the god with the consent of the whole community: the whole community goes to hell for this one thing, if left without repentance.

In every society, the devil will have something like this instituted, whether it be in the sacramental form of human sacrifice or other forms. Executing people for crimes whom everyone knows is innocent and yet consents to killing, leaving children or people who cannot help themselves to starve to death on the street without helping them, fighting unjust wars that the whole society consents to; the list goes on. If the whole country agrees to killing just one innocent person, and does not repent, then the whole country goes to hell for the death of this one person. The more innocent the victim is, and the more one is aware of what one is doing, the greater the crime.

Amazingly, even hunting witches can serve this purpose, because if the whole community consents to the murder of someone who they think is a witch, and yet lack much evidence beyond just thinking she is... then the whole community goes to hell for it.

The little girl in Africa with her ribs sticking out, ready to die, was first imagined by a mind who prayed to God for it. But if you think that this mind was thinking about harming her through this, then you are greatly mistaken. His target was not her, it was you.

She will die and probably go to heaven; but you and I and the rest of us in society, will look at the picture, shrug our shoulders and say there is nothing we can do, and go about our lives allowing for such things to exist, while the price is tallied on our souls. We can plainly see it, we know there are things we can do to stop this sort of thing from happening and most of us are not doing them, or not doing as much as we are able to reasonably do. Without the picture being shown to us, or without being told this girl exists, we can claim to be innocent, but afterwards, so long as we continue to do as we like in the face of such suffering, then we become his.

His thinking, his planning, is not like the way we would think. So many of us have no idea how badly he has beaten most of humanity. They think they are so strong, so smart, so wise, like they can do anything, etc. and he claps his hands and smiles for them, as he checks the clock waiting for their doom to come.

In modern times, abortion serves the same function. Provide an institutionalized killing within society, teach people even from a young age that the killing is correct, and take away the possibility of people to give excuses for it, and bring them all to hell; it is the same pattern. If the pro-life movement did not exist, the imaging of babies in the womb never occurred and everyone was completely ignorant of even the claim that the foetus was a child, then the devil would actually hate this. He wants the pro-life people to be there giving out their info, for the images of the babies in the womb to be published and for this information to be spread in the society, precisely so that the excuses for the sin can be taken away and the person who does it, the society that consents to it, etc. can all find their way to hellfire.

He does not support abortion because he wants to destroy the babies, he supports abortion because he wants to destroy **you**.

Just like the innocent man having his heart torn out at the top of the temple at Teotihuacan, the victim of abortion provides the same necessary niche within his kingdom. Without the killing of the innocent happening somewhere with your consent, without God being able to ask you 'where is your brother Abel?', then what could the devil accuse you with before the judgment seat of God?

If there was actually not a single abortion that occurred, but the whole society believed that it was happening and they all consented to it, he would be more pleased with this, than if abortion was happening regularly and the larger part of society was innocently unaware. He is more interested in reducing the number of abortions and getting more people to accept its existence, than he is interested in increasing the number of abortions and having society turn against it.

The final goal, however, is not abortion or human sacrifice, but it is the sin against the person of God Himself present in the Eucharist. This is something greater than those things. While there are people in our own time who are already pioneering this path by taking the Host in mortal sin (even those taking it daily), and many priests or lay people who knowingly consent to it, he is still quite far from getting the whole world with this one... that will have to wait until a much later time.

So, if you understood how this works, then you understand how his interest in witchcraft works as well. Whether by witchcraft or not, all his power, is actually channeled according to this line of thinking.

If he can replace human sacrifice of pagans with the murder and slavery of Indians by those eating Christ's body in the mass, then he will work his power in favour of this replacement. If he can replace the unjust treatment of women with the murder of the unborn, then he is all for it; it is a good trade-off for him. If he can replace the division of Christianity into so many churches with one united church that waters down its doctrines and allows people to do anything without fear of hell, he will support it. If he can bring the Antichrist into the world as a person who abolishes all poverty, all abortion, all war, all sickness, and all problems of any sort, but who in exchange just gets the whole world to eat the Eucharist daily in a state of mortal sin; then he will be excited by it.

He will give answers to the witch's magic according to how it suits these purposes above, but even still he can only work through the respective tionchar of different people depending on the vocations God gave to them. Even though he is limited by that constraint, he will do more for things that are going to pull more people to hell. Witchcraft therefore, becomes stronger or more powerful if in some way it serves this purpose.

If a witch, in her stupidity, wished to become as powerful as possible within the ephemeral kingdom, she would have to work under these terms.

If she wants to get more power in her witchcraft, she ought to think like this and be aiming for something that is going to help people to go to hell.

This is difficult to give examples for, because, truth be told, while God keeps His promises always, the devil certainly does not, hence there is absolutely no guarantee at all that the aimed-for results will come from any particular action. As a general rule, this is how his interest works in witchcraft, but if a person is consciously seeking to do witchcraft along these terms because they think that the things in this book are true, I can't promise that he is going to answer politely or as one hoped.

Lord, we pray that you free us from all of our sins and help our souls to be pure in your eyes. We pray that we do nothing that will lead people to hell, but help us to make all our deeds in this life to be things that lead people closer to heaven. We ask for these things, if it is your will, in Jesus' name, Amen

XIV: The Consequences of Witchcraft

What are the consequences of practicing witchcraft?

Like all sins, it deserves punishment, but God punishes different sins in different ways.

Pagan nations all eventually come to a ruin; every pagan society, with the exception of a few, fell under the domination of either Christians or Muslims who worship the true God. However, usually this has to do more with the fourth commandment than it does with the first (which is what witchcraft is principally touching). The lack of belief in the true God will cause people to violate the fourth commandment more because they don't think there is a God that is going to punish them for breaking the laws, rebelling against the government, lying to their parents, cheating their boss, disrespecting their teachers, etc., which inevitably dooms them to collectively become slaves (or something like it) of others. And this lack of belief in the true God is going to be held up by the witchcraft. Therefore the witchcraft can, in this way, bring about destruction to its society by weakening it. There are noted exceptions to this, particularly in pagan places where Confucius' thought had great dominance.

So, while witchcraft can doom the society in the above way, it may not necessarily do so. There are too many examples of very strong pagan states in history that lasted for long times, for us to think that that particular route is always the inevitable consequence. Egypt, Rome, Persia, Babylon, the great kingdoms of India, Imperial China, the Incas, the Aztecs, etc. The only way such states could become great was through adherence to the fourth commandment, and in East Asia, a pagan philosopher even deepened this adherence rather than lead them away from it.

Look at the mass of the pyramids, the stretch of the Great Wall; consider the stones of Incan Peru that were cut so precisely that no mortar was needed between them when building walls; consider the drainage systems of the ancient cities of the Indus Valley, the concrete aqueducts that brought water to roman cities or the heating systems in roman houses... all these things were only possible because of the cooperation of a complex society, and that cooperation can only occur when the fourth commandment is being obeyed.

Egypt flourished for thousands of years and it accomplished amazing things. They built obelisks, which could be 10-20 metres high (the largest, standing today at the Lateran Basilica in Rome was 30 metres) all cut from a single piece of stone, and people today are not sure how they did it. They built the pyramids and other monuments with massive stones which had to have been transported over long distances in order to get them to where the pyramid stood. They possessed so much knowledge of such things for that time period that some pseudo-scientific theories today try to suggest that maybe they had help from extraterrestrials, because it seems like too big of an advance for that time.

Eventually their civilization did collapse, or at least diminish, however. The prophet Ezekiel cursed Egypt and said that it would never be a great kingdom again. And, at least as far as how 'great kingdoms' are usually counted in the history books, since that time, it hasn't.

If a nation practices witchcraft, but it still follows the fourth commandment, then it is not going to fail like that, it will continue to be strong and powerful. And those nations did hold the fourth commandment in a certain important regard. East Asian societies were permeated by Confucian teachings that taught people to honour and obey superiors, whether it be parents, teachers or rulers. Roman society put great importance on duties of children to parents and they took education seriously, and the nature of its original political system was one that likely inspired genuine loyalty within the masses, because they fought for the state, since they saw it as representing the people. It was in later times when the system had become corrupt, when emperors were replaced so frequently by assassinations, that the state weakened and collapsed. Egyptians and other peoples honoured their kings as gods. To do so was idolatrous, but it likely influenced people to at least obey the laws and do the things necessary that made the state unified and strong.

So the fate of being ruled by others is not necessarily the penalty for witchcraft. In that case, then, what is the consequence of it?

If you try to curse people, then you may receive exactly what you wished upon others, and this can be a consequence of witchcraft for those who do this. But not all who practice witchcraft will perform such curses. Modern-day Wiccans openly reject it, to their credit.

So what is the consequence?

The real consequence which will come to anyone who practices and believes in this thing, is that she will eventually find herself living in a nightmare of her own creation.

If a little village in Africa believed in witchcraft and that magic could help you to get the boy to fall in love with you, help you to get the child you want, etc. They will also eventually find themselves believing that witchcraft can also be used to harm people. They will be suspicious of their neighbours, they do not know who is going to curse them, they will dig in their yard to see if there is some hexed item that is buried there... they will live in a world of fear and anxiety, dread and despair... created by their own belief system. There is no loving God that protects them from witchcraft, because they think the gods work their power through the witchcraft.

Consider what Paul wrote to the pagans living in the 1st century of the Roman empire in Ephesus.

Ephesians 2:12 remember that you were at that time separate from Christ, excluded from the commonwealth of Israel, and strangers to the covenants of promise, having no hope and without God in the world.

They lived in a world without hope. That was the penalty.

How was it without hope?

Imagine if all the Greek and Roman myths really were true. The universe really is governed by powers that enjoy the killing of innocents in the arena, that value power and glory over love and mercy, that are envious, that have hatred, that commit adultery, etc. They do not love you, they do not care about you, you are there to please them in their lusts or else they will hurt you.

These are the ultimate things in charge of reality, whom you must serve. And it shall be this way for eternity whether you are alive or in the afterlife. Think, if you can, that that really is the reality and contemplate it. Now, do you feel good? It is a pleasant reality to believe in? Do you want to live in that world?

This reality lets you do all sorts of different sins that you like to do, and yet ultimately, is this the thing that you want to be true?

Even if people who practice witchcraft believe in the true God, because they are Jews, Muslims or Christians, their world will still become dark like this if they practice witchcraft. If they think God is some kind of impersonal energy force that has power that can be tapped into by the witchcraft, then they ultimately don't believe in God, and they fall into the same category as the pagans, with the same consequences. Or maybe they think that God is like only one power, and witchcraft has some power apart from God that can be tapped into, and if so then they ultimately don't believe in God, and they fall into the same category as the pagans, with the same consequences.

In short: what is the consequence of witchcraft? How does God punish this sin?

The answer: it is to live in a world, created by your own and others imagination, in which the true loving God who wants you to join their family is not present, and something else is instead. The deepest desire in your heart cannot be fulfilled, because the One that can fulfill it does not really exist. And so the devil goes to God's throne and secures the punishment for you; he reads the sentence as follows: 'Continue casting your spells, burning your sacrifices and honouring the gods and spirits your sinful minds have invented. And then go live in this cruel, dark world of your own creation, which will leave you with no peace and confuse you into thinking that sin is the path to happiness, because living in that place is what you deserve.'

And this lack of hope and cruel world that exists in your imagination, will in turn lead you to easily fall into other sins. Because without hope of heaven or hope in God, you will be lead to think that the only way to find what you want is through sin, and so you will sin, and your sins will multiply and eventually destroy you, leading you to hell.

There is no one who loves human beings like God does. The moment they reject him in favour of the god or supernatural thing (or lack thereof) that their own minds have created, they have already lost hope, even if they didn't realize it. That is the penalty they must endure for it.

Lord, we pray that all those in the midst of pagan cultures and witchcraft will turn away from their sins and repent before it is too late. We pray that they may recognize the hollowness of the devil's promises. We ask for these things, if it is your will, in Jesus' name, Amen

XV: The Witch-hunt

This book has largely been an attempt to explain some of the general truths that surround the spiritual world. It has not gone into too much depth for how witchcraft, shamanism and other such things works as an institution in societies. People who are interested in learning about that could study from anthropologists who have done much more thorough research on that issue. This book has not dealt with the role of witchcraft as an institution, which is an anthropologist's proper domain, but it has instead tried to explain things which go beyond the abilities of what the anthropologist can answer.

An issue surrounding witchcraft, which deeply touches the anthropologist's work, is the issue of witch hunts. In many societies, including the modern day in many of the less developed parts of the world, this is a reality within their culture.

People might wonder: if witchcraft really is true (at least part of the time), and these people really can exist and harm others, then can we condemn societies that hunt witches? Would it not in fact be justifiable to go and hunt them ourselves?

This is actually an important question, and I want to

spend some space here giving an answer to it.

In the bible, Moses tells the people that they should not allow for a witch to live among them. This can be perhaps interpreted as meaning that they would kill or banish someone who was found to be practicing witchcraft.

In past times, the church encouraged temporal governments to use the power of the law and legal punishment to stop witchcraft from existing.

Moses also forbade paganism from existing at all in the midst of the Israelites. Any kind of idol was forbidden, and anyone who preached a foreign god to the Israelites could be executed. People in Israel were not even allowed to marry a person from one of the other countries that didn't believe in God, for fear that this would cause them to be lead away to worship foreign gods.

Witchcraft is essentially a kind of pagan religious activity, and hence banning it would seem to be necessary if you banned paganism as a whole, since allowing it would then be allowing something which you already banned.

The question of whether or not witches should be punished by the society for their witchcraft is essentially tied together into the same question as to whether the society ought to punish people who worship false gods or engage in paganism.

In answering this question, one must understand that laws ought to be there in order to punish people so that the rest of the society can be safe. If there is no threat to anyone, then you don't need a law to punish people, but if there is a threat to the society, then you do need a law to punish people.

For example, a little child who says he wants to kill people does not need a law to stop him, because his own parents can suitably suppress this threat from the child. However, if an adult were to be like this, you would need a law to stop him.

If a person disseminated ideas which was going to lead people to engage in some public violence, then that person needs to be stopped, but if this person disseminated the ideas and no one listens to him, then the state doesn't need to stop him.

In Moses' law, this principle is the same. Moses bans things in many places which are not actually bad in themselves, but they need to be banned in order to prevent the Israelites from going away from God and losing their faith. These laws were protecting the society's morals and protecting the souls of people from damnation.

Jesus said in the gospel that if your right hand causes you to sin, it is better to cut it off than to go down to hell with it; by the same logic, one must also say, that if a certain thing in the public society is leading people to hell, then it is the responsibility of the state to destroy it.

The church teaches that capital punishment is wrong if it is possible to incarcerate a person, but in Moses' time, the tribal bronze age civilization perhaps did not have the capacity to run an established judiciary with a prison system, and hence capital punishment would not be wrong in that context because the alternative was just letting the criminal go free, seeing as there was no place to hold him.

In modern states, where incarceration is possible and is already done, they have no excuse and they ought to ban capital punishment.

But a principle here must be understood, that it is the

right of the state to use the law to protect public morals, and if the person needs to be removed from the public in order to do so (by incarceration when prisons exist, and capital punishment if they do not exist), then there is nothing wrong with this action.

People can still rebel against God in secret. They can reject God in secret and hate Him in secret. But they would not be punished under Moses' laws, because they were not a danger to the faith of the community. Moses put all these restrictions upon the people of Israel because they were weak in faith, and there was a danger that such things could lead them away from God and down to perdition.

If the Israelites got married to pagans, but their faith was so strong that they never bowed down before the foreign gods, then there would have been no reason for Moses banning such marriages. If a person could preach foreign gods in Israel, but no one would ever listen to him and people would just laugh at him when he preached, then there would be no reason why you needed to put this person to death, because he presents no danger at all to the society.

From this perspective, we can then come to the

question for the modern-day. If the presence of books, CDs or other media about witchcraft (or any topic at all in fact where sin is being promoted) is likely to lead people away from God and down to hell and outlawing them could prevent this from happening, then the state should try to get rid of these things. If the presence of people practicing witchcraft (or any practice at all which is sinful) carries the same risk to the public, then it is the same answer.

But legal punishment is not the preferred answer. It is better to have a society that rejects these things on its own than to have a society that needs a state to outlaw these things in order to prevent people from being ensnared by them.

If people can be stopped from following these things by education, by influencing them through the media, or some other means that does not require anyone to be punished or go to jail, then those methods ought to be used rather than legal punishments. This is not just for witchcraft, but the same principle is true for all sorts of things in societies that carry the risk of leading people to hell.

Hence, the idea of searching for people doing witchcraft

in secret and stopping them is somewhat absurd, because if the society rejects them so much that they must be doing these things in secret, then you obviously do not need a law to punish them and thereby protect the rest of the society, seeing that no one is at risk of losing their morals because of this, since no one even knows that they are there. If the faith of the society really was so weak that allowing such a person to exist even in secret was a danger to the morals of others who came in contact with them, only then could you ever justify that kind of a witch-hunt.

It is only in the societies where the faith is weak, where the people do not love God enough so that such things are a threat to them, in which you need all sorts of legal controls to prevent bad influences from being spread around. The Israelites constantly complaining under Moses was a society like this, but not every society is like this.

In a huge number of societies, including parts of the world today, they prosecuted people for witchcraft on the basis of hearsay or unfounded suspicions. This has to be condemned for the same reason that one must condemn the prosecution of any person on a lack of evidence.

Sometimes they will even use supernatural evidence for such trials, but if this kind of evidence is inadmissible for normal cases going to court, then you know it is also inadmissible here as well. Who can claim that they had an infallible power from God to interpret supernatural evidence to judge a legal case? If Anne Catherine Emmerich could not tell the difference between her visions and her ordinary dreams, then what is the likelihood that the old man in the village in Africa going to be able to do this?

Some people might disagree with this and they may be thinking that all witchcraft is dealing with the devil, and therefore all witchcraft should be not be allowed. Even if the people are not going to be swayed away from their faith by the practice of witchcraft, it still must be banned because it uses the devil's power. And they have a point, because by allowing even these things you are allowing for people to communicate with the devil.

However, try to understand that every time any person anywhere commits a sin, you are also with the devil there too. The priest who has even just a little bit of pride, the sales clerk who breaks a little rule to get out of work early, the child who tells a little lie to his parents... the devil is in all of these things, because wherever sin is, the devil is there too. But you don't outlaw these things, even though the devil is present.

The witch is just openly acknowledging the person that everyone, including those who believe in God, are collectively listening to much of the time. If you want to outlaw witchcraft, because the devil is in it, then you could also outlaw every sin in existence and attach some legal penalty to it, because the devil is in those things too.

Now, some people may say in response to all of this, that it is not for this reason alone that they want witchcraft to be outlawed, but they are afraid that the witchcraft may be used to threaten them. They are thinking that people may use witchcraft to call down curses upon them and therefore to protect themselves they must punish the witches.

Witchcraft is able to achieve results and a person can get demonic power used to harm a person through witchcraft. But using the law to defend yourself from this may be impossible, seeing that this is a spiritual attack and you can't imprison the demons like you would a person. If you put the witch in jail, that is not going to stop her from being able to harm people with witchcraft. If you kill her, this still may not stop her.

As I wrote at the beginning, there is nothing that the

devil does without God's permission. There is nothing that witchcraft is able to do without first receiving approval from the throne of God. There is also no power in existence that is able to stop the demons from doing things in this world other than God. You can try all the laws you like, set up wherever institutions you think will work, create whatever technology you think will be useful and you are guaranteed that they will not stop the devil from engaging in his spiritual warfare.

If one wants to defend oneself from witchcraft, the logical course of action would be to turn to God in prayer and stay away from sin.

Not all witchcraft is done with cursing of people. The modern Wiccan religion in fact deserves some respect on this point, because they are forbidden to use their witchcraft to curse people or harm them in any way.

But there are many uses of witchcraft in the world that are used to put curses on people. Whether they work or not is decided at the throne of God.

Now, if you simply want justice applied to the people who are using witchcraft like this, then rather than using laws and states to punish them, rather than hunting them... wouldn't the logical thing to do rather be to pray to God and ask for justice?

If a person is using witchcraft to harm other people, isn't the most logical and best punishment to use a spiritual method in answer to a spiritual crime? Rather than burning them, hanging them or drowning them in lakes, if you need justice done, why not just pray to God for their punishment and do nothing else, just like how they used witchcraft to curse a person and did nothing else beyond this?

It is a sin to pray for something bad to happen to your enemy out of hatred for them. It is not a sin to ask for justice to be applied in the world out of love for human beings. Nothing happens in the physical world unless someone has prayed for it first.

If no one, either human or angelic, ever prayed for criminals to be punished, then no criminal ever would be punished. If no one ever prayed for evil people to receive what is due for them, then it would never come to them and they would live with impunity forever.

If you think it is wrong to pray to God and ask for punishment, then why would you think it right for human beings at any time to inflict punishments on other human beings for the sake of justice? If it is wrong to pray to God for those things, then it must also be wrong to actually do these things as well.

Hence, it is not a sin to ask for such things, but it must be done with love and truth.

How do you do so?

I suggest the following principles:

When you actually inflict legal punishments on a person it must also be done in love and truth. When you punish criminals, you do not do so selectively by applying punishment to those you don't like and sparing those you like， but rather you give the same law and standard to all. If you yourself violate the law, then you must also be punished by it. When you put a criminal in jail, you should work for his rehabilitation as being preferable to keeping him there forever. Even if they do not deserve it, you are willing to pay a price for them in order so that they can become better. This is the way that justice in the physical world ought to be, and when applying spiritual penalties it ought to be the same.

For example, I think people should never ask for a certain person to be punished that they can name. Rather if they want God to apply justice they should instead ask Him that all people who do such and such a sin without stopping may be punished, regardless of who they are. You must also ask for Him to apply punishment to yourself in whatever manner He knows is best for you, because you are His child and parents punish children when they need to do so. Also, when you pray for such things, do not simply ask for punishment but ask for mercy as well, and ask for God to help the person to get out of their sins and become better again.

And furthermore, the key ingredient of mercy: you also ask God that He will allow you to suffer for the sinners, should it be His will, even though they do not deserve it, so that they can receive mercy and be saved.

Lord, we know that you are a Just Judge and Merciful Redeemer. We acknowledge our own sins and beg you to cure us from them. Sin is our disease and suffering is our medicine. We pray that you cure us of our disease, bring us to never sin again and bring us to an even better state in the end than we were in originally. Hold our hands as you apply this medicine to us, and let us never forget that you love us in the midst of it. Now that we have taken the beam from our eyes, allow us now to ask you for others. For all those in the world who practice witchcraft to intentionally harm others, we pray that you likewise apply the same cure to them. Give them suffering as a medicine to cure them of their sin, make their curses against others reflect back upon them in justice. We also ask that you help to bring them to an even better state in the end than they were before they began to sin. We pray that you allow us to suffer for such people when you will it so that they may also be saved. We ask for these things, if it is your will, in Jesus' name, Amen

XVI: Note on Localities, Family Heritages, Nations and Images

One last note to end this piece which I want to mention here is the special relationships involving places, objects, images, etc. Which I have not talked about already.

Are different races and ethnicities different to other races and ethnicities in the question of tionchar?

Honestly, I am not sure. The Jews, being specially selected by God, probably were intended to have a different spiritual relationship with Him than other peoples of the world, but what that means in practice, I am not sure.

Perhaps He does intend for different peoples and ethnicities to have different relationships with him and thus gives them different tionchar.

The example of Abraham's descendants is a point to look at. Did it make a difference for the way that people related to God whether they were descended from Ishmael or from Isaac? It did make a difference, because He blessed them differently and Isaac inherited the original promise given to Abraham.

All races have their origin from Adam – from one human

being. And we human beings are all part of one giant extended family. What made the races different was simply that different descendants of Adam separated from one another and developed differently from one generation to the next down to the present.

Other than the example above, there are actually many cases in the bible where God blesses people differently on the basis of family heritage. Like different tribes of Israel being blessed in different ways, or different nations being blessed (or cursed) in different ways.

It would stand to reason then that if someone has a different relationship with God because his ancestor was Ishmael rather than Isaac, or because he was a Levite and not an Ephraimite... then therefore we could conclude that race and ethnicity can indeed mean a difference in tionchar.

Moses said that if you followed God's commandments, then He would bless your descendants down to the thousandth generation, but if you disobeyed them, then He would bring punishments on your descendants to the third or fourth generation. That statement in itself implies God treating people differently on the basis of race, because race is nothing more than different genealogical heritage from a long-term perspective.

If the ancestors of some people in Ireland served God,

but the ancestors of some people in India did not, then according to Moses' statement about blessing descendants for the sake of their ancestors' deeds, God is going to bless the people in Ireland in such a way that he is not going to bless the people in India.

If your relationship with God is affected by ancestry, then it would therefore follow that your tionchar is affected by race and ethnicity as well, since tionchar is nothing more than the way you were designed to have a relationship with God.

Now, if God makes His creation fairly evenly, one would expect that the places with the most number of people to also have the most number of people with the more unique forms of tionchar. Hence, Asia, with 60% of the world's population ought to also have the largest number of people with such tionchar and the most powerful of all witchcraft. Asia ought to have the largest number of wei'nu living among its population, or the largest number of males called to the priesthood, for the same reason.

Perhaps we can see clues to this too. Where did the world's great religions have their origin? Muhammad was from Arabia, Buddha came from either northern India or Nepal, Hinduism from India, Sikhism from

India/Pakistan, Daoism from China, Zoroastrianism from Iran, Bahai from Iran, Jainism from India, Confucianism from China, Shintoism from Japan. How many great world religions can you think of that originated from Africa, Europe or the Americas? There are a few (Christianity is not one of them, unless we were to count the different branches of Christianity that broke from the church), but it is comparatively much smaller than Asia.

Sometimes it happens that people will say that a particular place is cursed or haunted, or that a particular family has a curse running through it, etc.

There is a tendency which ought to be pointed out which is that, as Paul wrote, where sin abounds, grace abounds even more. The reverse is also true in a certain way: the more opportunities that God gives to a person or persons to receive grace, there will also be an increase in the devil's opportunity to tempt this person. Hence the places where the church is most established will also be the places that typically are open to experience the most temptations if people fail to take those graces that come from the church; partly for this reason perhaps the morals of the West are in such a bad state. For the same reason, the catholic priesthood will be subject to much harder temptations than most other people.

Furthermore, the days of the liturgical year in which people can acquire more graces, like on the solemnities (eg. Easter, the Assumption, All Saints Day, Christmas) will also be the time when the devil increases his temptations for those who fail to look for these graces. Oddly enough, we even celebrate Halloween (All Hallows Eve, or the eve before All Saints day) as a night for ghosts, monsters and demons; the reality is that the devil actually can and will increase his temptation at that time due to the superior graces that can be acquired on November 1st. However, the same is also true for the other solemnities, like on August 15th, January 1st, December 8th, June 29th, March 19th, etc.

Throughout this work I have put the devil as the person who is primarily being an intercessor with God to ask for the deception and ruin of human beings. However, the devil is not alone in this. There are a huge number of other demons that are with him who are doing essentially the same work of interceding with God to ask for the temptation, deception and ruin of human beings.

Furthermore, there is also to consider all the souls of the human beings who suffered eternal damnation.

When a person goes to hell, they still are capable of speaking to God, although they refuse to love Him and to share in His presence.

When a person dies they immediately see God, and God presents them with every word, thought and action they had in their lifetimes, and they see which things were good and which things were bad. If they have already completely let go of all the bad in their own lifetimes, then they look upon God and feel peace; this is their entrance into heaven.

If they did not make full correction for all those things, but they are sorry that they did them, then they look upon God and they feel great pain because they see how much God loves them and how bad they were to Him; they tell God how sorry they were, and God accepts their apology, but they still feel very great pain. These people are the souls in purgatory and they suffer terribly.

And another group of people, who make up most of the human race, see God judging all the bad things they did and rather than repent or change, they are filled with anger and despair. They see the person they hated and who they still hate, and this person takes off the mask and they see God's face behind it... and they think that if

God is really this person who they hated so much, then they don't want God. They prefer to suffer for eternity than to ever love someone who treats them like this. God tells them that they are not better than the person they looked down upon, and they refuse to accept it, and hate Him for being a God who is like this. God tells them that He didn't care for their fasts, their processions, their prayers and worship, because it was all for appearances and not for love of Him; and then they hate Him because He is so ungrateful for all that they did for Him. God tells people of a religion that their religion was wrong and the religion they hated was the true teaching, and they hate God for favouring the other religion over their own, and thus refuse to love Him. God shows them that their own mother went to hell, and they hate God for not thinking that their beloved mother was worthy of heaven, and thus depart from Him.

And so, they refuse to stay with Him, but depart from His presence. But once they leave, they can have no more peace, no more truth, and no more love, because outside of God there is no person and no place that can give those things to them. And they remain, like Cain, wandering in exile from His presence without peace forever. But even in that place they are, like Cain, still recipients of God's mercy and treated more lightly than their sins deserve.

These people are the souls in hell.

The way that people end this life on earth, whether repentant for their sins or not repentant, will also be the same way that they will feel when they stand before God's judgment seat.

Jesus said in the gospel, 'this is the judgment, that the light has come into the world, but men preferred darkness'. The Son of God came and they did not accept Him. The judgment at your death that sends you to heaven or hell is not God's choice, it is your choice. Do you really accept God and the Son He sent to save you or not? Most people will say, yes of course, but that is because they imagine Him to be a person that thinks the same way as they do, who agrees with them, who approves of them, who is just a reflection of their own ego and desires, etc. But when they actually see Him and the fullness of the Truth, they will refuse to love Him then, just as they did at the last moment of life. If they could not love the person that stood next to them in life, then they are not going to love God when that person takes off his mask and they see it was God all along. That is the judgment by which people enter the kingdom or not.

Most people, even most of the people who believe in

the Son of God, will choose to leave Him, because once they really see Him, they will not be able to accept Him, and like the devil, they will prefer to suffer than to love Him.

People don't really fully grasp this: God is here right now, in your life right now, behind the faces of all those you sin against. If you reject Him now, then when you actually see Him at your judgment, you will reject Him then too... because it is the same Person and the same question. People who sin gravely against Him but who say they would never reject God if they were given such a judgment are basically saying that they would never reject this idea in their head that they call God, but the real God they would reject. And it is the real God who is going to judge them, not the false thing they have created in their own imagination.

I would like to quote here Pope Francis' statement in his letter Amoris Laetitia: "No one can be condemned for ever, because that is not the logic of the Gospel! Here I am not speaking only of the divorced and remarried, but of everyone, in whatever situation they find themselves."

No person who goes to hell goes there because God refuses to forever forgive. As the Pope said, that is not the logic of the gospel. The people in hell go there, and they stay forever, by their own choice to reject God forever. People living in the world right now might have trouble believing how it is possible that so many souls in hell would choose to reject God forever if given such a choice, but that is only because the idea of God in the heads of people and the reality of God as a true Person are two completely different things.

God told Moses, that if He stayed with the people for just one day, He would destroy them all. That is because if God was actually there, the people would all sin against Him and oppose Him, and He would be obliged to make them suffer for their own sins, since the time was not right to pay a sacrifice on their behalf. Anne Catherine Emmerich said that if Jesus walked the world in the modern day, He would find just as many enemies and just as much opposition as He did 2000 years ago.

If God was walking in the world today, almost everyone would oppose Him. And if all the people in the world died today and saw God for who He really was, they would oppose Him there too and thereby be separated from His presence. That is the judgment God has upon the world.

In the life of human beings now, they choose to sin against the God who is here now through many different ways. When they die and see Him face to face, they will continue to do so and depart from God's presence by their choice to continue to do so.

As Jesus said in the gospel of John: 'this is the judgment that has come into the world'.

Once they see Him for who He really is, then all these people, whether Muslims, Jews, Protestants, Catholics, Buddhists, pagans, etc. abandon Him and will never want Him again for ever. They will never change their minds and go back again, no matter how much time is given them. And just like the devil, if any of them ever did change their minds, God would take them back... but if God knew that at some point after the judgment they were going to change, He would have given them more time in this life before their deaths so that this would have happened. There is no one after death who changes, and not because God fixed it, but because we did.

At the Second Coming, the angels will blow their trumpets and all the dead will rise to life. All the souls in hell will appear, and God will tell them that if any of them wishes to leave their torments and come have peace again, they are welcome to, and that all they have to do is repent of their sins and love Him. And every single one of them will say no and prefer to suffer forever than to accept Him. And they will all fall into the lake of fire, but the sparks of the fire will come from no other place than their own empty hearts.

Sometimes many Christians propose an idea of universal salvation, and they hope that all souls, including even the devil, will be saved in the end. This is a heresy, but the truth is that God, in the deepest part of His Heart, is the first person who would wish that this heresy was true. You have no idea how badly He wished that it were true. But love that is forced is not love, and love that is bribed is not loved; as the Song of Songs said, if one were to buy love, one would be roundly mocked. God did not decide that this should be a heresy, rather it is us human beings who made it a heresy rather than a true doctrine.

These souls in hell not only hate God, but they reject everything that belongs to God. They become monsters, suffering greatly and yet filled with hatred towards God and towards everyone else in the universe. Even the people they knew in life, even their own family members, they will hate with a deep hatred and want them to come and join them in the suffering they are experiencing. They become like an image of Satan; like him, they cannot stand the idea that the people they knew in life will pass a test that they failed.

There are various movies with 'zombie apocalypse' depicted in them where everyone turns into a monster that is a twisted version of their former selves, and they are lusting after getting the healthy people to join them and become monsters too. The truth is that this is not entirely fictional, and the Holy Spirit, who is moving and planting seeds in all cultures, may be inspiring something through it; all people who go to hell are going to become monsters, they will not have bodies in hell, but in the final resurrection they will come back and we will see them all (billions of them) in the flesh as the monsters they have become. Original sin, from which all other sins and the end of hellfire stems from, is propagated through the flesh, it is not attained through seeing a bad example; the zombie infection is similar. In the movies, you see people of all different places and walks of life, from the policeman, to the doctor, to the store clerk, getting infected and becoming a monster; the reality is just like this, the people you see driving their cars on the street, the students in the classrooms, the librarian, the street vendor, the people you see and meet every day... one day these people will become the most hideous monsters imaginable. And just like how in the movie, almost everyone becomes a zombie, and only a remnant are still clean, so also in reality most people are going to become these monsters in hell, while trying to get everyone else to become monsters and join them.

So, these damned souls will pray to God and ask God specifically for their own family members, their work colleagues, their neighbours, etc. to come down and join them. Like Satan they will pray to God that these people will suffer temptation and deception, and God may grant it for the same reason that he grants the devil's prayers for these things.

In this way, things which had relation with such people when they were alive will become the primary subject of their hatred once they go to hell. The people they didn't know in life, they will not pray as much for, but rather they will focus their attention on those they knew. Similarly, they will also focus their attention on the places that are more familiar to them, the jobs and institutions that are more familiar to them, etc.

So, for example a police officer who died and went to hell, will pray to God that his own colleagues in the police force will also be subject to the temptations he went through, because he hates them now and wants them to join them. And God sees that his colleagues, like most of humanity does not love Him, and He allows the devil or perhaps he even allows the soul of the dead police officer to influence his former colleagues. And so they are tempted to stop catching real criminals and instead to use their time to go around getting bribes from people, so that when they die, they can come down and join him.

However, he will not be able to do very much. Just like

the devil, the souls of the damned will only be permitted to bother the living inasmuch as the living can resist and no further than that. Hence, for example, the colleagues of the dead police officer could simply follow their consciences rather than the evil thing they desire to do, and they would be almost completely safe from the invisible hatred of their dead colleague.

Another example: in a city where people worshipped pagan gods in ancient times and performed lewd sexual theatre shows in honour of these gods, had many people who went to hell for this reason. But the souls of these people continually want living people to follow the road they did to hell, so they continue to try to get permission from God to tempt people in the place they lived in this way. Eventually the people who are living listen to the voices long dead, and they create a sexual revolution that embraces all the perversity that had brought damnation to their ancestors who lived in the same place thousands of years before. And their ancestors' spirits are even permitted to teach them to reject Christianity as an evil religion, just as their ancestors did when it was persecuted in the pre-Christian period.

The soul never ceases to exist. The person that existed at one time in one place still exists today, but you simply cannot see this person with your eyes. But the person will still try to influence the world, and will succeed only if the world willingly cooperates.

Hence, because the number of the dead souls is very high, virtually every place in the world, every home, every hill, every rock, every occupation, every family, every descendant, will be touched by this problem. The souls of the damned, depending on who they are, will seek to intercede in different ways according to what they were in life.

It is perhaps better for a culture to remove any kind of honour for them. For this reason, people should not build statues or monuments to dead people, hang up portraits in honour of them, put their faces on their money, etc. unless the person is known to be in either heaven or purgatory- because if they are in hell, then you might as well just build a statue to Satan, hang up a portrait of a demon, put the face of the devil on your money...because in hell, the human souls residing there will be the same as him. We perhaps do not really fully understand what the vast majority of the dead souls in history look like at this moment in the present. The vast majority of people who lived in the past are at this moment the most hideous monsters imaginable, filled with hatred and sin, while bearing not even the tiniest trace of love. The same people who were even founding fathers of nations, great philosophers or writers, explorers, scientists, etc. are at the moment you are reading this, the most evil creatures you can possibly imagine. They have already destroyed their former selves and lost any goodness or virtue they once possessed in the world. Like the zombies in the movie, they become monstrous versions of their past selves.

The person they were in life is not the same person they are now. This is what is not understood.

Putting their faces in textbooks or museums to teach people about who they are for educational purposes is perhaps not a problem, but rather giving them places of honour, teaching them as good examples to follow, making them the subject of public admiration, etc. This is perhaps a problem.

These people all still exist today, and they are extremely evil; the statues and images depicting them are not what they look like now.

Because these damned souls will have a tendency of seeking to harm the people who have a connection with them, therefore the people who honour them, especially those who honour them and yet are aware of their sins, will also perhaps become their target and they will try hard to bring them to 'follow their example' to come and join them in hellfire.

Even people who are thought of as though they were

paragons of virtue in the nations they lived in, are still suspect, because you do not know their hidden lives and what was really in their hearts. In many places people honour heroes who openly did evil and they even celebrate the evil as though it were good; for example, the founders of the United States committed the sin of revolution, which is not permitted by God's law because He ordained the governing authorities to rule people and condemned rebellion (part of the fourth commandment)- and yet they are honoured as heroes for their sin. If honouring them attracts their attention, honouring them for the sin that they committed perhaps attracts their attention even more. If any of them went to hell in the end, one must be very wary about the great honour bestowed on them.

For example, what if they were in hell and inspired the Americans to fight a civil war, to deeply hate people of rival political ideas or rival parties as though it were a normal part of democracy to have such hatred, to spread war around the world in the name of democracy and political rights, to use the name of democracy and rights to have abortion, obscenities and every kind of sin, etc... all because they want to bring more of the living along the same path to darkness that they followed. And there are crazed individuals, who are diagnosed as insane, and yet perhaps are possessed by these dead souls from the American revolution, and the evil spirits dominating these living persons convince them to think the government is evil and trying to control them, and they persuade them to shoot people or blow up government buildings in a new 'revolution for liberty'. I do not know if that is what has happened or not, nor do I know where the souls of such people are now, but I wish to use this simply as an example of what this dynamic could look like in the real world when the living give honour to a dead person who is now a very evil monster. Perhaps the US founding fathers are all in heaven or purgatory- I do not know.

But one must recognize that all the dead in past times are still here, and they touch the world and affect it, although we may not consciously realize how they do it. Hitler is still here somewhere, so is Charlemagne, so is Francis Drake, so is Jean-Paul Sartre, so is Napoleon, so is Nero, so is Gandhi, so is Muhammad, so is Elvis Presley. Unlike in this life, however, wherein people are most often shades of grey, the people who are dead are either black or white.

I am really hesitant about writing about this, because my imagination is not trustworthy enough to condemn or judge people. However, because there is the real possibility that honouring such persons has something to do with the misfortunes in the present, I will write a number of possible 'suspects' to consider, but who are in no way being assumed as guilty.

Stalin died in 1953, a few months later the Korean War ended and North Korea began its permanent isolation from the rest of the world from that time up until today.

Interest in Martin Luther's books revived greatly in Germany after the defeat in World War I. The last book that Luther wrote in his life, before he finally died, was entitled *On the Jews and their lies* in which he called for their synagogues to be destroyed and for them to be openly attacked by the public. Luther's preaching and use of the media of his time upset the spiritual order, Hitler's use of public speaking and media turned the world upside-down. Many people wonder what it was in Germany that was able to create such a thing as what happened in the 20th century.

Hitler admired Genghis Khan. Genghis Khan fought his enemies by using horse archers that devastated battlefields because they fought against enemies who were not used to this kind of mobile advantage in the battlefield. Genghis Khan and his descendants treated rebellious populations with annihilation. Hitler had the same mind towards the Warsaw uprising or similar events, and he fought the war using mobile armour and technology that gave a great advantage over his enemies.

Hitler is admired among many in the Muslim world who hate Israel. Mein Kampf, the protocols of the learned elders of Zion, and other materials circulated by the Nazis can be found sold in Muslim countries today, and many people in these countries have the spirit with them that calls for the destruction of Israel.

Outside of the tombs of saints there are many miracles that get reported from time to time and many people have spiritual revivals when they go on pilgrimage to those places. Within the vicinity of Mao's body in Tiananmen Square thousands of people were massacred in 1989 who called for democracy.

Toyotomi Hideyoshi wanted to conquer China through Korea and Manchuria in the late 16th century, and he launched his invasion but he failed. Japan did not attempt to attack another country again until the 19th century. When they did, they went after China and went through Korea first and had all the same dreams of an empire over Asia that were abandoned after Toyotomi Hideyoshi died and seemingly departed from history.

Qin Shihuang united China, became its first emperor and ruled it brutally in order to keep it together. Without sacrificing human rights, they thought the country could not keep itself together. Mao Zedong was compared to Qin Shihuang when he united a country torn apart by foreign invasion and chaos following the collapse of the Qing dynasty, and he himself boasted that he surpassed Qin Shihuang in brutality. The modern

Chinese state also sacrifices human rights in order to keep national unity and order.

Islamic State appeared three years after Bin Laden's death.

Hugo Chavez's had great admiration of Simon Bolivar. The taking of Marilyn Monroe's name by Marilyn Manson (as well as Charles' Manson's name, but he isn't dead).

I write the possibilities above not because I assume them to be true, but merely because I wish to put them forward as possibilities to consider when thinking about this question of how souls in hell may influence the world now. I must again affirm that this is entirely speculative and not reliable at all.

In any event, unless we know people to be in heaven or purgatory, I think the rule ought to be that all such public honours to anyone should be taken away. The unfortunate reality is that most people who lived and died in past history are monsters in hell now who will do everything they can to harm us, hence we ought to be careful about who we honour.

If a person is a saint recognized by the authority of

God's church then we can feel safe in honouring them. But even the masses who are in purgatory are also safe to be honoured because although they are suffering, they also have no hatred for the living and they love the living. The souls in purgatory do not sin anymore, hence they are completely safe to give public honour. But we don't have a list of who they are.

If we want to do this, then we can pray for it. And I suspect such prayers will be in the first category of prayers (the ones that are God's will to grant) because our wish here is that we can honour only those who truly ought to be honoured.

You can say this prayer together with me:

Lord, we pray that ourselves, the church and the world will have a greater awareness of which souls who have left this world are in damnation and which are not. And help us to have greater honour in this world for those in heaven and to eliminate honour in this world for those in hell. We ask for these things, if it is your will, in Jesus' name, Amen

All the souls in heaven will seek to help people on Earth to get to heaven, and they pay the most attention to the people, families, places, occupations, institutions and things that have the most relation to them.

Hence, a person who knew a martyr in life, will have that martyr pray for them after they die. Even the person who kills the martyr will have this martyr pray for them in a special way.

Maria Goretti was murdered by a young man who wanted to rape her in 1902. The young man went to prison, but in prison he had dreams of her and he repented of what he did, and after he got out of prison he told others to reject pornography because it was the source of his sin. She was in heaven and she loved him, even though he was her killer, and because he had this relation to her, she wanted to bring him to heaven too. Like the opposite of the damned police officer above who wants to bring his colleagues to hell.

Whatever the saints were in life, they will continue to be after they die, and they will try to intercede for the world according to what talents they possessed. The souls in hell do the opposite, and try to bring people to hell, and intercede for the world according to the talents they possessed.

So, a nation, for example, which had so many monks that lived their lives in holy seclusion contemplating the deeper truths will have these monks praying for their nation. It is not hard to read some of the great Russian writers and see the spirit of someone in the nation's past who contemplated deeply on the Truth of God.

Compare Anton Chekhov's short story 'the Bet' with the life of Anthony the Great in Egypt; do you realize that Chekhov's story is describing the life of St Anthony so perfectly? Anton was probably named after him (his birthday was January 17th in the Russian calendar, which is Anthony's feast day) and Anthony perhaps prayed for Anton in his life, but maybe Anton never consciously realized the inspiration. It is a long-held tradition that the saint whose name you are baptized under will intercede for you for the rest of your life.

I feel even like I should quote some of the dialogue in the story here and ask you whether you think it was Chekov or Anthony the Great who was saying this:

""And I despise your books, I despise wisdom and the blessings of this world. It is all worthless, fleeting, illusory, and deceptive, like a mirage. You may be proud, wise, and fine, but death will wipe you off the face of the earth as though you were no more than mice burrowing under the floor, and your posterity, your history, your immortal geniuses will burn or freeze together with the earthly globe.

"You have lost your reason and taken the wrong path. You have taken lies for truth, and hideousness for beauty. You would marvel if, owing to strange events of some sorts, frogs and lizards suddenly grew on apple and orange trees instead of fruit, or if roses began to smell like a sweating horse; so I marvel at you who exchange heaven for earth. I don't want to understand you."

The character who had spent fifteen years in solitary confinement preferred the prison over all the riches in the world, and renounced the millions he had been promised if he won the bet by escaping at the last moment. The character of Anthony the Great, who preferred living in isolation from the world out in the desert to be away from temptations and closer to God is being described so perfectly in the story.

The Amerindians of the Americas who embraced a less civilized existence that was closer to nature will pray for the people who live in their home now. Why Americans are the way they are, why things like hunting, fishing, outdoor sports, are so popular as hobbies in this part of the world than the rest of the world I often wonder if it had something to do with the prayers of the original residents of the place for those who live there now.

They replaced the original inhabitants, but the original inhabitants live on still by praying for these people now inhabiting their land and making them more like themselves than the more refined European cultures their ancestors came from.

The modern state of Israel successfully defended itself

against greater numbers that sought its destruction in war many years ago, similar to the exploits of David in the bible- the same person is perhaps still there helping them.

Saladin, while he died a Muslim, was said by many to live an upright life. It is hard to know if he is heaven or not, but I sometimes imagined if the Kurds fighting back in resistance to protect themselves people who believe that God wants them to kill and destroy could have received help from him, because he was Kurdish.

If Confucius is in heaven, perhaps it adds to the explanation of the respect to parents in East Asia inspired by his teachings.

The martyrs of Uganda were killed by a homosexual king, and their country is subject to much international attack because it puts laws against homosexual practice.

When Joan of Arc was liberating Orleans, she said that St Louis (King Louis IX of France, who died two centuries earlier) had prayed for the city and for that reason it was being saved.

Gandhi died on January 30th 1948, and it was the same year several months later that Mother Teresa began going on the streets of Calcutta to do her ministry among the poor. He was perhaps with her.

Gandhi cited his own inspiration within the religious teachings of Christ and the Hindu scriptures as well as various individuals. Among these individuals was Leo Tolstoy, the famous writer, who was a Russian aristocrat that freed his serfs, rejected war and thought that the church had gone far from what Jesus Christ had taught. Gandhi said he loved Christ, but he hated Christians and he embraced the non-violent teachings of Christ and wanted an India where all people were brothers and sisters together rather than separated by caste. Perhaps he was with Gandhi.

Martin of Tours was a roman soldier in France in the 4th century, who refused to fight because he felt it was against his religion as a Christian, and then the commander was angry with him, reminding him of his military oath. Martin insisted that a Christian could not kill, and the commander mocked his religion. Martin proposed to charge the enemy without weapons or armour, to which the commander happily agreed. But before he could do so, the other side made peace. The commander, who was the future emperor Julian the apostate, would reject the Christian religion when he became emperor and use the blood of pagan sacrifices to wash himself in order to 'undo' his baptism, because he hated Christianity, including all of its peace-loving notions. He would die while fighting a war in Persia, but Martin would live to be bishop of Tours, just as Christ said to Peter on the Mount of Olives 'those who live by the sword will perish by the sword'. Martin of Tours' feast day is November 11th, it was on the same day in 1918 that the guns silenced on the Western Front and the First World War ended.

The Virgin Mary, appeared at Fatima in 1917 and said another world war would come because of the sins of the world and that people needed to pray for peace. Perhaps it was the praying for peace that brought this war to an end. America declared war on December 8th 1941, the solemnity of the Immaculate Conception. The atomic bomb was first used in war on August 6th 1945, the feast of the Transfiguration, when we remember Jesus showing His glory in dazzling light. The war ended on August 15th, 1945, with Japan's unconditional surrender, which as Catholics know, is the Assumption of Mary to heaven.

Pope John Paul II, the apostle of Mary, consecrated the world along with all the other bishops in a public ceremony in Rome, in accordance with the request of Mary at Fatima, who had called specifically for the consecration of Russia because from Russia errors were going to spread over the world. She said to the visionaries at Fatima that Russia needed to be consecrated in this way to bring about peace. The Pope consecrated not only Russia, but the whole world. The date the pope chose was March 25th 1984, the feast of the Annunciation.

On December 25th 1991, Mikhail Gorbachev publicly announced his resignation, saying that his office no longer existed and that all political powers were now turned over to Boris Yeltsin. That night, the Soviet flag at the Kremlin came down and was replaced with the Russian flag.

The angel announced to Mary that she would bear God's Son, and we remember this on March 25th, and we remember the birth of God's Son on December 25th.

The massive Sagrada Familia church in Barcelona was planned by Anton Gaudi who died almost a century before it could be completed. He didn't have enough resources and finances to complete the church, but he had faith and said that St Joseph would finish the church. The church was finally consecrated and made open for mass by Pope Benedict XVI, whose baptismal name is Joseph.

Therese de Lisieux, the wei'nu of Jesus life prior to His preaching, wrote that she once prayed for a condemned murderer in Paris who was going to be executed and she didn't want him to go to hell. She hoped for some sign that her prayer was heard and that this man would repent before the end. When she opened the newspapers after his execution, it said that the moment before he died, there was a cross nearby and the murderer grabbed it and kissed it before he was executed.

The wei'nu of Jesus' Mercy, St Faustina, died in Poland in the late 30s. The Nazi governor of Poland, Hans Frank, at the Nuremburg trial openly repented of the enormous evil he did and believed that God's mercy was great enough even for him. He and Albert Speer were the only ones to admit their own guilt. He was the only person to be hanged there with a smile on his face as he entered the room. His last words before execution were: "I am thankful for the kind treatment during my captivity and I ask God to accept me with mercy". Perhaps like Therese, she had done the same for him from heaven.

Lawrence of Brindisi had as his baptismal name, Giulio Cesare (Julius Caesar). Lawrence was a Capuchin friar that had great skills at public preaching. In 1601, he was in Hungary with the army of the Holy Roman Empire as it was preparing to battle with the Ottoman Turks. The Imperial army had 18,000 soldiers and the Turks had 80,000, and Lawrence made a speech to the soldiers to encourage them and to tell them that God was on their side. He then went on a horse, and holding a crucifix up in his hand, he went in front of the army and led it against the Turks. The Turks were defeated, and they lost 30,000 men. The Turks regrouped and attacked again a few days later, and Lawrence did the same with holding the crucifix in front of the army, while on horseback, and they defeated them again. Julius Caesar was definitely not a holy man in his life, but it is possible he didn't suffer eternal damnation and still got to heaven in the end. Perhaps in the moments after he was stabbed he looked at his friends who did this and forgave them, preferring to let go of what they had done to him than to let go of them, and so when he saw God he likewise was accepted by the One who preferred to let go of the evil done against Him than to let go of the beloved sinner He created. Perhaps it was his redeemed and cleansed spirit with Lawrence at the battle and who helped Lawrence in his public speaking and orations and to give him victory in battle, just like how Caesar had been a great orator and general in life; or maybe it was just a coincidence Lawrence was baptized with his name.

John Paul II was canonized in 2014, only 9 years after his death, thus being one of the fastest papal canonizations of all time. This was due to a huge popularity surrounding the late Pope. The Pope that canonized him is named Francis. St Francis of Assisi died in 1226 and was canonized only two years later by the Pope in 1228, also because of a big personality cult. The modern Pope Francis also has developed a massive personality cult, just like the Francis of that time.

Albert Einstein, who lived in Germany for most of his life, shared the same name as Albert the Great, although his parents perhaps named him that name for a different reason. Albert the Great was a German Dominican university professor in the 13th century who is one of the most important founders of what would later become science. Among his students was St Thomas Aquinas. He wrote so many books and had such deep knowledge of natural things in his time.

Coincidentally or not, the birthplaces of both of them are in fact less than 40 kilometres from each other in Germany. Perhaps the first Albert was praying for the second one. When Einstein handed in his German passport and renounced his citizenship after Hitler took office, perhaps the first Albert was with him and would have done the same.

The truth is that there is nothing in the world, in history, science, geography, geology, etc. that happens coincidentally or without a meaning behind it. There are always people praying for these things with an intelligent purpose. We just do not have the eyes to see it.

Because they intercede for what has relation to them, it is good to honour them, even just to put up pictures of them, put them on money, put quotations of their writings in places of honour, etc. It will bring blessings with it.

They will be able to do far more than what the damned souls can do, fortunately.

What they want the most for us is that we come and join them. They love us so much... it is hard to describe how great this love is. You could even be their murderer and they desperately want you to be forgiven, and to come up to live with them as their brother or sister. Even if we call them saints in life, what they look like now is ten thousand times more amazing than what they looked like in life. They want nothing more than for us to come and join them.

They want us to be happy, but they also want us to have the greatest happiness of all. The souls in hell are willing to put up with us being happy for a while, if it means eternal condemnation for us, and the souls in heaven are willing to put up with us bearing the cross and being unhappy for a while, if it means eternal life for us.

As the story of Job can teach, the greatest blessing the soul can possess is neither wealth, family, health or any comfort this world can offer... but the greatest blessing is to have love inside oneself. To have love in your heart is a greater gift than anything else the created world has, and if you understand this, then you possess wisdom and you can pass the test given to you in this life.

Therefore, turn your mind and heart to God and pray, endlessly pray, asking not simply to be freed from any bodily afflictions or worldly misfortunes, but beg God to ask Him that you can have the greatest blessing of all, which is not to be loved by others but to possess love oneself.

Lord, we thank you for the blessing of being able to communicate with you. Just as Mary brought God into the world, so is prayer the way that we receive the grace to love, and we pray you for the grace to love just as you have loved us. We ask for these things, if it is your will, in Jesus' name, Amen

All Glory to God

www.ingramcontent.com/pod-product-compliance
Lightning Source LLC
Chambersburg PA
CBHW060611290526
45793CB00001B/1